CONTENTS

ANSWER KEY

CHAPTER 1

1.1. – ORDER OF OPERATIONS

1. $5+3\cdot2=\underline{11}$

2. $2\cdot3-(-3)=\underline{9}$

3. $-5\cdot5-(-8)\cdot2=\underline{-9}$

4. $-2-5-(-2)+2=\underline{-3}$

5. $(-2)(-5)-(-2)\cdot2=\underline{14}$

6. $25\cdot2-7=\underline{43}$

7. $15+4/2=\underline{17}$

8. $14/7+3\cdot6=\underline{20}$

9. $5/5-30/2\cdot5=\underline{-74}$

10. $1+4/2-8/4\cdot5=\underline{-7}$

11. $20/4/2+4=\underline{13/2}$

12. $12\cdot(2+3)=\underline{60}$

13. $5(3\cdot2/3\cdot2)+2=\underline{22}$

14. $1/2+3/2=\underline{2}$

15. $6/3-20/10=\underline{0}$

16. $5(1+3\cdot2)+2/2-8/4=\underline{34}$

17. $(15+3)\cdot2-2=\underline{34}$

18. $0/5+3\cdot2=\underline{6}$

19. $5/0+3\cdot2=\underline{\text{Undefined}}$

20. $(1+1)\cdot(2-2)\cdot(4\cdot5\cdot5)=\underline{0}$

21. $(5+3)\cdot2=\underline{16}$

22. $(5\cdot3)\cdot2=\underline{30}$

23. $5\cdot(3\cdot2)=\underline{30}$

24. $5\cdot3\cdot2=\underline{30}$

25. $100/2^2+21/3=\underline{32}$

26. $(2+1)^2/3+13=\underline{16}$

27. $2(3^2-4/2)^2-1\cdot3=\underline{95}$

28. $3(1-4/2^2)^2-4^2/3=\underline{-16/3}$

29. $10(2^4/2-1^2+1)/2=\underline{40}$

30. $2+3(2-20/2^2)^2-(5^2+3)/2=$

31. $5/0=\underline{\text{Undefined}}$

32. $0/4=\underline{0}$

33. $0/0=\underline{\text{Undefined}}$

34. $(2+4)\cdot5^2-2/2=\underline{149}$

35. $-1\cdot5^2-2^2+(-2)^{3-1\cdot2}=\underline{-31}$

36. $\left(-2^2-2\right)^2\cdot(-2)^{1-1}=\underline{36}$

37. $(4-5\cdot2)/2-1=\underline{-4}$

1.2. – DECIMALS AND FRACTIONS

Write as decimals:

1. $\dfrac{1}{10} = \underline{0.1}$

2. $\dfrac{1}{100} = \underline{\quad 0.01}$

3. $\dfrac{1}{1000} = \underline{\quad 0.001}$

4. $\dfrac{1}{10000} = \underline{0.0001}$

5. $\dfrac{2}{10} = \underline{0.2}$

6. $\dfrac{5}{100} = \underline{0.05}$

7. $\dfrac{-31}{1000} = \underline{\quad -0.031}$

8. $\dfrac{766}{10000} = \underline{0.0766}$

9. $\dfrac{55}{10} = \underline{5.5}$

10. $\dfrac{101}{100} = \underline{1.01}$

11. $\dfrac{-335}{1000} = \underline{-0.335}$

12. $\dfrac{20000}{10000} = \underline{2}$

13. $\dfrac{1}{2} = \underline{0.5}$

14. $\dfrac{1}{5} = \underline{0.2}$

15. $\dfrac{1}{4} = \underline{0.25}$

16. $\dfrac{1}{3} = \underline{0.333\ldots}$

17. $\dfrac{1}{8} = \underline{0.125}$

18. $\dfrac{1}{9} = \underline{0.111\ldots}$

19. $\dfrac{2}{5} = \underline{0.4}$

20. $\dfrac{2}{4} = \underline{0.5}$

21. $\dfrac{3}{5} = \underline{0.6}$

22. $\dfrac{4}{5} = \underline{0.8}$

23. $\dfrac{3}{4} = \underline{0.75}$

24. $\dfrac{7}{5} = \underline{1.4}$

25. $\dfrac{5}{4} = \underline{1.25}$

26. $\dfrac{9}{5} = \underline{1.6}$

27. $\dfrac{2}{9} = \underline{0.222\ldots}$

28. $\dfrac{1}{20} = \underline{0.02}$

29. $\dfrac{3}{20} = \underline{0.06}$

30. $\dfrac{8}{5} = \underline{1.6}$

Write the decimals as fractions

31. $0.3 = \dfrac{3}{10}$

32. $0.2 = \dfrac{2}{10}$

33. $0.1 = \dfrac{1}{10}$

34. $0.01 = \dfrac{1}{100}$

35. $0.02 = \dfrac{2}{100}$

36. $0.11 = \dfrac{11}{100}$

37. $0.26 = \dfrac{26}{100}$

38. $1.3 = \dfrac{13}{10}$

39. $1.42 = \dfrac{142}{10}$

40. $0.011 = \dfrac{11}{1000}$

41. $0.312 = \dfrac{312}{1000}$

42. $0.16 = \dfrac{16}{100}$

43. $1.4 = \dfrac{14}{10}$

44. $2.043 = \dfrac{2043}{1000}$

45. $43.3 = \dfrac{433}{10}$

46. $4.12 = \dfrac{412}{100}$

47. $1.302 = \dfrac{1302}{1000}$

48. $1.111 = \dfrac{1111}{1000}$

49. $102.32 = \dfrac{10232}{100}$

50. $2.346 = \dfrac{2346}{1000}$

Perform the operations; give the answer as a decimal and fraction:

51. $50 \cdot 0.1 = \underline{5}$

52. $85 \cdot 0.01 = \underline{0.85}$

53. $45 \cdot 0.001 = \underline{0.045}$

54. $6 \cdot 0.0001 = \underline{0.0006}$

55. $5123 \cdot 0.001 = \underline{5.123}$

56. $435 \cdot 0.01 = \underline{4.35}$

57. $15 \cdot 0.001 = \underline{0.015}$

58. $-236 \cdot 0.0001 = \underline{-0.236}$

59. $1228 \cdot 0.1 = \underline{122.8}$

60. $1085 \cdot 0.01 = \underline{10.85}$

61. $4500 \cdot 0.001 = \underline{4.5}$

62. $0.16 \cdot 0.0001 = \underline{0.000016}$

63. $12 \cdot 1.2 = \dfrac{12}{1} \cdot \dfrac{12}{10} = \dfrac{144}{10} = 1.44$

64. $25 \cdot 0.22 = \dfrac{25}{1} \cdot \dfrac{22}{100} = \dfrac{550}{100} = 5.5$

65. $2.5 \cdot 1.8 = \dfrac{25}{10} \cdot \dfrac{18}{10} = \dfrac{450}{100} = 4.5$

66. $7.2 \cdot 8.8 = \dfrac{72}{10} \cdot \dfrac{88}{10} = \dfrac{6336}{100} = 63.36$

67. $0.15 \cdot 2.01 = \dfrac{15}{100} \cdot \dfrac{201}{100} = \dfrac{3015}{10000} = 0.3105$

68. $87.5 \cdot 0.2 = \dfrac{875}{100} \cdot \dfrac{2}{10} = \dfrac{1750}{1000} = 17.5$

69. $31.5 \cdot 0.3 = \dfrac{315}{10} \cdot \dfrac{3}{10} = \dfrac{945}{100} = 9.45$

70. $0.215 \cdot 1.38 = \dfrac{215}{1000} \cdot \dfrac{138}{100} = \dfrac{29670}{100000} = 0.2967$

71. $0.5 \cdot 1.23 = \dfrac{5}{10} \cdot \dfrac{123}{100} = \dfrac{615}{1000} = 0.615$

72. $1.02 \cdot 2.5 = \dfrac{102}{100} \cdot \dfrac{25}{10} = \dfrac{2550}{1000} = 2.55$

73. $31.7 \cdot 0.18 = \dfrac{317}{10} \cdot \dfrac{18}{100} = \dfrac{5706}{1000} = 5.706$

74. $21.2 \cdot 1.13 = \dfrac{212}{10} \cdot \dfrac{113}{100} = \dfrac{23956}{1000} = 23.956$

75. $0.42 \cdot 5.56 = \dfrac{42}{100} \cdot \dfrac{556}{100} = \dfrac{23352}{10000} = 2.3352$

76. $3.1 \cdot 0.642 = \dfrac{31}{10} \cdot \dfrac{642}{1000} = \dfrac{19902}{10000} = 1.9902$

77. $13.7 \cdot 8.9 = \dfrac{137}{10} \cdot \dfrac{89}{10} = \dfrac{12192}{100} = 12.192$

78. $1.07 \cdot 0.03 = \dfrac{107}{100} \cdot \dfrac{3}{100} = \dfrac{321}{10000} = 0.0321$

Perform the operations; give the answer as a decimal and fraction:

79. $\dfrac{1}{0.1} = \underline{10}$

80. $\dfrac{5}{0.01} = \underline{500}$

81. $\dfrac{-56}{0.001} = \underline{-56000}$

82. $\dfrac{-2.3}{0.01} = \underline{-230}$

83. $\dfrac{3}{0.1} = \underline{30}$

84. $\dfrac{0.55}{0.01} = \underline{55}$

85. $\dfrac{-31.6}{0.001} = \underline{-31600}$

86. $\dfrac{0.023}{0.01} = \underline{2.3}$

87. $\dfrac{15}{0.01} = \underline{1500}$

88. $\dfrac{-215}{0.01} = \underline{-21500}$

89. $\dfrac{-45.6}{0.001} = \underline{-45600}$

90. $\dfrac{-12.3}{0.01} = \underline{-1230}$

91. $\dfrac{1}{0.02} = \dfrac{1}{\left(\dfrac{2}{100}\right)} = \left(\dfrac{100}{2}\right) = 50$

92. $\dfrac{-2}{0.03} = \dfrac{-2}{\left(\dfrac{3}{100}\right)} = \left(-\dfrac{200}{2}\right) = -100$

93. $\dfrac{-4.6}{0.05} = \dfrac{-4.6}{\left(\dfrac{5}{100}\right)} = \left(-\dfrac{460}{2}\right) = -230$

94. $\dfrac{-1.3}{0.06} = \dfrac{-1.3}{\left(\dfrac{6}{100}\right)} = \left(\dfrac{-130}{6}\right)$

95. $\dfrac{1}{0.25} = \dfrac{1}{\left(\dfrac{25}{100}\right)} = \left(\dfrac{100}{25}\right) = 4$

96. $\dfrac{-2}{0.9} = \dfrac{-2}{\left(\dfrac{9}{100}\right)} = \left(\dfrac{-200}{9}\right)$

97. $\dfrac{-4.1}{0.2} = \dfrac{-4.1}{\left(\dfrac{2}{10}\right)} = \left(\dfrac{-41}{2}\right)$

98. $\dfrac{-1.3}{0.05} = \dfrac{-1.3}{\left(\dfrac{5}{100}\right)} = \left(\dfrac{-130}{5}\right) = -26$

99. $\dfrac{1}{0.015} = \dfrac{1}{\left(\dfrac{15}{1000}\right)} = \left(\dfrac{1000}{15}\right) = \dfrac{200}{3}$

100. $\dfrac{-12}{0.6} = \dfrac{-12}{\left(\dfrac{6}{10}\right)} = \left(\dfrac{-120}{6}\right) = 20$

101. $\dfrac{-14}{0.003} = \dfrac{-14}{\left(\dfrac{3}{1000}\right)} = \left(\dfrac{-1400}{3}\right)$

102. $\dfrac{-0.3}{0.02} =$

$\dfrac{\left(-\dfrac{3}{10}\right)}{\left(\dfrac{2}{100}\right)} = \left(-\dfrac{3}{10}\right)\left(\dfrac{100}{2}\right) = -15$

103. 0.2 units on the left of −1: $\underline{-1.2}$
104. 0.5 units on the left of −2: $\underline{-2.5}$
105. 0.3 units on the right of −1: $\underline{-0.7}$
106. 0.4 units on the right of −2: $\underline{-1.6}$
107. 0.8 units on the left of −9: $\underline{-9.8}$
108. 0.2 units on the left of 0: $\underline{-0.2}$
109. 0.9 units on the right of −9: $\underline{-8.1}$
110. 0.2 units on the right of −5: $\underline{-4.8}$
111. 0.21 units on the left of −1: $\underline{-1.21}$
112. 0.51 units on the left of −2: $\underline{-1.51}$
113. 0.34 units on the right of −1: $\underline{-0.66}$
114. 0.06 units on the right of −10: $\underline{-9.94}$
115. 0.11 units on the right of −1: $\underline{-0.89}$
116. 0.01 units on the right of −2: $\underline{-1.99}$
117. 0.34 units on the right of 9: $\underline{9.34}$
118. 0.06 units on the right of 10: $\underline{10.06}$
119. 0.17 units on the right of −9: $\underline{-8.83}$
120. 0.78 units on the left of −3: $\underline{-3.78}$

121. 0.01 units on the left of −7: $\underline{-7.01}$
122. 0.02 units on the right of −1: $\underline{-0.98}$
123. 0.002 units on the right of −10: $\underline{-9.998}$
124. 0.111 units on the right of −1: $\underline{-0.889}$
125. 0.021 units on the right of −2: $\underline{-1.979}$
126. 0.4 units on the right of 9: $\underline{9.4}$
127. 0.03 units on the right of 10: $\underline{10.03}$
128. 0.202 units on the right of −9: $\underline{-8.798}$
129. Close to 2 on its left: $\underline{1.999}$ right: $\underline{2.001}$
130. Close to 1 on its left: $\underline{0.999}$ right: $\underline{1.001}$
131. Close to 0 on its left: $\underline{-0.001}$ right: $\underline{0.001}$
132. Close to −1 on its left: $\underline{-1.001}$ right: $\underline{-0.999}$
133. Close to −7 on its left: $\underline{-7.001}$ right: $\underline{-6.999}$
134. Close to −12 on its left: $\underline{-12.001}$ right: $\underline{-11.999}$
135. Close to −2 on its left: $\underline{-2.001}$ right: $\underline{-1.999}$
136. Close to −10 on its left: $\underline{-10.001}$ right: $\underline{-9.999}$
137. Close to 9 on its left: $\underline{8.999}$ right: $\underline{9.001}$
138. Close to 100 on its left: $\underline{99.999}$ right: $\underline{100.001}$

139. The numbers between 3 and 3.1: $\underline{3.01, 3.06}$. Fractions: $\left(\dfrac{301}{100}\right), \left(\dfrac{306}{100}\right)$

140. The numbers between 6.2 and 6.3: $\underline{6.21, 6.25}$. Fractions: $\left(\dfrac{621}{100}\right), \left(\dfrac{625}{100}\right)$

141. The numbers between 6.2 and 6.21: $\underline{6.201, 6.202}$. Fractions: $\left(\dfrac{6201}{1000}\right), \left(\dfrac{6202}{1000}\right)$

142. The numbers between −5.2 and −5.3: $\underline{-5.21, -5.22}$. Fractions: $\left(-\dfrac{521}{100}\right), \left(-\dfrac{522}{100}\right)$

143. The numbers between 0.25 and 0.251: $\underline{0.2501, 0.2502}$. Fractions: $\left(\dfrac{2501}{10000}\right), \left(\dfrac{2502}{10000}\right)$

144. The numbers between 1.11 and 1.111: $\underline{1.1101, 1.1102}$. Fractions: $\left(\dfrac{11101}{10000}\right), \left(\dfrac{11102}{10000}\right)$

145. The numbers between 0.21 and 0.22: $\underline{0.211, 0.212}$. Fractions: $\left(\dfrac{211}{1000}\right), \left(\dfrac{212}{1000}\right)$

146. The numbers between 5.99 and 5.999: $\underline{5.991, 5.992}$. Fractions: $\left(\dfrac{5991}{1000}\right), \left(\dfrac{5992}{1000}\right)$

147. The numbers between 6 and 6.01: <u>6.001, 6.002</u>. Fractions: $\left(\dfrac{6001}{1000}\right),\left(\dfrac{6002}{1000}\right)$

148. The values are: 11.2, 12, 12.4

149. The values are: 4.72, 4.77, 4.86

150. The values are: -0.62, -0.57, -0.5

151. Fractions greater than 1:
$$\frac{7}{6},\frac{35}{34},\frac{21}{7},\frac{10001}{10000}$$

152. A fraction will be greater than 1 if <u>the numerator is greater than the denominator</u>

153. Fractions greater than 2:
$$\frac{50}{26},\frac{20}{7},\frac{20001}{10000}$$

154. A fraction will be greater than 2 if <u>the numerator is greater than twice the denominator</u>

155. Fractions greater than 5: $\dfrac{47}{9},\dfrac{100}{6},\dfrac{28}{3}$

156. A fraction will be greater than 5 if <u>the numerator is greater than 5 times the denominator</u>

157. Fractions smaller than $\dfrac{1}{2}$: $\dfrac{1}{3},\dfrac{23}{51}$

158. A fraction will be smaller than $\dfrac{1}{2}$ if: <u>the denominator is more than twice the numerator</u>

159. Fractions smaller than $\dfrac{1}{3}$: $\dfrac{2}{7},\dfrac{24}{75},\dfrac{3}{11}$

160. A fraction will be smaller than $\dfrac{1}{3}$ if: <u>the denominator is more than 3 times the numerator</u>

161.
$$\frac{1}{2}=\frac{2}{4}=\frac{3}{6}=\frac{a}{2a}=...=0.5$$
$$\frac{1}{3}=\frac{2}{6}=\frac{3}{9}=\frac{a}{3a}=...=0.333...$$
$$\frac{1}{4}=\frac{2}{8}=\frac{3}{12}=\frac{a}{4a}=...=0.25$$
$$\frac{7}{4}=\frac{14}{8}=\frac{21}{12}=\frac{7a}{4a}=...=1.75$$
$$\frac{2}{3}=\frac{4}{6}=\frac{16}{24}=\frac{2a}{3a}=...=0.666...$$
$$\frac{11}{8}=\frac{22}{16}=\frac{33}{24}=\frac{11a}{8a}=...=1.375$$
$$\frac{a}{b}=\frac{8a}{8b}=\frac{ka}{kb}$$
$$\frac{3a}{a}=\frac{6}{2}=3$$
$$\frac{a+2}{2+a}=\frac{10a+20}{20+10a}=1$$
$$\frac{x}{7x}=\frac{1}{7}$$
$$\frac{1+a}{a-1}=\frac{2+2a}{2a-2}$$

Fill the blank with: <,> or =:

162. $\dfrac{1}{2}>\dfrac{1}{3}$

163. $\dfrac{1}{3}>\dfrac{1}{4}$

164. $\dfrac{2}{5}<\dfrac{3}{7}$

165. $\dfrac{5}{8}<\dfrac{7}{11}$

166. $\dfrac{12}{7}>\dfrac{13}{8}$

167. $\dfrac{21}{8}>\dfrac{13}{5}$

168. $\dfrac{35}{8}>\dfrac{17}{4}$

169. $\dfrac{a}{b}<\dfrac{a+1}{b+1}$, $b>a>0$

170. $\dfrac{a}{b-1}>\dfrac{a+1}{b+1}$, $b>a>0$

171. $\dfrac{1}{n+1}<\dfrac{1}{n}$, $n\geq 0$

172. $\dfrac{1}{n^2}<\dfrac{1}{n}$, $n\geq 1$

173. $n^2<n, 0\leq n\leq 1$

174. $\dfrac{1}{n^2}>\dfrac{1}{n}, 0\leq n\leq 1$

175. $\dfrac{1}{a}>\dfrac{1}{b}, a<b$

176.

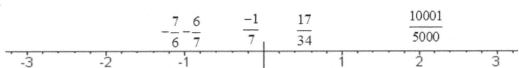

177.

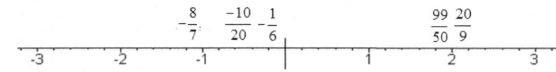

$$-\frac{8}{7} \qquad \frac{-10}{20} \quad -\frac{1}{6} \qquad\qquad\qquad \frac{99}{50} \quad \frac{20}{9}$$

178.

$$-\frac{3}{2} \quad -\frac{4}{5} \qquad\qquad \frac{9}{8} \qquad\qquad \frac{5}{2} \quad \frac{100}{33}$$

179.

$$-\frac{9}{3} \qquad -\frac{66}{32} \quad -\frac{7}{5} \qquad \frac{1}{10} \quad \frac{2}{3}$$

180.

$$-\frac{7}{8} -\frac{6}{13} \quad \frac{11}{21}$$
$$-2\frac{100}{17\ 501}$$

181.

$$-\frac{10}{6} \quad -\frac{8}{7} \quad \frac{-102}{200} \qquad\qquad \frac{181}{90} \quad \frac{189}{60}$$

182.

$$-\frac{5}{2} \qquad -\frac{6}{5} \qquad \frac{33}{100}\frac{2}{5} \quad \frac{90}{80}$$

183.

$$-\frac{3}{1} -\frac{10}{4} \qquad -\frac{2}{10} \qquad \frac{64}{33}\frac{21}{10}$$

184.

$$-\frac{37}{12} -\frac{12}{5} -\frac{6}{3} \qquad\qquad \frac{11}{10} \quad \frac{11}{6}$$

Calculate:

185. $\quad 1+\dfrac{2}{3} = \dfrac{5}{3}$

186. $\quad \dfrac{5}{6}+\dfrac{2}{3} = \dfrac{10}{6}$

187. $\quad \dfrac{2}{7}-\dfrac{1}{6} = \dfrac{5}{42}$

188. $\quad 5\cdot\dfrac{3}{8}-\dfrac{2}{12} = \dfrac{41}{24}$

189. $\quad \left(\dfrac{2}{14}-\dfrac{3}{7}\right)\cdot\dfrac{2}{9} = \dfrac{-4}{14}\cdot\dfrac{2}{9} = \dfrac{-8}{126}$

190. $\quad \left(\dfrac{7}{2}-\dfrac{4}{3}\right)\cdot\dfrac{1}{5} = \dfrac{13}{6}\cdot\dfrac{1}{5} = \dfrac{13}{30}$

191. $\quad \dfrac{5}{6}+\dfrac{2}{3} = \dfrac{9}{6}$

192. $\quad \dfrac{1}{a}+\dfrac{1}{a} = \dfrac{2}{a}$

193. $\dfrac{1}{d} + d = \dfrac{1+d^2}{d}$

194. $\dfrac{1}{a} + \dfrac{a}{1} = \dfrac{1+a^2}{a}$

195. $\dfrac{1}{b+1} + b = \dfrac{1+b(b+1)}{b+1}$

196. $\dfrac{a}{b} + \dfrac{1}{b} = \dfrac{a+1}{b}$

197. $\dfrac{a}{b} + \dfrac{d}{b} = \dfrac{a+d}{b}$

198. $\dfrac{a}{c} + \dfrac{d}{b} = \dfrac{ab+cd}{cb}$

199. $\dfrac{a+b}{b} + \dfrac{d}{b} = \dfrac{a+b+d}{b}$

200. $\dfrac{\left(\dfrac{a}{b}\right)}{b} = \dfrac{a}{b^2}$

201. $\dfrac{a}{\left(\dfrac{a}{b}\right)} = b$

202. $\dfrac{\left(\dfrac{b}{a}\right)}{b} = \dfrac{1}{a}$

203. $\dfrac{\left(\dfrac{b}{a}\right)}{1} = \dfrac{b}{a}$

204. $\dfrac{\left(\dfrac{1}{a}\right)}{b} = \dfrac{1}{ab}$

205. $\dfrac{\left(\dfrac{b}{1}\right)}{b} = 1$

206. $\dfrac{1}{\left(\dfrac{a}{b}\right)} = \dfrac{b}{a}$

207. $\dfrac{\left(\dfrac{a}{b}\right)}{\left(\dfrac{a}{b}\right)} = 1$

208. $\dfrac{\left(\dfrac{b}{a}\right)}{\left(\dfrac{a}{b}\right)} = \dfrac{b^2}{a^2}$

209. $\dfrac{\left(\dfrac{a}{1}\right)}{\left(\dfrac{a}{b}\right)} = b$

210. $\dfrac{\left(\dfrac{a}{b}\right)}{\left(\dfrac{1}{b}\right)} = a$

211. $\dfrac{\left(\dfrac{c+1}{d}\right)}{\left(\dfrac{1}{d}+d\right)} = \dfrac{\left(\dfrac{c+1}{d}\right)}{\left(\dfrac{1+d^2}{d}\right)} = \left(\dfrac{c+1}{1+d^2}\right)$

212. $\dfrac{1}{\left(\dfrac{1}{d}+d\right)} + d =$

$\dfrac{1}{\left(\dfrac{1+d^2}{d}\right)} + d = \left(\dfrac{2d+d^3}{1+d^2}\right)$

213. $\dfrac{1-d}{(d+2)} + \dfrac{2}{d} =$

$\dfrac{d(1-d)+2(d+2)}{(d+2)d}$

214. $\dfrac{1}{d} + \dfrac{2}{d^2} + \dfrac{1}{d^3} = \dfrac{d^2+2d+1}{d^3}$

215. $\dfrac{2}{3} + \dfrac{3a}{c} - \dfrac{b}{2} = \dfrac{4c+18a-3cb}{6c}$

216. $\dfrac{\left(\dfrac{4}{b}-\dfrac{a}{7}\right)}{2} = \dfrac{\left(\dfrac{28-ab}{7b}\right)}{2} = \dfrac{28-ab}{14b}$

217. $\dfrac{a}{c(c+1)} + \dfrac{d}{c+1} = \dfrac{a+dc}{c(c+1)}$

218. $\dfrac{2x}{\left(\dfrac{2x+2}{3+x}\right)} + \dfrac{\left(\dfrac{x+1}{x-2}\right)}{x-3} =$

$$\frac{2x(3+x)}{2x+2}+\frac{x+1}{(x-2)(x-3)}=\frac{2x(3+x)+(x+1)(2x+2)}{(2x+2)(x-2)(x-3)}$$

234. $\dfrac{3}{\left(\dfrac{a}{7}\right)}=\dfrac{21}{a}$

219. $\dfrac{\left(2x+\dfrac{1}{x}\right)}{\left(1+\dfrac{1}{x}\right)}=\dfrac{\left(\dfrac{2x^2+1}{x}\right)}{\left(\dfrac{x+1}{x}\right)}=\left(\dfrac{2x^2+1}{x+1}\right)$

235. $\dfrac{6}{\left(\dfrac{8}{3}\right)}=\dfrac{9}{4}$

220. $\dfrac{12}{2a}\times\dfrac{a+1}{6}=\dfrac{(a+1)}{a}$

221. $\dfrac{12}{2a}\div\dfrac{a}{6}=\dfrac{36}{2a^2}$

236. $\dfrac{\left(\dfrac{4}{3}\right)}{\left(\dfrac{3}{4}\right)}=\dfrac{16}{9}$

222. $3\times\dfrac{4}{3}=4$

223. $3\div\dfrac{4}{3}=\dfrac{9}{4}$

237. $\dfrac{\left(\dfrac{2}{3}\right)}{\left(\dfrac{4}{5}\right)}=\dfrac{6}{5}$

224. $12-\dfrac{4}{3}=\dfrac{32}{3}$

225. $a\times\dfrac{b}{3c}=\dfrac{ab}{3c}$

238. $\dfrac{\left(\dfrac{2}{3}\right)}{\left(\dfrac{2}{3}\right)}=1$

226. $\dfrac{b}{3a}\div 3a=\dfrac{b}{3a^2}$

227. $\dfrac{b}{3a}\times 3a=b$

239. $\left(\dfrac{a}{b}\right)\cdot\left(\dfrac{c}{a}\right)=\dfrac{c}{b}$

240. $\left(\dfrac{2}{c}\right)\cdot\left(\dfrac{c}{7}\right)=\dfrac{2}{7}$

228. $\dfrac{\left(\dfrac{1}{3}+\dfrac{2}{5}\right)}{\left(\dfrac{5}{3}-\dfrac{1}{3}\right)}=\dfrac{\left(\dfrac{11}{15}\right)}{\left(\dfrac{4}{3}\right)}=\dfrac{33}{60}=\dfrac{11}{20}$

241. $\left(\dfrac{b+1}{3}\right)\cdot\left(\dfrac{2}{b}\right)=\dfrac{2(b+1)}{3b}$

242. $\left(\dfrac{z+1}{z-2}\right)\cdot\left(\dfrac{4}{z+1}\right)=\dfrac{4}{z-2}$

229. $\dfrac{\left(\dfrac{b}{3c}\right)}{2}=\dfrac{b}{6c}$

243. $\left(\dfrac{3a+6}{5}\right)\cdot\left(\dfrac{1}{a+2}\right)=\dfrac{3}{5}$

244. $\left(\dfrac{2c-4}{c}\right)\cdot\left(\dfrac{2c}{4c-8}\right)=1$

230. $\dfrac{\left(\dfrac{1}{2}\right)}{2\left(\dfrac{2}{3c}\right)}=\dfrac{3c}{8}$

245. $\dfrac{1}{\left(\dfrac{2}{4}\right)}\cdot\left(\dfrac{2}{3}\right)=\dfrac{4}{3}$

231. $\dfrac{\left(\dfrac{1}{2}\right)}{2}=\dfrac{1}{4}$

246. $\dfrac{\left(\dfrac{3}{4}\right)}{\left(\dfrac{a}{2}\right)}\cdot\left(\dfrac{2}{3}\right)=\dfrac{1}{a}$

232. $\dfrac{\left(\dfrac{2}{7}\right)}{3}=\dfrac{2}{21}$

233. $\dfrac{2}{\left(\dfrac{2}{7}\right)}=\dfrac{1}{7}$

247. $\dfrac{\left(\dfrac{1}{a}\right)}{\left(\dfrac{2}{a}\right)}+2=\dfrac{5}{2}$

248. $\dfrac{\left(x+\dfrac{1}{x}\right)}{\left(1-\dfrac{1}{x}\right)}=\dfrac{x^2+1}{x-1}$

249. $\dfrac{\left(\dfrac{1}{1+x}+1\right)}{\left(x-\dfrac{2}{x}\right)}=\dfrac{x(2+x)}{(x^2-2)(1+x)}$

250. $\dfrac{\left(\dfrac{x}{3}-2\right)}{\left(2-\dfrac{2+x}{3}\right)}=\dfrac{x-6}{4-x}$

251. $\dfrac{2x}{\left(\dfrac{2}{3+x}\right)}+\dfrac{\left(\dfrac{2}{x}\right)}{x+3}=\dfrac{(x(3+x))^2+2}{x(x+3)}$

252. $\dfrac{a-b}{\left(1-\dfrac{a}{b}\right)}=\dfrac{a-b}{\left(\dfrac{b-a}{b}\right)}=-b$

253. $\dfrac{2}{(1-a)}+\dfrac{2}{a(1-a)}=\dfrac{2(a+1)}{a(1-a)}$

254. $\dfrac{a}{(3+a)^2}+\dfrac{2}{(a+3)}=\dfrac{3a+6}{(3+a)^2}$

255. $\dfrac{1}{(1-x)^3}+\dfrac{2}{(1-x)^2}=\dfrac{3-2x}{(1-x)^3}$

256. $\dfrac{1}{(1-x)^3}+\dfrac{2}{x(1-x)^2}=\dfrac{2-x}{x(1-x)^3}$

257. $\dfrac{1}{(1-x)(2-x)}+\dfrac{2}{x(1-x)^2}=$

$\qquad =\dfrac{-x^2-x+4}{x(1-x)^2(2-x)}$

258. $\dfrac{2}{(1-x)x}+\dfrac{2}{x^2(1-x)^2}=$

$\qquad =\dfrac{-2x^2+2x+2}{x^2(1-x)^2}$

259. $\dfrac{a^2+1}{a}-\dfrac{a+1}{a^2+a}=$

$\dfrac{(a^2+1)(a+1)-(a+1)}{a(a+1)}=\dfrac{(a^2)(a+1)}{a(a+1)}=a$

260. $\dfrac{a+x}{x}-\dfrac{y+1}{xy}+\dfrac{2}{y}=\dfrac{ay+xy-y-1+2x}{xy}$

261. $\dfrac{a+x}{a-x}\div\dfrac{a+x}{x-a}=\dfrac{a+x}{a-x}\cdot\dfrac{x-a}{a+x}=-1$

262. $\dfrac{a+x}{a^2-x^2}-\dfrac{a-x}{x-a}=\dfrac{a+x+a^2-x^2}{a^2-x^2}$

263. $\left(\dfrac{2c-4}{c}\right)\div\left(\dfrac{4c^2+16}{c^2}\right)=\dfrac{2c^2-4c}{4c^2+16}$

264. $\left(\dfrac{6xy+2}{3y}\right)\div\left(\dfrac{3xy+1}{6y^5}\right)=\dfrac{(6xy+2)6y^4}{3(3xy+1)}=4y^4$

265. $\left(\dfrac{x^2-z^2}{xyz}\right)+\left(\dfrac{z-x^2}{xy}\right)=\dfrac{x^2-zx^2}{xyz}=\dfrac{x(1-z)}{yz}$

True or False:

266. $\dfrac{a+b}{c}=\dfrac{a}{c}+\dfrac{b}{c}$ True

267. $\dfrac{a+b}{c+d}=\dfrac{a}{c}+\dfrac{b}{d}$ False

268. $\dfrac{a+b}{a}=1+\dfrac{b}{a}$ True

269. $\dfrac{a-b}{b-a}=-1$ True

270. $\dfrac{a}{c+d}=\dfrac{a}{c}+\dfrac{a}{d}$ False

271. $\dfrac{c-d}{d}=c$ False

272. $\dfrac{c-d}{d}=-1+c$ True

273. $\dfrac{ab}{ad}=\dfrac{b}{d}$ True

274. $\dfrac{a(c-d)}{a}=c-d$ True

275. $\dfrac{ac-d}{c-d} = a$ *False*

276. $\dfrac{2a+d}{d-2a} = -1$ *False*

Fill the blank to make the fractions equal:

277. $\dfrac{a}{3} = \dfrac{2a}{6}$

278. $\dfrac{a-b}{4} = \dfrac{3a-3b}{12}$

279. $\dfrac{a}{b} = \dfrac{2a}{2b}$

280. $\dfrac{1}{a} = \dfrac{3}{3a}$

281. $\dfrac{1}{3} = \dfrac{a}{3a}$

282. $\dfrac{a-b}{a-b} = 1$

283. $\dfrac{2-a}{-2} = \dfrac{a-2}{2}$

284. $\dfrac{2a}{b} = \dfrac{8a}{4b}$

285. $\dfrac{x^2}{2xy} = \dfrac{2xy}{4y^2}$

286. $\dfrac{2a}{7x} = \dfrac{2ax}{14x^2}$

1.3. – PERCENTAGES

1. A percentage is <u>a way to represent a part of a whole</u> we sometimes use <u>a fraction</u> or a <u>decimal number</u> to represent it.

2. Find (write the expression and simplify it to get a final answer):

   a. 1% of 900 = <u>9</u>
   b. 2% of 900 = <u>18</u>
   c. 3% of 900 = <u>27</u>
   d. 10% of 900 = <u>90</u>
   e. 15% of 900 = <u>135</u>
   f. 20% of 900 = <u>180</u>
   g. 25% of 900 = <u>225</u>
   h. 35% of 900 = <u>315</u>
   i. 100% of 900 = <u>900</u>
   j. 101% of 900 = <u>909</u>
   k. 110% of 900 = <u>990</u>
   l. 120% of 900 = <u>1080</u>
   m. 125% of 900 = <u>1125</u>
   n. 140% of 900 = <u>1260</u>
   o. 200% of 900 = <u>1800</u>
   p. 300% of 900 = <u>2700</u>

3. Find (write the expression and simplify it to get a final answer):

   a. 1% of 50 = <u>0.5</u>
   b. 2% of 50 = <u>1</u>
   c. 10% of 70 = <u>7</u>
   d. 15% of 90 = <u>13.5</u>
   e. 20% of 110 = <u>22</u>
   f. 25% of 350 = <u>87.5</u>
   g. 35% of 1100 = <u>385</u>
   h. 100% of 125 = <u>125</u>
   i. 101% of 520 = <u>525.2</u>
   j. 110% of 130 = <u>143</u>
   k. 120% of 122 = <u>146.4</u>
   l. 125% of 250 = <u>312.5</u>
   m. 140% of 9100 = <u>12740</u>
   n. 200% of 240 = <u>480</u>
   o. 300% of 120 = <u>360</u>
   p. A% of M = $\underline{\dfrac{AM}{100}}$

4. His score $\dfrac{130}{200} = \dfrac{65}{100} = 65\%$

5. $\dfrac{17}{20} = 0.85 = 18\%$

6. Her score $\dfrac{70}{80} = 0.875 = 87.5\%$

7.
$$P_{shaded} = \frac{\left(\frac{90}{100}x\right) \cdot \left(\frac{90}{100}x\right)}{x^2} = \frac{81}{100} = 81\%$$
$$P_{NotShaded} = 100 - 81 = 19\%$$

8.
$$P_{NotShaded} = \frac{\pi\left(\frac{x}{2}\right)^2}{x^2} = \frac{\pi}{4} \approx 0.785 = 78.5\%$$
$$P_{Shaded} = 100 - 78.5 = 21.5\%$$

9.
$$A_{Big} = xy$$
$$A_{small} = \left(\frac{40}{100}x\right)\left(\frac{60}{100}x\right) = \frac{24}{100}xy$$
$$P_{NotShaded} = \frac{\left(\frac{24}{100}xy\right)}{xy} = \frac{24}{100} = 24\%$$
$$P_{Shaded} = 100 - 24 = 76\%$$

10.

a.
$$P_{Brown} = \frac{15}{80} = 0.1875 = 18.75\%$$
$$White = \frac{15}{100} \cdot 80 = 12\, cookies$$
$$P_{Black} = \frac{80 - 12 - 15}{80} = \frac{53}{80} = 0.6625 = 66.25\%$$

b.
$$P_{Brown} = \frac{13}{78} \approx 0.167 = 16.7\%$$
$$P_{White} = \frac{10}{78} \approx 0.128 = 12.8\%$$
$$P_{Black} = \frac{51}{78} = 0.654 = 65.4\%$$

11. His benefit $\dfrac{1000}{4000} = \dfrac{25}{100} = 25\%$

12. Her lost $\dfrac{1000}{4000} = \dfrac{25}{100} = 25\%$

13. The percentage of it that is shaded: 50%

14. The percentage of it that is shaded: $\dfrac{1}{8} = \dfrac{12.5}{100} = 12.5\%$

15. The percentage of the circle that is

Shaded: $\dfrac{20}{360} = \dfrac{1}{18} \approx 0.0556 = 0.556\%$ Not Shaded: $\dfrac{340}{360} = \dfrac{17}{18} \approx 0.944 = 9.44\%$

16. The percentage of the circle that is

Shaded: $\dfrac{30}{100} \cdot \dfrac{60}{100} = \dfrac{18}{100} = 18\%$ Not Shaded: 82%

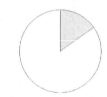

17. $\dfrac{20}{100} \cdot \dfrac{75}{100} 40 = \dfrac{600}{100} = 6$ *Students*

18. The amount. $\dfrac{10}{100} \cdot \dfrac{40}{100} x = 40$; $x = 1000$

19. The amount. $\dfrac{60}{100} \cdot \dfrac{40}{100} x = 20$; $x = \dfrac{2000}{24}$ *euros*

20. 10% of 20% of 30% of 200. $\dfrac{10}{100} \cdot \dfrac{20}{100} \cdot \dfrac{30}{100} \cdot 200 = 1.2$

21. 20% of 30% of 30% of 300. $\dfrac{20}{100} \cdot \dfrac{30}{100} \cdot \dfrac{30}{100} \cdot 300 = 1.8$

22. Find 80% of 120% of 400. $\dfrac{80}{100} \cdot \dfrac{120}{100} \cdot 400 = 384$

23. Find 90% of 130% of 70% 500. $\dfrac{90}{100} \cdot \dfrac{130}{100} \cdot \dfrac{70}{100} \cdot 500 = 409.5$

24. The amount. $\dfrac{20}{100} \cdot \dfrac{20}{100} x = 5$; $x = 125 euros$

25. The amount. $\dfrac{10}{100} \cdot \dfrac{30}{100} \cdot \dfrac{5}{100} x = 50$; $x = 33333.333... euros$

26. $20\pi = \dfrac{40}{100} \cdot \dfrac{90}{100} \pi R^2$; $\sqrt{\dfrac{2000}{36}} = R ; R \approx 7.45cm$

INCREASE OR DECREASE BY A PERCENTAGE

27. The price of a shirt is A $.

		e. 1.08A	j. 1.58A	o. 2.1A
a. 1.01A		f. 1.1A	k. 1.9A	p. 3A
b. 1.02A		g. 1.18A	l. 2A	q. 3.28A
c. 1.03A		h. 1.3A	m. 2.01A	r. 4A
d. 1.05A		i. 1.5A	n. 2.08A	

28. The price of a shirt is A $.

a. 0.99A	d. 0.95A	g. 0.82A	j. 0.42A
b. 0.98A	e. 0.92A	h. 0.7A	k. 0.1A
c. 0.97A	f. 0.90A	i. 0.5A	l. 0

m. Can't be it means negative price.

n. Can't be it means negative price.

29.

a. 1.1

b. 1.25

c. 1.072

d. 0.88

e. 0.65

f. 0.949

g. 0

h. 2

i. 3

j. $1+\dfrac{M}{100}=\dfrac{100+M}{100}$

k. $1-\dfrac{S}{100}=\dfrac{100-S}{100}$

30. $B\dfrac{110}{100}\cdot\dfrac{90}{100}=\dfrac{99}{100}B$, so overall change is 1% decrease.

31. $C\dfrac{120}{100}\cdot\dfrac{70}{100}=\dfrac{84}{100}C$ so overall change is 16% decrease.

32. $D\dfrac{80}{100}\cdot\dfrac{140}{100}=\dfrac{112}{100}D$ so overall change is 12% increase

33. $E\dfrac{70}{100}\cdot\dfrac{150}{100}=\dfrac{105}{100}E$ so the overall change is 5% increase.

34. $E\left(\dfrac{104}{100}\right)^{80}=E(1.04)^{80}$

36. $M\left(\dfrac{97.5}{100}\right)^{10}=M(0.975)^{10}$

35. $M\left(\dfrac{88}{100}\right)^{10}=M(0.88)^{10}$

37. $M\left(\dfrac{100+x}{100}\right)^{n}=M\left(1+\dfrac{x}{100}\right)^{n}$

BIGGER OR SMALLER BY A PERCENTAGE

38. Find the percentage by which:

a. 5 is bigger than 4:
$$\dfrac{5-4}{4}=\dfrac{1}{4}=0.25=25\%$$

b. 4 is smaller than 5:
$$\dfrac{5-4}{5}=\dfrac{1}{5}=0.2=20\%$$

c. 11 is bigger than 10:
$$\dfrac{11-10}{10}=\dfrac{1}{10}=0.1=10\%$$

d. 10 is smaller than 11:
$$\dfrac{11-10}{11}=\dfrac{1}{11}\approx0.091=9.1\%$$

e. 51 is bigger than 50 :
$$\dfrac{51-50}{50}=\dfrac{1}{50}=0.02=2\%$$

f. 40 is smaller than 45:
$$\dfrac{45-40}{45}=\dfrac{5}{45}\approx0.0889=8.89\%$$

g. A is bigger than B:
$$\dfrac{A-B}{B}=\dfrac{A}{B}-1$$

h. x is smaller than y:
$$\dfrac{y-x}{y}=1-\dfrac{y}{x}$$

39. Given that the long side of the shaded rectangle is 70% of x and that its short side is 60% of y. Find the percentage of the big rectangle that is shaded.

$$P_{shaded}=\dfrac{\left(\dfrac{70}{100}x\right)\cdot\left(\dfrac{60}{100}y\right)}{xy}=\dfrac{42}{100}=42\%$$

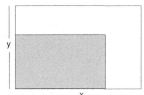

40. Given that the side length of the square is two thirds of the short side of the rectangle find:

a. The area of the shapes in terms of x.

Rectangle: $A = 3x^2$ Square: $A = \left(\dfrac{2}{3}x\right)^2 = \dfrac{4}{9}x^2$

b. The percentage of the area of the rectangle that is shaded and not shaded.

$$P_{NotShaded} = \frac{\left(\dfrac{4}{9}x^2\right)}{3x^2} = \frac{4}{27} \approx 0.148 = 14.8\%$$

$$P_{Shaded} = \frac{\left(3x^2 - \dfrac{4}{9}x^2\right)}{3x^2} = \frac{\left(\dfrac{23}{9}x^2\right)}{3x^2} = \frac{23}{27} \approx 0.852 = 85.2\%$$

c. Area of the square is <u>smaller</u> than the <u>area</u> of the rectangle.

$$A_{Smaller} = \frac{\left(3x^2 - \dfrac{4}{9}x^2\right)}{3x^2} = \frac{\left(\dfrac{23}{9}x^2\right)}{3x^2} = \frac{23}{27} \approx 0.852 = 85.2\%$$

d. <u>Perimeter</u> of the square is <u>smaller</u> than the <u>perimeter</u> of the rectangle.

$$P_{Smaller} = \frac{\left(8x - \dfrac{8}{3}x\right)}{8x} = \frac{16}{24} \approx 0.667 = 66.7\%$$

41. Given the diagram in which a rectangle is located inside a square. The side length of the square is 2x. The rectangle's long side is 80% of the side of the square. The short side of the rectangles is 30% less of the side of the square.

a. The area of the square in terms of x. $A = 4x^2$

b. Side lengths of rectangle in terms of x.

$a = \dfrac{80}{100} \cdot 2x = \dfrac{16x}{10}$ $b = \dfrac{70}{100} \cdot 2x = \dfrac{14x}{10}$

c. Area of rectangle in terms of x.

$A = \dfrac{16x}{10} \cdot \dfrac{14x}{10} = \dfrac{224x^2}{100}$

d. Using the previous parts the percentage of the area that is not shaded.

$$P_{NotShaded} = \frac{\left(\dfrac{224x^2}{100}\right)}{4x^2} = \frac{224}{400} = \frac{56}{100} = 56\%$$

e. The <u>area</u> of the square is **bigger** than the <u>area</u> of the rectangle.

$$A_{bigger} = \frac{\left(4x^2 - \dfrac{224x^2}{100}\right)}{\left(\dfrac{224x^2}{100}\right)} = \frac{176}{224} \approx 0.786 = 78.6\%$$

f. <u>Perimeter</u> of the rectangle is **smaller** than the <u>perimeter</u> of the square.

$$P_{Smaller} = \frac{8x - 6x}{8x} = \frac{1}{4} = 0.25 = 25\%$$

18

2. Ricardo drives to work 40% less than Rhona. Rhona drives to work 10% more than Alex who drives 400 km per week.

    a. How many km does Rhona drive to work per week?

$$Rhona_{drives} = \frac{110}{100} \cdot 400 = 440 km$$

    b. How many km does Ricardo drive to work per week?

$$Ricardo_{drives} = \frac{60}{100} \cdot 440 = 264 km$$

    c. By what percentage does Ricardo drive more or **less** than Alex?

$$P_{less} = \frac{(400 - 264)}{400} = \frac{136}{400} = \frac{34}{100} = 34\%$$

RATIO AND PROPORTION

42. The ratio between 2 and 5 is the same as between <u>40</u> and a 100.

43. The ratio between 3 and 7 is the same as between <u>15</u> and 35.

44. The ratio between 2 and 12 is the same as between 6 and <u>36</u>

45. The ratio 1:3:7 is the same as <u>2:6:14</u>

46. Divide 120 in the ratio 2:3 $\frac{120}{5} = 24;$ $\frac{2}{3} = \frac{2 \cdot 24}{3 \cdot 24} = \frac{48}{72}$

47. Divide 140 in the ratio 3:4 $\frac{140}{7} = 20;$ $\frac{3}{4} = \frac{3 \cdot 20}{4 \cdot 20} = \frac{60}{80}$

48. Divide 180 in the ratio 2:3:4 $\frac{180}{9} = 20;$ $2:3:4 = 2 \cdot 20:3 \cdot 20:4 \cdot 20 = 40:60:80$

49. Divide 360 in the ratio 2:5:8 $\frac{360}{15} = 24;$ $2:5:8 = 2 \cdot 24:5 \cdot 24:8 \cdot 24 = 48:120:192$

50. Divide 30 in the ratio 1:2:3 $\frac{30}{6} = 5;$ $1:2:3 = 1 \cdot 5:2 \cdot 5:3 \cdot 5 = 5:10:15$

51. The diagram representing an apartment has the scale 1:50. The dimensions of a bedroom in the diagram are 5 x 8 cm. Find the dimensions, perimeter and area of the bedroom.

    $Dimensions: 5:8 = 5 \cdot 50:8 \cdot 50 = 250:400$ $Area: 250 \cdot 400 = 100000 cm^2 = 10 m^2$

    $Perimeter: 2(250 + 400) = 1300 cm = 13 m$

52. The ingredients needed to make a cake half as big.

$$2:1:3 = 2 \cdot \frac{1}{2}:1 \cdot \frac{1}{2}:3 \cdot \frac{1}{2} = 1:\frac{1}{2}:\frac{3}{2}$$

53. The amount of pasta each one of the family members will eat.

    $1:1:2:2$ $\frac{600}{6} = 100$ $1 \cdot 100:1 \cdot 100:2 \cdot 100:2 \cdot 100 = 100:100:200:200$

54. The scale of a map is 1:800000. Find the real distance represented by:

    a. 1 cm $1:800000 cm = 8 km$

    b. 9 cm $1:800000 = 9:9 \cdot 800000 = 9:7200000 = 72 km$

    c. Distance in the map that represent 10km $\frac{1000000 cm}{800000} = \frac{10}{8} = 1.25 cm$

    d. Distance in the map that represent 50km $\frac{5000000 cm}{800000} = \frac{50}{8} = 6.25 cm$

1.4. – PRIME NUMBERS AND FACTORS GCD AND LCM

1. A prime number is <u>a number that can be divided only by itself and by 1</u>
2. Write 5 examples of prime numbers: <u>7, 13, 17, 19, 41</u>
3. Write 5 examples of numbers that are not prime: <u>4, 6, 9, 15, 100</u>
4. Write down the prime factors of the following numbers:

a. 3: <u>3 (prime)</u>
b. 4: <u>2,2</u>
c. 5: <u>3 (prime)</u>
d. 6: <u>2,3</u>
e. 8: <u>2,2,2</u>
f. 9: <u>3,3</u>
g. 10: <u>5, 2</u>
h. 15: <u>5, 3</u>
i. 11: <u>11</u>
j. 12: <u>3,4</u>
k. 13: <u>13 (prime)</u>
l. 18: <u>2,3,3</u>
m. 20: <u>2,2,5</u>
n. 21: <u>3,7</u>
o. 22: <u>11, 2</u>
p. 23: <u>23 (prime)</u>

q. 24: <u>2,2,2,3</u>
r. 25: <u>5, 5</u>
s. 26: <u>13, 2</u>
t. 27: <u>3,3,3</u>
u. 28: <u>7,2,2</u>
v. 29: <u>29 (prime)</u>
w. 30: <u>2,3,5</u>
x. 40: <u>2,2,2,5</u>
y. 45: <u>3,3,5</u>
z. 52: <u>2,2,13</u>
aa. 66: <u>2,3,11</u>
bb. 70: <u>2,5,7</u>
cc. 76: <u>2,2,19</u>
dd. 78: <u>2,3,13</u>
ee. 80: <u>2,2,2,2,5</u>
ff. 81: <u>3,3,3</u>

gg. 82: <u>2,41</u>
hh. 83: <u>83 (prime)</u>
ii. 84: <u>2,2,3,7</u>
jj. 85: <u>5,17</u>
kk. 88: <u>2,2,2,11</u>
ll. 90: <u>2,3,3,5</u>
mm. 92: <u>2,2,23</u>
nn. 100: <u>2,2,5,5</u>
oo. 110: <u>2,5,11</u>
pp. 200: <u>2,2,2,5,5</u>
qq. 210: <u>3,7,2,5</u>
rr. 1000: <u>2,2,2,5,5,5</u>
ss. 550: <u>2,5, 5,11</u>
tt. 442: <u>2,13,17</u>

Write down 3 multiples of the following numbers:

1. 9: <u>18, 27, 90</u>
2. 5: <u>10,15,45</u>
3. 2: <u>5,8,20</u>
4. 23: <u>46, 69, 92</u>
5. 25: <u>100, 125, 2500</u>
6. 20: <u>100, 120, 2000</u>
7. 10: <u>20, 30, 1000</u>
8. 150: <u>300, 3000, 450</u>

GREATEST COMMON DIVISOR (GCD)

5. The greatest common divisor of 6 and 8: <u>2</u>
6. The greatest common divisor of 7 and 9: <u>1</u>
7. The greatest common divisor of 8 and 12: <u>4</u>
8. The greatest common divisor of 12 and 10: <u>2</u>
9. Find the greatest common divisor of 9 and 15: <u>3</u>
10. Find the greatest common divisor of 18 and 20: <u>2</u>
11. Find the greatest common divisor of 30 and 25: <u>5</u>
12. The greatest common divisor of 120 and 20: <u>20</u>
13. The greatest common divisor of 42 and 14: <u>14</u>
14. The greatest common divisor of 100 and 13: <u>1</u>
15. The greatest common divisor of 22 and 20: <u>2</u>
16. The greatest common divisor of 220 and 310:
$$220 = 2^2 \cdot 5 \cdot 11; \quad 310 = 2 \cdot 5 \cdot 31 \qquad \underline{\text{so GCD is 10}}$$
17. The greatest common divisor of 68 and 90:
$$68 = 2^2 \cdot 17; \quad 90 = 2 \cdot 3^2 \cdot 5 \qquad \underline{\text{so GCD is 2.}}$$
18. The greatest common divisor of 512 and 360:
$$512 = 2^9; \quad 360 = 2^3 \cdot 3^2 \cdot 5 \qquad \underline{\text{so GCD is 8}}$$
19. The greatest common divisor of 640 and 312:
$$640 = 2^7 \cdot 5; \quad 312 = 2^3 \cdot 39 \qquad \underline{\text{so GCD is 8}}$$

LEAST COMMON MULTIPLE (LCM)

20. Find the least common multiple of 6 and 8: $2^3 \cdot 3 = 24$

21. Find the least common multiple of 7 and 9: $7 \cdot 3^2 = 63$

22. Find the least common multiple of 12 and 8: $2^3 \cdot 3 = 24$

23. Find the least common multiple of 15 and 14: $2 \cdot 7 \cdot 3 \cdot 5 = 210$

24. Find the least common multiple of 18 and 10: $2 \cdot 3^2 \cdot 5 = 90$

25. The least common multiple of 12 and 10: $2^2 \cdot 3 \cdot 5 = 60$

26. The least common multiple of 120 and 20: $2^3 \cdot 3 \cdot 5 = 120$

27. The least common multiple of 42 and 14: $2 \cdot 3 \cdot 7 = 42$

28. The least common multiple of 100 and 13: $2^2 \cdot 5^2 \cdot 13 = 1300$

29. The least common multiple of 22 and 20: $2^2 \cdot 5 \cdot 11 = 220$

30. The least common multiple of 220 and 310: $2^2 \cdot 5 \cdot 11 \cdot 31 = 6820$

     $220 = 2^2 \cdot 5 \cdot 11; \quad 310 = 2 \cdot 5 \cdot 31$

31. The least common multiple of 68 and 90: $2^2 \cdot 3^2 \cdot 5 \cdot 17 = 3060$

     $68 = 2^2 \cdot 17; \quad 90 = 2 \cdot 3^2 \cdot 5$

32. The least common multiple of 512 and 360: $2^9 \cdot 3^2 \cdot 5 = 23040$

     $512 = 2^9; \quad 360 = 2^3 \cdot 3^2 \cdot 5$

33. The least common multiple of 640 and 312: $2^7 \cdot 5 \cdot 39 = 24960$

     $640 = 2^7 \cdot 5; \quad 312 = 2^3 \cdot 39$

1.5. – TYPES OF NUMBERS

Natural Numbers (N): $N = \{1, 2, 3, 4...\}$

Integers (Z): $Z = \{...-4, -3, -2, -1, 0, 1, 2, 3, 4...\}$

Rational Numbers (Q): $Q = \{\dfrac{a}{b}, a, b \in Z\}$

Numbers that **can** be written as <u>fractions</u> being both the numerator and the denominator <u>integers</u>.

Examples: $\dfrac{1}{1}, \dfrac{2}{3}, \dfrac{-7}{3}, \dfrac{4}{-1}, \dfrac{0}{2}, 0.55, 0.121212...$

Irrational Numbers (Q'): $Q' \neq \{\dfrac{a}{b}, a, b \in Z\}$ Numbers that <u>cannot</u> be written as fractions, being both the <u>numerator</u> and the <u>denominator</u> integers.

Examples: $\pi, \sqrt{2}, e...$

Real Numbers (R): $R = Q + Q'$ (Rationals and Irrationals)

Exercises:

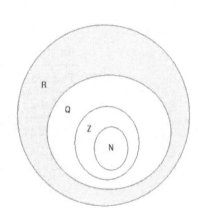

1. Natural numbers are contained in the <u>Integer</u> numbers.
2. Integer numbers are contained in the <u>Rational</u> numbers
3. Rational numbers are contained in the <u>Real</u> numbers.
4. Irrational numbers are located <u>in the outermost ring</u>.
5. Shade the area in which the irrational numbers are located:
6. True or False:
   a. All Natural numbers are Integers: <u>True</u>
   b. All Real numbers are Natural: <u>False</u>
   c. All Rational numbers are Real: <u>True</u>
   d. All Real numbers are Rational: <u>False</u>
   e. All Integer numbers are Rational: <u>True</u>
   f. All Real numbers are Irrational: <u>False</u>
   g. Some Irrational numbers are Real and some are not: <u>False</u>
   h. Some Irrational numbers are Integers: <u>False</u>
   i. Some integers are negative: <u>True</u>
   j. Some Irrationals are negative: <u>True</u>
   k. Some Natural numbers are negative: <u>False</u>
7. Fill the chart with yes or no (follow the example):

Number	Natural	Integer	Rational	Real
-2	no	yes	yes	yes
Π	no	no	no	yes
$-3.121212....$	no	no	yes	yes
-15.16	no	no	yes	yes
$\sqrt{3}$	no	no	no	yes
$-2\dfrac{2}{5}$	no	no	yes	yes
$\sqrt[3]{8}$	yes	yes	yes	yes

8. Fill the numbers column with appropriate numbers and yes or no. Follow the example.

Number	Natural	Integer	Rational	Real
−1	no	yes	yes	yes
0.1	no	no	yes	yes
Does not exist	yes	yes	yes	no
$\sqrt{2}$	no	no	no	yes
$\dfrac{1}{2}$	no	no	yes	yes
0	no	yes	yes	yes
0.333...	no	no	yes	yes
Does not exist		yes	no	

4. Convert the following numbers into the form: $\dfrac{n}{m}$

1. $0.333... = \dfrac{1}{3}$

2. $1.111... = \dfrac{10}{9}$

3. $5.3 = \dfrac{53}{10}$

4. $5.2828... = \dfrac{523}{99}$

5. $-2.3535... = \dfrac{233}{99}$

6. $42.67 = \dfrac{4267}{100}$

7. $12.355355... = \dfrac{12343}{999}$

8. $-31.44 = \dfrac{-3144}{100}$

9. $0.125125... = \dfrac{125}{99}$

10. $3.22332233... = \dfrac{32230}{2930}$

11. $1115.36 = \dfrac{111536}{100}$

12. $122.53 = \dfrac{12253}{100}$

13. $1.123123... = \dfrac{1122}{999}$

14. $1.22565656... = \dfrac{12134}{9900}$

15. $1.5696969... = \dfrac{1554}{990}$

16. $5.540404040... = \dfrac{5485}{990}$

5. Given the following diagram:
Write the following numbers in the appropriate location in the diagram:

a. 2.2
b. −5
c. 3
d. $\dfrac{1}{3}$
e. 5
f. −3.3
g. 1.111…
h. $\dfrac{1}{\sqrt{3}}$
i. 2π
j. $1+2\pi$
k. $\sqrt{2}+3$
l. $\dfrac{4}{2}$

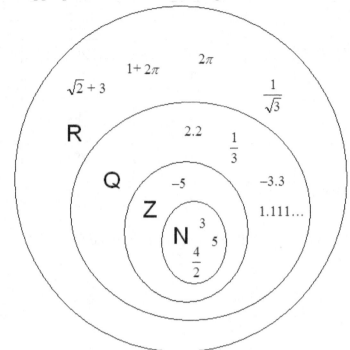

6. Circle the right option. The number −2 is:
    a. Integer and Natural.
    b. Positive
    c. Integer and Rational
    d. Natural and Real
    e. Natural and Rational
    f. None of the above

7. Circle the right option. The number 3.41414141….. is:
    a. Integer and Natural.
    b. Natural
    c. Integer and Real
    d. Rational and Integer
    e. Rational
    f. None of the above

8. Circle the right option. The number 3.41 is:
    a. Integer and Natural.
    b. Integer
    c. Rational and Real
    d. Integer and Real
    e. Rational and negative
    f. None of the above

9. Circle the right option. The number $\sqrt{31}$ is:
    a. Integer and Natural.
    b. Integer
    c. Decimal
    d. Integer and Real
    e. Rational
    f. Irrational

10. Circle the right option. The number 5 is:
    a. Natural.
    b. Integer
    c. Real
    d. Integer and Natural
    e. Rational and Natural
    f. All of the above

1.6. – ROOTS

Simplify as much as possible:

1. $\sqrt{0} = \underline{0}$

2. $\sqrt{1} = \underline{\pm 1}$

3. $\sqrt{4} = \underline{\pm 2}$

4. $\sqrt{9} = \underline{\pm 3}$

5. $\sqrt{16} = \underline{\pm 4}$

6. $\sqrt{25} = \underline{\pm 5}$

7. $\sqrt{-1} = \underline{\text{Does not exist}}$

8. $\left(\sqrt{4}\right)^2 = \underline{4}$

9. $\left(\sqrt{5}\right)^2 = \underline{5}$

10. $\left(\sqrt{532}\right)^2 = \underline{532}$

11. $\left(\sqrt{a}\right)^2 \left(\sqrt[n]{a}\right)^n = \underline{a^2}$

12. $\sqrt{0.01} = \sqrt{\dfrac{1}{100}} = \pm\dfrac{1}{10}$

13. $\sqrt{0.25} = \sqrt{\dfrac{1}{4}} = \pm\dfrac{1}{2}$

14. $\sqrt{2.25} = \sqrt{\dfrac{9}{4}} = \pm\dfrac{3}{2}$

15. $\sqrt{\dfrac{a^2}{9}} = \pm\dfrac{a}{3}$

16. $\sqrt{\dfrac{8}{200}} = \sqrt{\dfrac{1}{25}} = \dfrac{1}{5}$

17. $\sqrt{3} + \sqrt{3} = 2\sqrt{3}$

18. $\sqrt{2} + \sqrt{2} + \sqrt{2} = \underline{3\sqrt{2}}$

19. $\sqrt{2} + \sqrt{8} + \sqrt{2} = \underline{4\sqrt{2}}$

20. $\sqrt{4} + \sqrt{2} + \sqrt{8} = \underline{3\sqrt{2} + 2}$

21. $\sqrt{9} + \sqrt{12} + \sqrt{27} = \underline{6\sqrt{3} + 3}$

22. $\sqrt{50} + \sqrt{75} + \sqrt{12} = \underline{5\sqrt{2} + 7\sqrt{3}}$

23. $\sqrt{3} + \sqrt{75} = \underline{6\sqrt{3}}$

24. $\sqrt{32} - \sqrt{128} = \underline{-4\sqrt{2}}$

25. $\sqrt{27} + \sqrt{81} + \sqrt{48} = \underline{7\sqrt{3} + 9}$

26. $\sqrt{200} + \sqrt{50} - \sqrt{18} = \underline{12\sqrt{2}}$

27. $\sqrt{20} + \sqrt{80} - \sqrt{125} = \underline{-\sqrt{5}}$

28. $\sqrt{10}\sqrt{10} = \underline{10}$

29. $\sqrt{2}\sqrt{8} = \underline{4}$

30. $\sqrt{3}\sqrt{9}\sqrt{3} = \underline{9}$

31. $\dfrac{\sqrt{200}}{\sqrt{2}} = \underline{10}$

32. $\dfrac{\sqrt{72}}{\sqrt{2}} = \underline{6}$

33. $\dfrac{\sqrt{75}}{\sqrt{5}} = \underline{\sqrt{15}}$

34. $\sqrt{3}\dfrac{\sqrt{24}}{\sqrt{2}} = \underline{6}$

35. $\sqrt{a}\sqrt{a} = a$

36. $\sqrt{a} + \sqrt{a} = 2\sqrt{a}$

Rationalize the denominator:

37. $\dfrac{1}{\sqrt{2}} = \left(\dfrac{1}{\sqrt{2}}\right) \cdot \left(\dfrac{\sqrt{2}}{\sqrt{2}}\right) = \dfrac{\sqrt{2}}{2}$

38. $\left(\dfrac{3}{\sqrt{5}+1}\right) \cdot \left(\dfrac{\sqrt{5}-1}{\sqrt{5}-1}\right) = \dfrac{3\left(\sqrt{5}-1\right)}{4}$

39. $\left(\dfrac{-7}{\sqrt{5}-2}\right) \cdot \left(\dfrac{\sqrt{5}+2}{\sqrt{5}+2}\right) = \dfrac{7\left(\sqrt{5}+2\right)}{1} = 7\left(\sqrt{5}+2\right)$

40. $\dfrac{\sqrt{2}+3}{-5}$, Denominator already rational

41. $\left(\dfrac{\sqrt{2}+3}{\sqrt{6}-5}\right)\cdot\left(\dfrac{\sqrt{6}+5}{\sqrt{6}+5}\right)=\dfrac{\left(\sqrt{2}+3\right)\left(\sqrt{6}+5\right)}{-19}$

42. $\left(\dfrac{\sqrt{2}}{\sqrt{6}+\sqrt{3}}\right)\cdot\left(\dfrac{\sqrt{6}-\sqrt{3}}{\sqrt{6}-\sqrt{3}}\right)=\dfrac{\sqrt{2}\left(\sqrt{6}-\sqrt{3}\right)}{3}$

43. $\left(\dfrac{\sqrt{2}-1}{2\sqrt{5}-\sqrt{3}}\right)\cdot\left(\dfrac{2\sqrt{5}+\sqrt{3}}{2\sqrt{5}+\sqrt{3}}\right)=\dfrac{\left(\sqrt{2}-1\right)\left(2\sqrt{5}+\sqrt{3}\right)}{17}$

44. $\left(\dfrac{-1}{2\sqrt{a}+b}\right)\cdot\left(\dfrac{2\sqrt{a}-b}{2\sqrt{a}-b}\right)=\left(\dfrac{-2\sqrt{a}+b}{4a-b^2}\right)$

45. $\left(\dfrac{3\sqrt{a}-2b}{2\sqrt{a}+\sqrt{b}}\right)\left(\dfrac{3\sqrt{a}-2b}{2\sqrt{a}-\sqrt{b}}\right)=\left(\dfrac{9a-12b\sqrt{a}+4b^2}{4a-b}\right)$

Rationalize the numerator:

46. $\dfrac{\sqrt{4}}{\sqrt{5}}=\dfrac{2}{\sqrt{5}}$

47. $\left(\dfrac{3-\sqrt{2}}{\sqrt{5}+1}\right)\cdot\left(\dfrac{3+\sqrt{2}}{3+\sqrt{2}}\right)=\dfrac{7}{\left(\sqrt{5}+1\right)\left(3+\sqrt{2}\right)}$

48. $\left(\dfrac{-7}{\sqrt{5}-2}\right)$, Numerator already rational

49. $\left(\dfrac{\sqrt{2}+3}{\sqrt{6}-5}\right)\left(\dfrac{\sqrt{2}-3}{\sqrt{2}-3}\right)=\dfrac{-7}{\left(\sqrt{6}-5\right)\left(\sqrt{2}-3\right)}$

50. $\left(\dfrac{\sqrt{2}}{\sqrt{x}+\sqrt{3}}\right)\cdot\left(\dfrac{\sqrt{2}}{\sqrt{2}}\right)=\dfrac{2}{\sqrt{2}\left(\sqrt{x}+\sqrt{3}\right)}$

51. $\left(\dfrac{\sqrt{b}-a}{2\sqrt{a}-\sqrt{3}}\right)\cdot\left(\dfrac{\sqrt{b}+a}{\sqrt{b}+a}\right)=\dfrac{b-a^2}{\left(2\sqrt{a}-\sqrt{3}\right)\left(\sqrt{b}+a\right)}$

52. $\left(\dfrac{-3\sqrt{7}+8}{2\sqrt{5}+7}\right)\cdot\left(\dfrac{-3\sqrt{7}-8}{-3\sqrt{7}-8}\right)=\dfrac{-1}{\left(2\sqrt{5}+7\right)\left(-3\sqrt{7}-8\right)}$

53. $\left(\dfrac{\sqrt{a}-2\sqrt{b}}{2\sqrt{a}+\sqrt{b}}\right)\cdot\left(\dfrac{\sqrt{a}+2\sqrt{b}}{2\sqrt{a}+\sqrt{b}}\right)=\left(\dfrac{a-4b}{4a+4\sqrt{ab}+b}\right)=$

1.7. – INTERVAL NOTATION AND INEQULITIES

1. Represent the following Intervals on the real line:

   a. $x \in (2, 5]$

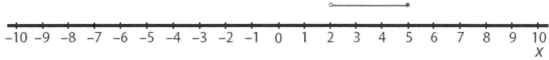

   b. $x \in (3,6)$

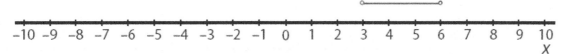

   c. $x \in [-5,9]$

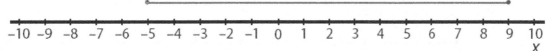

   d. $x \in [-8,-1)$

   e. $x \in [-\infty,-1)$

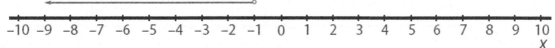

   f. $x \in [-\infty,6]$

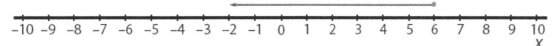

   g. $x \in (6, \infty]$

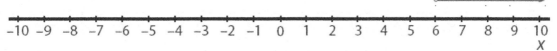

   h. $\{\, x \mid 7 < x < 9\}$

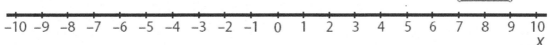

   i. $\{\, x \mid -7 < x < -2\}$

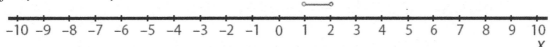

   j. $\{\, x \mid 1 < x < 2\}$

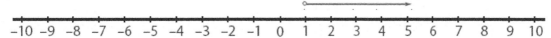

   k. $\{\, x \mid \infty < x < 2\}$ Not Possible

   l. $\{\, x \mid 1 < x < \infty\,\}$

2. Write each one of the Intervals using all types of notations:

a. $x \in (4, 5) = 4 \leq x \leq 5$

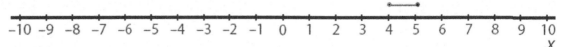

b. $x \in (-\infty, 5) = x < 5$

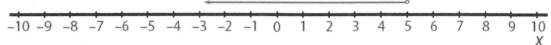

c. $x \in (4, 5) = 4 < x < 5$

d. $x \in (3, \infty] = 3 < x$

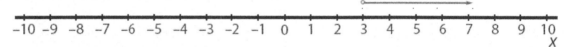

e. $x \in]{-}5,9] = -5 < x \leq 9$

f. $x \in [-8,-1[= -8 \leq x < -1$

g. $\{ x \mid 7 < x < 9 \} = x \in (7, 9)$

h. $\{ x \mid -7 < x < -2 \} = x \in (-7, -2)$

3. Solve the following inequalities and shade the solution on the given diagram:

a.
$-x \leq 3$
$x \geq -3$

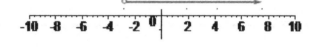

b.
$5 - x \leq 2$
$x \geq 3$

c.
$8 - 2x \leq 3$
$x \geq \dfrac{5}{2}$

d.
$-2x \leq 4 + x$
$x \geq -\dfrac{4}{3}$

e.
$7 + x \leq x + 3$ Never
$7 \leq 3$

f. $-2x \leq 2x+1$

$x \geq -\dfrac{1}{4}$

g. $-2x \leq 2x$

$x \geq 0$

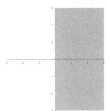

h. $-5x+3 \leq 2x-1$

$x \geq \dfrac{4}{7}$

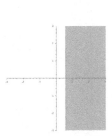

i. $7x \leq 4+7x+1$

$0 \leq 5, \forall x \in \mathbb{R}$

j. $\dfrac{x}{2} \leq x+1$

$x \geq -2$

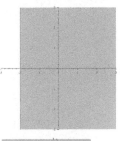

k. $\dfrac{x}{3} \leq \dfrac{x}{6}+1$

$x \leq 6$

l. $\dfrac{x-4}{6} \leq x-1$

$x \geq \dfrac{2}{5}$

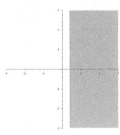

m. $\dfrac{2-x}{3} \leq \dfrac{x}{5}-3$

$x \geq \dfrac{55}{8}$

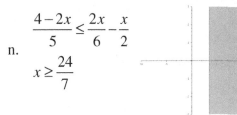

n. $\dfrac{4-2x}{5} \leq \dfrac{2x}{6}-\dfrac{x}{2}$

$x \geq \dfrac{24}{7}$

o. $\dfrac{-2x}{5}-3 \leq \dfrac{x-2}{4}-\dfrac{x-1}{2}$

$x \geq -20$

p. $\dfrac{y+4}{6} \leq y-1$

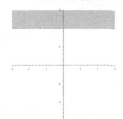

q. $\dfrac{2-2y}{3} \leq \dfrac{y}{4}-1$

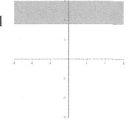

r. $\dfrac{4-y}{5} \leq \dfrac{y}{2}-y$

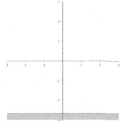

s. $\dfrac{-2y}{5} - 1 \le y - \dfrac{y-1}{2}$

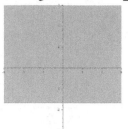

$-2 \le 2x \le 1$

t. $-1 \le x \le \dfrac{1}{2}$

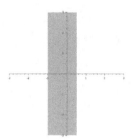

$-8 \le \dfrac{-6x+3}{4} \le 7$

u. $\dfrac{35}{6} \ge x \ge -\dfrac{25}{6}$

4. Solve the inequalities:

$-2 \le -\dfrac{5y}{3} + y \le 0$

a. $-6 \le -2y \le 0$

$3 \ge y \ge 0$

$-3 \le -\dfrac{4x}{3} + x \le 0$

b. $-9 \le -x \le 0$

$9 \ge x \ge 0$

$-2 \le -\dfrac{5-y}{3} + \dfrac{y}{2} + 1 \le 1$

$-12 \le -10 + 2y + 3y \le 0$

c. $-2 \le 5y \le 10$

$-\dfrac{2}{5} \le 5y \le 2$

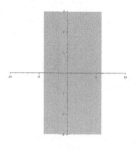

$-10 \le 4y + 2 \le 9$

v. $-3 \le y \le \dfrac{7}{4}$

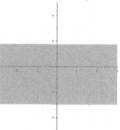

$0 \le \dfrac{y+2}{3} \le 2$

w. $-2 \le y \le 4$

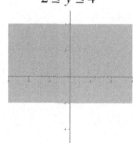

$-3 \le \dfrac{x}{6} - \dfrac{5x}{3} \le 0$

d. $-18 \le x - 10x \le 0$

$-18 \le -9x \le 0$

$2 \ge x \ge 0$

$-1 \le \dfrac{x}{8} - \dfrac{5x+1}{2} + \dfrac{x}{4} \le 1$

$-8 \le x - 20x - 4 + 2x \le 8$

e. $-4 \le -17x \le 12$

$\dfrac{4}{17} \ge x \ge -\dfrac{12}{17}$

$0 \le \dfrac{x}{6} - \dfrac{5x+2}{3} + \dfrac{x}{4} \le 2$

$0 \le 2x - 20x - 8 - 3x \le 24$

f. $8 \le 21x \le 32$

$\dfrac{8}{21} \le 21x \le \dfrac{32}{21}$

5.

   a. Solve $2x \leq 2$ $x \leq 1$ b. Solve $-x < -2$. $x \geq 2$

   c. Represent both solutions on the real line:

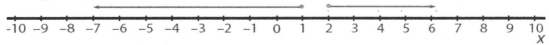

   d. State their intersection: <u>None</u>

5.

   a. Solve $2x - 2 \leq 2$ $x \leq 2$ b. Solve $-3x + 1 > -2$. $x < 1$

   c. Represent both solutions on the real line:

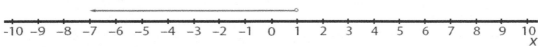

   d. State their intersection: $x \in (-\infty, 1)$

6.

   a. Solve $x - 2 \leq -5$ $x \leq -3$ b. Solve $-2x + 14 \leq -2$. $x \geq 8$

   c. Represent both solutions on the real line:

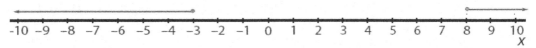

   d. State their intersection: <u>None</u>

7.

   a. Solve $3x - 7 \leq 2$ $x < 3$ b. Solve $-x < -2$. $x > 2$

   c. Represent both solutions on the real line:

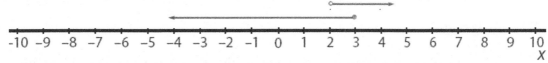

   d. State their intersection: $x \in (2, 3]$

8.

   a. Solve $5x - 2 \leq 2$ $x \leq \dfrac{4}{5}$ b. Solve $-2x + 1 > -2$. $x < \dfrac{3}{2}$

   c. Represent both solutions on the real line:

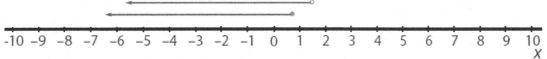

   d. State their intersection: $x \in (-\infty, \dfrac{4}{5}]$

9.

   a. Solve $5x - 2 \leq -12$ $x \leq -2$ b. Solve $-2x - 3 \leq -2$. $x \geq -\dfrac{1}{2}$

   c. Represent both solutions on the real line:

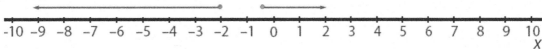

   d. State their intersection: <u>None</u>

1.8. – EXPONENTS

Product:

$a^0 = 1$

$a^1 = a$

$a^2 = a \times a$

$a^3 = a \times a \times a$

...

$a^3 a^2 = a \cdot a \cdot a \bullet a \cdot a = a^5$

$$a^m a^n = a^{m+n}$$

Division:

$\dfrac{a^5}{a^3} = \dfrac{a \cdot a \cdot a \cdot a \cdot a}{a \cdot a \cdot a} = \dfrac{a \cdot a}{1} = a^2$

$$\dfrac{a^m}{a^n} = a^{m-n}$$

$\dfrac{a^2}{a^5} = \dfrac{a \cdot a}{a \cdot a \cdot a \cdot a \cdot a} = \dfrac{1}{a \cdot a \cdot a} = \dfrac{1}{a^3} = a^{-3}$ **Power:**

$(a^2)^3 = (a^2)(a^2)(a^2) = a^6$

$$(a^m)^n = a^{mn}$$

$\left(\dfrac{a^2}{b}\right)^3 = \left(\dfrac{a^2}{b}\right)\left(\dfrac{a^2}{b}\right)\left(\dfrac{a^2}{b}\right) = \left(\dfrac{a^6}{b^3}\right)$

$$\left(\dfrac{a^m}{b^k}\right)^n = \left(\dfrac{a^{mn}}{b^{kn}}\right)$$

Radicals:

$(a^3)^{\frac{1}{2}} = a^{\frac{3}{2}} = \sqrt[2]{a^3} = \sqrt{a^3}$

$(a^4)^{\frac{1}{7}} = a^{\frac{4}{7}} = \sqrt[7]{a^4}$

$$(a^m)^{\frac{1}{n}} = a^{\frac{m}{n}} = \sqrt[n]{a^m}$$

Exercises

Write in all possible forms and evaluate without using a calculator (follow example):

1. $4^{-1} = \dfrac{1}{4} = 0.25$

2. $10^0 = \underline{1}$

3. $10^1 = \underline{10}$

4. $10^3 = \underline{1000}$

5. $10^{-1} = \dfrac{1}{10} = 0.1$

6. $10^{-2} = \dfrac{1}{100} = 0.01$

7. $10^{-3} = \dfrac{1}{1000} = 0.001$

8. $10^{-4} \quad \dfrac{1}{10000} = 0.0001$

9. $2^0 = 1$

10. $2^1 = 2$

11. $2^{-1} = \dfrac{1}{2} = 0.5$

12. $2^{-2} = \dfrac{1}{2^2} = \dfrac{1}{4} = 0.25$

13. $2^{-3} = \dfrac{1}{2^3} = \dfrac{1}{8} = 0.125$

14. $2^{-4} = \dfrac{1}{2^4} = \dfrac{1}{16} = 0.0625$

15. $(-1)^0 = \underline{1}$

16. $-1^0 = -1$

17. $(-1)^1 = -1$

18. $-1^1 = -1$

19. $(-1)^{-1} = \dfrac{1}{-1} = -1$

20. $-1^2 = -1$

21. $(-1)^2 = 1$

22. $-1^2 = -1$

23. $(-1)^{-2} = \dfrac{1}{(-1)^2} = \dfrac{1}{1} = 1$

24. $-1^{-2} = -\dfrac{1}{1^2} = -\dfrac{1}{1} = -1$

25. $(-3)^0 = 1$

26. $(-3)^1 = -3$

27. $-3^1 = -3$

28. $(-3)^2 = 9$

29. $-3^2 = -9$

30. $(-3)^{-1} = \dfrac{1}{(-3)^1} = \dfrac{1}{-3} = -\dfrac{1}{3}$

31. $-3^{-1} = -\dfrac{1}{3^1} = -\dfrac{1}{3}$

32. $(-3)^{-2} = \dfrac{1}{(-3)^2} = \dfrac{1}{9}$

33. $-3^{-2} = -\dfrac{1}{3^2} = -\dfrac{1}{9}$

34. $9^{\frac{1}{2}} = \sqrt{9} = \pm 3$

35. $16^{\frac{3}{4}} = \left(2^4\right)^{\frac{3}{4}} = 2^3 = 8$

36. $(3^{-1})^2 = 3^{-2} = \dfrac{1}{3^2} = \dfrac{1}{9}$

37. $(-8^{-3})^{\frac{2}{3}}$

$(-1)^{\frac{2}{3}}\left(2^{-9}\right)^{\frac{2}{3}} = \sqrt[3]{(-1)^2}\left(2^{-6}\right) = \dfrac{1}{64}$

38. $27^{-\frac{4}{3}} = 3^{-4} = \dfrac{1}{81} =$

39. $125^{-\frac{1}{3}} = 5^{-1} = \dfrac{1}{5} =$

40. $16^{\frac{3}{4}} = 2^3 = 8 =$

41. $(3^{-1})^2 = 3^{-2} = \dfrac{1}{9} =$

42. $(-8^{-3})^{\frac{2}{3}} = (-1)^{\frac{2}{3}} \cdot (8^{-3})^{\frac{2}{3}} = 1 \cdot 8^{-2} = \dfrac{1}{64}$

43. $(-27^{-1})^{\frac{2}{3}} = (-1)^{\frac{2}{3}} \cdot (27^{-1})^{\frac{2}{3}} = 1 \cdot 3^{-2} = \dfrac{1}{9}$

44. $(16^{-1})^{-\frac{3}{2}} = (2^{-4})^{-\frac{3}{2}} = 2^6 = 64$

45. $\left(\dfrac{1}{2}\right)^0 = 1$

46. $\left(\dfrac{1}{2}\right)^1 = \dfrac{1}{2}$

47. $\left(\dfrac{1}{2}\right)^{-1} = \dfrac{1}{\left(\dfrac{1}{2}\right)} = 2$

48. $\left(\dfrac{1}{2}\right)^2 = \dfrac{1}{4}$

49. $\left(\dfrac{1}{2}\right)^{-2} = \dfrac{1}{\left(\dfrac{1}{2}\right)^2} = 4$

50. $\left(\dfrac{3}{5}\right)^0 = 1$

51. $\left(\dfrac{3}{4}\right)^1 = \dfrac{3}{4}$

52. $\left(\dfrac{2}{5}\right)^{-1} = \dfrac{1}{\left(\dfrac{2}{5}\right)} = \dfrac{5}{2}$

53. $\left(\dfrac{5}{11}\right)^2 = \dfrac{25}{121}$

54. $\left(\dfrac{a}{b}\right)^{-1} = \dfrac{1}{\left(\dfrac{a}{b}\right)} = \dfrac{b}{a}$

55. $\left(\dfrac{1}{b}\right)^{-1} = \dfrac{1}{\left(\dfrac{1}{b}\right)} = b$

56. $b^{-1} = \dfrac{1}{b}$

57. $\left(\dfrac{-11}{2}\right)^{-2} = \dfrac{4}{121}$

58. $\left(\dfrac{3}{-2}\right)^{1} = -\dfrac{3}{2}$

59. $\left(\dfrac{-12}{\sqrt{2}}\right)^{-1} = -\dfrac{\sqrt{2}}{12}$

60. $\left(\dfrac{5\sqrt{2}}{11}\right)^{2} = \dfrac{50}{121}$

61. $\left(\dfrac{-2\sqrt{5}}{2}\right)^{-2} = \dfrac{1}{5}$

62. $\left(\dfrac{3+5\sqrt{2}}{-2}\right)^{2} = \dfrac{53+30\sqrt{2}}{4}$

63. $\left(\dfrac{-12}{2-\sqrt{2}}\right)^{-2} = \dfrac{6-4\sqrt{2}}{144}$

64. $\left(\dfrac{5+\sqrt{2}}{11}\right)^{2} = \dfrac{27+10\sqrt{2}}{121}$

65. $\left(\dfrac{-2-\sqrt{5}}{2+\sqrt{2}}\right)^{-2} = \dfrac{9+4\sqrt{5}}{6+4\sqrt{2}}$

66. $\left(\dfrac{-27}{8}\right)^{\frac{2}{3}} = \dfrac{9}{4}$

67. $\left(\dfrac{16}{9}\right)^{\frac{3}{4}} = \left(\dfrac{2^4}{3^2}\right)^{\frac{3}{4}} = \dfrac{2^3}{3^{\frac{3}{2}}} = \dfrac{8}{\sqrt{27}}$

68. $\left(\dfrac{1}{2}\right)^{\frac{3}{2}} =$

69. $\left(\dfrac{9}{16}\right)^{\frac{1}{2}} =$

70. $\left(\dfrac{8}{27}\right)^{-\frac{1}{3}} =$

71. $a^{-2} =$

72. $a^{-\frac{1}{2}} =$

73. $a^{-\frac{2}{7}} =$

74. $5^{27}5^{-29} = 5^{-2} = \dfrac{1}{25}$

75. $4^{27}2^{-49} = 2^5 = 32$

76. $9^{12}3^{-20} = 3^4 = 81$

77. $a^7a^{-9} =$

78. $(-125)^{\frac{2}{3}} =$

79. $(-125)^{\frac{2}{3}} =$

$(-1)^{\frac{2}{3}}(5^3)^{\frac{2}{3}} = \sqrt[3]{(-1)^2}\cdot 5^2 = \sqrt[3]{1}\cdot 5^2 = 25$

80. $\dfrac{5^{10}}{5^2} = 5^8$

81. $\dfrac{3^1}{9^{\frac{1}{2}}}3^{-\frac{1}{2}} = 3^{1-\frac{1}{2}-1} = 3^{-\frac{1}{2}} = \dfrac{1}{\sqrt{3}}$

82. $\dfrac{\sqrt{2}\cdot 4^2}{2^{\frac{3}{4}}}2^{-\frac{1}{2}} = 2^{\frac{1}{2}+4-\frac{1}{2}-\frac{3}{4}} = 2^{\frac{13}{4}}$

83. $\dfrac{a^{-1}}{a^{-2}} = a$

84. $\sqrt{\dfrac{a^{-10}}{a^{-12}}} = a$

85. $\sqrt{\sqrt{a}} = a^{\frac{1}{4}}$

86. $\sqrt{a\sqrt{a}} = \sqrt{a^{\frac{1}{2}+1}} = a^{\frac{3}{4}}$

87. $a\sqrt[3]{\sqrt{a}} = a^{1+\frac{1}{6}} = a^{\frac{7}{6}}$

88. $\dfrac{1}{\sqrt[4]{\sqrt{\sqrt{a}}}} = a^{-\frac{1}{16}}$

89. $\sqrt{\sqrt{\sqrt[7]{a^2}}} = a^{\frac{1}{14}}$

90. $\sqrt[3]{\sqrt{a\sqrt{a^2}}} = a^{\frac{1}{4}}$

91. $\dfrac{2\sqrt{a}}{\sqrt{2a}} = \dfrac{2}{\sqrt{2}} = \sqrt{2}$

92. $\dfrac{\sqrt{a}}{\sqrt[3]{a}} = a^{\frac{1}{2}-\frac{1}{6}} = a^{\frac{1}{3}}$

93. $\dfrac{a\sqrt{a}}{\sqrt[5]{a}} = a^{\frac{3}{2}-\frac{1}{10}} = a^{\frac{7}{5}}$

94. $\dfrac{\sqrt{8}\sqrt{a}}{\sqrt{2a}} = 2a^{-\frac{1}{2}}$

95. $\sqrt{\dfrac{\sqrt{a}a^{-1}}{a\sqrt{a^{-2}}}} = a^{-\frac{1}{4}}$

96. $\dfrac{a}{\sqrt{2a^{-1}}} = \dfrac{a^{\frac{3}{2}}}{\sqrt{2}}$

97. $\dfrac{\sqrt{\dfrac{1}{a}}}{\sqrt{aa^{-2}}} = a^0 = 1$

98. $\left(\dfrac{2}{5}\right)^3 \times \left(\dfrac{5}{3}\right)^3 = \dfrac{2^3 5^3}{5^3 3^3} = \dfrac{8}{27}$

99. $\left(\dfrac{4}{7}\right)^2 \div \left(\dfrac{9}{7}\right)^2 = \dfrac{2^4 7^2}{7^2 3^4} = \dfrac{16}{81}$

100. $\left(\dfrac{2}{5}\right)^3 \cdot \left(\dfrac{3}{5}\right)^{-4} = \dfrac{2^3 3^{-4}}{5^3 5^{-4}} = \dfrac{8 \cdot 5}{81} =$

$= \dfrac{40}{81}$

101. $\left(\dfrac{3}{4}\right)^5 \div \left(\dfrac{9}{64}\right)^2 = \dfrac{3^5 \cdot 2^{12}}{2^{10}3^4} = 3 \cdot 2^2 = 12$

102. $\left(\dfrac{7}{5}\right)^7 \div \left(\dfrac{49}{125}\right)^3 = \dfrac{7^7 \cdot 5^6}{5^7 7^6} = \dfrac{7}{5}$

103. $\left(\dfrac{2^{-3}}{3^{-2}}\right)^3 \cdot \left(\dfrac{4}{27}\right)^2 = \dfrac{2^{-9} \cdot 2^4}{3^{-6}3^6} =$

$= 2^{-5} = \dfrac{1}{32}$

104. $\left(\dfrac{4^2}{5^{-1}}\right)^3 \cdot \left(\dfrac{25^{-1}}{64}\right)^2 = \dfrac{2^{12}5^{-4}}{5^{-3}2^{12}} =$

$= 5^{-1} = \dfrac{1}{5}$

105. $\left(\dfrac{3^{-5}}{4^2}\right)^2 \div \left(\dfrac{9^{-2}}{2^3}\right)^3 = \dfrac{3^{-10}2^9}{2^8 3^{-18}} =$

$= 2 \cdot 3^8$

106. $\left(\dfrac{5^4}{7^{-3}}\right)^2 \div \left(\dfrac{25^{-1}}{49}\right)^{-3} = \dfrac{5^8 5^{-6}}{7^{-6}7^6} =$

$= 5^2 = 25$

107. $2^{-1} + 2 = \dfrac{1}{2} + 2 = \dfrac{5}{2}$

108. $3^{-1} - 3^{-2} = \dfrac{1}{3} - \dfrac{1}{9} = -\dfrac{2}{9}$

109. $5^{-1} - 5^{-2} = \dfrac{1}{5} - \dfrac{1}{25} = \dfrac{4}{25}$

110. $3^{-3} + 2^{-2} = \dfrac{1}{27} + \dfrac{1}{4} = \dfrac{31}{108}$

111. $3^{-2} + 4^{-2} = \dfrac{1}{9} + \dfrac{1}{4} = \dfrac{13}{36}$

112. $7^{-2} + 2^{-2} = \dfrac{1}{49} + \dfrac{1}{4} = \dfrac{53}{196}$

113. $8^{-2} - 3^{-2} = \dfrac{1}{64} - \dfrac{1}{9} = -\dfrac{55}{576}$

114. $7^{-2} - 2^{-3} = \dfrac{1}{49} - \dfrac{1}{8} = -\dfrac{41}{392}$

115. $a^{-1} + a^{-1} = \dfrac{1}{a} + \dfrac{1}{a} = \dfrac{2}{a}$

116. $ba^{-1} + a^{-1} = \dfrac{b}{a} + \dfrac{1}{a} = \dfrac{b+1}{a}$

117. $2x^{-1} + x^{-2} = \dfrac{2}{x} + \dfrac{1}{x^2} = \dfrac{2x+1}{x^2}$

118. $a^{-1} - ba^{-1} = \dfrac{1}{a} - \dfrac{b}{a} = \dfrac{1-b}{a}$

119. $(ba)^{-1} + a^{-1} = \dfrac{1}{ab} + \dfrac{1}{a} = \dfrac{1+b}{ab}$

120. $\dfrac{1}{x} + x^{-2} = \dfrac{1}{x} + \dfrac{1}{x^2} = \dfrac{x+1}{x^2}$

121. $ba^{-1} + (ba)^{-1} = \dfrac{b}{a} + \dfrac{1}{ab} = \dfrac{b^2+1}{ab}$

122. $\dfrac{a+a}{3a} = \dfrac{2}{3}$

123. $\dfrac{2a+a}{5\sqrt{a}} = \dfrac{3}{5} a^{-\frac{1}{2}}$

124. $\dfrac{a^2 + a^3}{2a} = \dfrac{a + a^2}{2}$

125. $\dfrac{4b^{-1}a^2}{2ba^{-1}} = 2a^3 b^{-2}$

126. $\dfrac{4b^{-3}}{\sqrt{2b}} = 2^{\frac{3}{2}} b^{-\frac{7}{2}}$

127. $\dfrac{9b^{-\frac{1}{2}}a^2}{27^{-1}b^{-1}a} = 3^5 ab^{\frac{1}{2}}$

128. $\dfrac{4b^{-1}a^5 a^2}{8ba^{-1}} = 2^{-1} a^8 b^{-2}$

129. $\dfrac{\sqrt[4]{a^2} + \sqrt{a}}{\sqrt{2a}} = \dfrac{2}{\sqrt{2}} = \sqrt{2}$

130. $\dfrac{b\sqrt[3]{a} + ba^{\frac{1}{3}}}{a\sqrt{b}} = \dfrac{2ba^{\frac{1}{3}}}{a\sqrt{b}} = 2\sqrt{b}a^{-\frac{2}{3}}$

131. $\dfrac{3^{-2}}{9^{\frac{2}{3}}} 27^{\frac{5}{4}} = 3^{-2+\frac{15}{4}-2} = 3^{-\frac{1}{4}} = \dfrac{1}{\sqrt[4]{3}}$

132. $\dfrac{4^{-4}\sqrt{2}}{8^{-\frac{2}{3}}} 16^{\frac{3}{4}} = 2^{-8+\frac{1}{2}+3+2} = 2^{-\frac{5}{2}} =$

$= \dfrac{1}{\sqrt{2^5}} = \dfrac{1}{\sqrt{32}}$

133. $\sqrt{5}\,\dfrac{25^2 5^{-1}}{25^{\frac{4}{3}}} 5^{\frac{1}{4}}\sqrt[3]{5} = 5^{\frac{1}{2}+4-1+\frac{1}{4}+\frac{1}{3}-\frac{8}{3}} = 5^{\frac{17}{12}}$

134. $\dfrac{4^{-2}2^{-4}}{16^2(\sqrt[6]{16^4})} 8^{\frac{1}{4}}2^{-1} = 2^{-4-4+\frac{3}{4}-1-8-\frac{8}{3}} = 2^{-\frac{227}{12}}$

135. $x\sqrt{x}\sqrt{3} = \sqrt{3}x^{\frac{3}{2}} = \sqrt{3x^3}$

136. $x\sqrt{x} + \sqrt{2x} = x^{\frac{3}{2}} + \sqrt{2}\cdot x^{\frac{1}{2}}$

137. $\dfrac{1}{x\sqrt{x}} = x^{-\frac{3}{2}}$

138. $\dfrac{x\sqrt[3]{x}}{\sqrt{x}} = x^{1+\frac{1}{3}-\frac{1}{2}} = x^{\frac{7}{6}} = \sqrt[6]{x^7}$

139. $\dfrac{\sqrt{2x}}{x\sqrt{4x}} = \dfrac{1}{x\sqrt{2}} = 2^{-\frac{1}{2}}x^{-1}$

140. $\dfrac{\sqrt{3x}}{x+x^2} = \dfrac{\sqrt{3x}}{x(1+x)} = \dfrac{\sqrt{3}}{\sqrt{x}(1+x)}$

141. $\dfrac{\sqrt{3x}}{\sqrt[3]{3x^2}} = 3^{\frac{1}{6}}x^{-\frac{1}{6}} = \sqrt[6]{\dfrac{3}{x}}$

142. $\dfrac{\sqrt{25x^2}}{\sqrt[3]{5x^3}} = 5^{\frac{2}{3}} = \sqrt[3]{25}$

143. $s^n s^{2n} s^2 = s^{3n+2}$

144. $a^{2k}ba^3 b^{2k}a = a^{2k+4}b^{2k+1}$

145. $\dfrac{3^n}{9^n} 27^n = 3^{n+3n-2n} = 3^{2n}$

146. $\dfrac{3^{2n+1}}{81^{n-2}} 27^{2n} = 3^{2n+1+6n-4n+8} = 3^{4n+9}$

147. $\dfrac{6^n}{8^{2n}}24^{3n}=3^{n+3n}2^{n+9n-6n}=3^{4n}2^{4n}=6^{4n}$

148. $\dfrac{2^n}{8^{n+1}}16^{n-2}=2^{n+4(n-2)-3(n-1)}=2^{2n-5}$

149. $\dfrac{5^{-n}}{125^{2n-2}}5^{-n+2}=5^{-n-n+2-3(2n-2)}=5^{-8n+8}$

150. $\dfrac{12^{2n+1}}{48^{3n-1}}\div 36^{4n}=$

$3^{2n+1-8n-3n+1}2^{4n+2-8n-12n+4}=$

$3^{2-9n}2^{6-16n}$

151. $\dfrac{x^{-n}}{x^{2n-2}}x^{-n+5}=x^{-4n+7}$

152. $\dfrac{2x^{-n+1}}{2^2 x^{3n+2}}x^{n+5}=2^{-1}x^{-3n+4}$

153. $\dfrac{2yx^{-2n+3}}{2^5 y^{-1}x^{-4n+2}}x^{-2n+1}=2^{-4}x^2 y^2$

154. $\dfrac{4^2 y^2 x^{-3} z}{2^2 xz^2 y^{-1}x}x^{-2}z^2=2^2 x^{-7}y^3 z$

155. $\dfrac{4^2 y^2 (x^{-2}z^2)^{-2}}{(2^2 x)^3 z^2 y^{-1}x}x^{-2}z^2=2^{-2}x^{-1}y^3 z^{-4}$

156. $\dfrac{4^{-2}y^3 (x^{-2}z^3)^{-1}}{(2^{-3}x)^{-3}z^{-2}y^{-1}x}xz^2=2^{-13}x^5 y^4 z$

157. $\left(\dfrac{a}{b^2}\right)^2 \div \left(\dfrac{a^{-1}}{b^3}\right)^{-3}\cdot\left(\dfrac{1}{b}\right)^3=a^{-1}b^2$

158. $\left(\dfrac{ab}{b^2}\right)^{-2}\div\left(\dfrac{(2ba)^{-1}}{b^3}\right)^{-3}\cdot\left(\dfrac{2}{b}\right)^3=a^{-5}b^{-13}$

159. $\dfrac{a^{-2}b^n (a^{-2n}b^3)^{-1}}{(b^{-3n}a)^3 \sqrt{ab^{-1}}}==$

$=a^{-2+2n-3-\frac{1}{2}}b^{n-3+9n+1}=a^{-\frac{11}{2}+2n}b^{10n-2}$

160. $\dfrac{a^{-2}b^n (a^{-2n}b^2)^n}{(b^{-3n}a)^n a^{-2n}b^n}==$

$=a^{-2-2n^2-n+2n}b^{n+2n+3n^2-n}=a^{-2n^2+n-2}b^{3n^2+2n}$

161. $\dfrac{3^n a^{-2}b^n (a^{-2n}b^3)^{n+1}}{(9^n b^{-2n}a)^n a^{-2n}b^{n+2}}=$

$=3^{n-2n^2}a^{-2n^2-n-2}b^{2n^2+3n+1}$

162. $\dfrac{3^n + 3^{n+1}}{3^{n-1}}=\dfrac{3^n(1+3)}{\left(3^n\cdot\dfrac{1}{3}\right)}=12$

163. $\dfrac{4^n + 4^{n-1}}{2^{n-2}}=\dfrac{2^{2n}(1+\dfrac{1}{4})}{\left(2^n\cdot\dfrac{1}{4}\right)}=5\cdot 2^n$

164. $\dfrac{7^{2n} + 7^{2n-1}}{7^{2n-2}}=\dfrac{7^{2n}(1+\dfrac{1}{7})}{\left(7^{2n}\cdot\dfrac{1}{49}\right)}=56$

165. $\dfrac{7^{3n-1} - 7^{3n}}{7^{2n-2}}=$

$=\dfrac{7^{3n}(\dfrac{1}{7}-1)}{\left(7^{2n}\cdot\dfrac{1}{49}\right)}=-42\cdot 7^n=-6\cdot 7^{n+1}$

166. $\dfrac{3^n + 3^{n+1}}{3^{n-1} + 3^n}=\dfrac{3^n(1+3)}{3^n(\dfrac{1}{3}+1)}=3$

167. $\dfrac{2^n + 2^{n-1}}{2^{n-2} + 2^{n-1}}=\dfrac{2^n(1+\dfrac{1}{2})}{2^n(\dfrac{1}{4}+\dfrac{1}{2})}=2$

1.9. – EQUATIONS

1st Degree (Linear Equations)

1. $\dfrac{x}{12} = 5$

   $x = 60$

2. $\dfrac{x}{7} + 2 = 5$

   $x = 21$

3. $\dfrac{2x}{7} + 2 = 5 - 3x$

   $x = \dfrac{21}{23}$

4. $\dfrac{2x}{7} + \dfrac{2}{5} = -2x + 1$

   $x = \dfrac{21}{80}$

5. $\dfrac{2x-1}{x} = 3$

   $x = -1$

6. $\dfrac{x+2}{2x} = 5$

   $x = \dfrac{2}{9}$

7. $\dfrac{x-2}{2x-1} = 6$

   $x = \dfrac{4}{11}$

8. $\dfrac{2x-2}{x+1} = -2$

   $x = 0$

9. $\dfrac{2x}{7} + 1 = \dfrac{-5x}{7}$

   $x = -1$

10. $\dfrac{2x}{7} + 4 = \dfrac{3x}{2}$

    $x = \dfrac{56}{17}$

11. $\dfrac{2}{x} - 3 = \dfrac{3}{2x}$

    $x = \dfrac{1}{6}$

12. $\dfrac{2}{x-2} - 3 = \dfrac{3}{x-2}$

    $x = \dfrac{5}{3}$

13. $\dfrac{-2}{x} = \dfrac{3}{x-2}$

    $x = \dfrac{4}{5}$

14. $\dfrac{4}{x+1} = \dfrac{4}{x+2}$

    $No \quad Solution$

15. $\dfrac{2}{x+1} = \dfrac{4}{x+2}$

    $x = 0$

16. $-\dfrac{2}{2x+1} - 2 = \dfrac{4}{2x+1}$

    $x = -2$

17. $\dfrac{x}{2} - \dfrac{x}{5} = 3$

    $3x = 30$

    $x = 10$

18. $\dfrac{2}{x} + \dfrac{3}{5} = 3$

    $x = \dfrac{5}{6}$

19. $\dfrac{2x-7}{2} - \dfrac{3x}{5} = x$

    $10x - 35 - 6x = 10x$

    $x = -\dfrac{35}{6}$

20. $1 - \dfrac{1}{x} = 7 - \dfrac{3x+1}{x}$

    $x - 1 = 7x - 3x - 1$

    $x = 0, Not \quad Valid$

    $No \quad Solution$

21. $3 - \dfrac{2x}{x-2} = 7 - \dfrac{2x+1}{x-2}$

    $3x - 6 - 2x = 7x - 14 - 2x - 1$

    $x = \dfrac{9}{4}$

22. $\dfrac{2-x}{x-2} = 1$

    $x = 0$

23. $\dfrac{2-x}{x-2} = -1$

    $0 = 0, True \quad \forall x \in \mathbb{R}$

24. $\dfrac{5-7x}{3x-2} = -1 + \dfrac{5}{3x-2}$

    $5 - 7x = -3x + 2 + 5$

    $x = -\dfrac{1}{2}$

25. $\dfrac{15-x}{3-x} = 7 - \dfrac{5x}{3-x}$

    $x = \dfrac{6}{11}$

26. $3x = 2$

Isolate x

1. $\dfrac{4}{x}=\dfrac{a}{x+6}$

   $x=\dfrac{24}{a-4}$

2. $\dfrac{14}{x+2}=\dfrac{a}{x+2}-a$

   $x=-\dfrac{14+a}{a}$

3. $\dfrac{2}{x+3}-a=\dfrac{a+b}{x+3}$

   $x=\dfrac{2-b-4a}{a}$

4. $\dfrac{5}{2x+1}-3a=\dfrac{b}{2x+1}$

   $x=\dfrac{5-b-3a}{6a}$

5. $\dfrac{-2x}{a+3}=\dfrac{x+2}{2a-1}$

   $x=-\dfrac{2a+6}{5a+5}$

6. $\dfrac{-5x+1}{2a}=\dfrac{bx}{3a+2}$

   $x=\dfrac{3a+2}{15a+2ab+10}$

7. $\dfrac{a}{x+2}=\dfrac{b}{x+2}-b+1$

   $x=-\dfrac{a+b+2}{b+1}$

8. $\dfrac{b}{2x-4}-3=\dfrac{b}{2x-4}-b+1$

   $No\ \ Solution$

9. $\dfrac{1}{ax+2}=\dfrac{b}{x+a}$

   $x=\dfrac{a-2b}{ba-1}$

10. $\dfrac{1}{ax+2}=\dfrac{b}{ax+2}-3$

    $x=\dfrac{b-7}{3a}$

11. $3\dfrac{x}{ax+2}=3$

    $x=\dfrac{6}{1-3a}$

12. $-3\dfrac{2x}{ax+3}=b$

    $x=-\dfrac{3b}{ab+6}$

13. $\dfrac{2x-3}{2ax+5}=-3b$

    $x=\dfrac{3-15b}{6ab+2}$

14. $\dfrac{x}{ax+2}=\dfrac{2}{a}-3$

    $x=-\dfrac{4-6a}{3a^2-a}$

15. $\dfrac{bx}{x+2}=3-b$

    $x=\dfrac{6-2b}{2b-3}$

16. $\dfrac{b+x}{x-3}=\dfrac{b}{x-3}+a$

    $x=\dfrac{-3a}{1-a}$

17. $\dfrac{bx}{a}=2x+8$

    $x=\dfrac{8a}{b-2a}$

18. $\dfrac{ax+b}{dx+2}=c-g$

    $x=\dfrac{2g-2c+b}{dc-gd-a}$

19. $\dfrac{1}{x+2}+\dfrac{1}{b}=2$

    $x=\dfrac{3b-2}{1-2b}$

20. $\dfrac{1-a}{x}+\dfrac{2a}{x}=2b$

    $x=\dfrac{1+a}{2b}$

21. $x-\dfrac{2+ax}{b}=2x+3$

    $x=\dfrac{-3a-2}{a+b}$

22. $\dfrac{7-2ax}{x+1}=2+b$

    $x=\dfrac{5-b}{2+b+2a}$

23. $\dfrac{3-2x}{2x-3}=a$

    $3-2x=2xa-3a$

    $x=\dfrac{3+3a}{2+2a}=\dfrac{3}{2},Not\ \ Valid$

24. $\dfrac{-2}{x-1}=\dfrac{2a}{x-1}-a$

    $x=\dfrac{2+3a}{a}$

25. $\dfrac{3}{a-2x}=\dfrac{b}{2x-a}-c$

    $x=\dfrac{3+b+ac}{2c}$

26. $\dfrac{x+1}{xa}-1=\dfrac{a+1}{a^2}-1$

39

2nd degree (Quadratic equations)

a. Solve the following equations using the "complete the square method".
b. Check your answers using the quadratic formula.
c. Write the factorized expression.

1. $x^2 - 4x + 1 = 3$

$(x-2)^2 - 4 + 1 = 3$

$x = \pm\sqrt{6} + 2$

$(x-(\sqrt{6}+2))(x-(-\sqrt{6}+2)) = 0$

2. $x^2 - 4x + 1 = -3$

$(x-2)^2 - 4 + 1 = -3$

$x = 2$

$(x-2)(x-2) = 0$

3. $x^2 - 4x + 1 = -13$

$(x-2)^2 - 4 + 1 = -13$

No Solution

4. $x^2 + 6x + 2 = 2$

$(x+3)^2 - 9 + 2 = 2$

$x = 0, -6$

$(x)(x+6) = 0$

5. $x^2 + 6x + 2 = -10$

$(x+3)^2 - 9 + 2 = -10$

No Solution

6. $x^2 + 8x + 3 = -10$

$(x+4)^2 - 16 + 3 = -10$

$(x+4)^2 = 3$

$x = \pm\sqrt{3} - 4$

$\left(x-(\sqrt{3}-4)\right)\left(x-(-\sqrt{3}-4)\right) = 0$

7. $x^2 - 12x - 2 = 3$

$(x-6)^2 - 36 - 2 = 3$

$(x-6)^2 = 41$

$x = \pm\sqrt{41} + 6$

$\left(x-\left(\sqrt{41}+6\right)\right)\left(x-\left(-\sqrt{41}+6\right)\right) = 0$

8. $x^2 - 2x - 5 = 3$

$(x-1)^2 - 1 - 5 = 3$

$(x-1)^2 = 9$

$x = \pm 3 + 1$

$(x+2)(x-4) = 0$

9. $x^2 - 3x - 5 = 3$

$\left(x-\dfrac{3}{2}\right)^2 - \dfrac{9}{4} - 5 = 3$

$x = \dfrac{3}{2} \pm \dfrac{\sqrt{41}}{2}$

$\left(x-\left(\dfrac{3}{2}+\dfrac{\sqrt{41}}{2}\right)\right)\left(x-\left(\dfrac{3}{2}-\dfrac{\sqrt{41}}{2}\right)\right) = 0$

10. $x^2 - 4x - 5 = 3$

$(x-2)^2 - 4 - 5 = 3$

$(x-2)^2 = 12$

$x = \pm\sqrt{12} + 2$

$\left(x-\left(\sqrt{12}+2\right)\right)\left(x-\left(-\sqrt{12}+2\right)\right) = 0$

11. $x^2 - 3x - 3 = -3$

$\left(x - \dfrac{3}{2}\right)^2 - \dfrac{9}{4} - 3 = -3$

$x = 0, 3$

$(x)(x - 3) = 0$

12. $x^2 - 3x - 4 = -1$

$\left(x - \dfrac{3}{2}\right)^2 - \dfrac{9}{4} - 4 = -1$

$x = \dfrac{3}{2} \pm \dfrac{\sqrt{21}}{2}$

$\left(x - \left(\dfrac{3}{2} + \dfrac{\sqrt{21}}{2}\right)\right)\left(x - \left(\dfrac{3}{2} - \dfrac{\sqrt{21}}{2}\right)\right) = 0$

13. $x^2 - 7x - 5 = 3$

$\left(x - \dfrac{7}{2}\right)^2 - \dfrac{49}{4} - 5 = 3$

$x = 8, -1$

$(x + 1)(x - 8) = 0$

14. $x^2 + x - 3 = 2$

$\left(x + \dfrac{1}{2}\right)^2 - \dfrac{1}{4} - 3 = 2$

$x = -\dfrac{1}{2} \pm \dfrac{\sqrt{21}}{2}$

$\left(x - \left(-\dfrac{1}{2} + \dfrac{\sqrt{21}}{2}\right)\right)\left(x - \left(-\dfrac{1}{2} - \dfrac{\sqrt{21}}{2}\right)\right) = 0$

15. $x^2 - 2x + 4 = 5$

$(x - 1)^2 - 1 + 4 = 5$

$x = 1 \pm \sqrt{2}$

$\left(x - \left(1 + \sqrt{2}\right)\right)\left(x - \left(1 - \sqrt{2}\right)\right) = 0$

16. $x^2 + 3x - 1 = 3$

$\left(x + \dfrac{3}{2}\right)^2 - \dfrac{9}{4} - 1 = 3$

$x = 1, -4$

$(x - 1)(x + 4) = 0$

17. $x^2 + 7x - 3 = 2$

$\left(x + \dfrac{7}{2}\right)^2 - \dfrac{1}{4} - 3 = 2$

$x = -\dfrac{7}{2} \pm \dfrac{\sqrt{69}}{2}$

$\left(x - \left(-\dfrac{7}{2} + \dfrac{\sqrt{69}}{2}\right)\right)\left(x - \left(-\dfrac{7}{2} - \dfrac{\sqrt{69}}{2}\right)\right) = 0$

18. $x^2 + 8x = 0$

$(x + 4)^2 - 16 = 0$

$x = 0, 4$

$(x)(x - 4) = 0$

19. $x^2 - 7x = 0$

$\left(x - \dfrac{7}{2}\right)^2 - \dfrac{49}{4} = 0$

$x = 0, 7$

$(x)(x - 7) = 0$

20. $-x^2 + 10x + 4 = -1$

$-\left(\left(x - 5\right)^2 - 25\right) + 4 = -1$

$(x - 5)^2 = 30$

$x = 5 \pm \sqrt{30}$

$\left(x - \left(5 + \sqrt{30}\right)\right)\left(x - \left(5 - \sqrt{30}\right)\right) = 0$

21. $2x^2 - 10x - 2 = 0$

$2\left(\left(x - \dfrac{5}{2}\right)^2 - \dfrac{25}{4} - 1\right) = 0$

$x = \dfrac{5}{2} \pm \dfrac{\sqrt{29}}{2}$

$2\left(x - \left(\dfrac{5}{2} + \dfrac{\sqrt{29}}{2}\right)\right)\left(x - \left(\dfrac{5}{2} + \dfrac{\sqrt{29}}{2}\right)\right) = 0$

22. $3x^2 - 9x - 6 = 0$

$3\left(\left(x - \dfrac{3}{2}\right)^2 - \dfrac{9}{4} - 2\right) = 0$

$x = \dfrac{3}{2} \pm \dfrac{\sqrt{17}}{2}$

$3\left(x - \left(\dfrac{3}{2} + \dfrac{\sqrt{17}}{2}\right)\right)\left(x - \left(\dfrac{3}{2} - \dfrac{\sqrt{17}}{2}\right)\right) = 0$

23. $-4x^2 - 2x - 6 = 1$

$-4\left(\left(x + \dfrac{1}{4}\right)^2 - \dfrac{1}{16} + \dfrac{7}{4}\right) = 0$

$x = No\ \ Solution$

24. $2x^2 - x - 1 = 2$

$2\left(\left(x - \dfrac{1}{4}\right)^2 - \dfrac{1}{16} - \dfrac{3}{2}\right) = 0$

$x = \dfrac{1}{4} \pm \dfrac{\sqrt{13}}{4}$

$2\left(x - \left(\dfrac{1}{4} + \dfrac{\sqrt{13}}{4}\right)\right)\left(x - \left(\dfrac{1}{4} - \dfrac{\sqrt{13}}{4}\right)\right) = 0$

25. $-5x^2 + 2x - 11 = -2$

$-5\left(\left(x - \dfrac{1}{5}\right)^2 - \dfrac{1}{25} + \dfrac{9}{5}\right) = 0$

$x = No\ \ Solution$

26. $-2x^2 - 2x = 0$

$-2\left(\left(x + \dfrac{1}{2}\right)^2 - \dfrac{1}{4}\right) = 0$

$x = 0, -1$

$-2(x)(x + 1) = 0$

27. $4x^2 - 2x = 0$

$4\left(\left(x - \dfrac{1}{4}\right)^2 - \dfrac{1}{16}\right) = 0$

$x = 0, \dfrac{1}{2}$

$4(x)\left(x - \dfrac{1}{2}\right) = 0$

28. $-2x^2 - 3 = -5$

$-2x^2 = -2$

$x = \pm 1$

$-2(x - 1)(x + 1) = 0$

29. $6x^2 - 7x = 0$

$6\left(\left(x - \dfrac{7}{12}\right)^2 - \dfrac{49}{144}\right) = 0$

$x = 0, \dfrac{7}{6}$

$6(x)\left(x - \dfrac{7}{6}\right) = 0$

30. $2x^2 - 6x = 0$

$2\left(\left(x - \dfrac{3}{2}\right)^2 - \dfrac{9}{4}\right) = 0$

$x = 0, 3$

$2(x)(x - 3) = 0$

31. $(2x - 1)(x - b) = 0$

Rational equations 2nd degree

1. $\dfrac{3}{x^2-4}=2$

$x=\pm\dfrac{\sqrt{22}}{2}$

2. $\dfrac{2}{x^2-2x+1}=1$

$x=1\pm\sqrt{3}$

3. $-\dfrac{2}{x^2-2x+3}=1$

No Solution

4. $\dfrac{x}{x^2-4}=2$

$x=-\dfrac{1}{4}\pm\dfrac{\sqrt{65}}{4}$

5. $\dfrac{x}{x-4}=5$

$x=5$

6. $\dfrac{x^2}{x^2-4x}=2$

$x=8$

7. $\dfrac{x^2-1}{x-5}=2$

No Solution

8. $\dfrac{x}{x-4}+\dfrac{2}{x-4}=5$

$x=\dfrac{11}{2}$

9. $\dfrac{x}{x-4}+\dfrac{2}{x+3}=-2$

$x=-\dfrac{1}{2}\pm\dfrac{\sqrt{393}}{6}$

10. $\dfrac{x-1}{2x-2}-\dfrac{2x-1}{x+3}=3$

$x=-\dfrac{13}{9}$

11. $\dfrac{x}{3x+2}-\dfrac{2x-1}{2x+3}=7$

$x=-\dfrac{89}{92}\pm\dfrac{\sqrt{561}}{92}$

12. $\dfrac{1}{x}+\dfrac{2}{x^2}=3$

$x=1,-\dfrac{2}{3}$

13. $\dfrac{2}{x^3}-\dfrac{3}{x^2}=5$

$x=1,2$

14. $\dfrac{1}{x-1}+\dfrac{2}{x^2-1}=2$

$x=\dfrac{1}{4}\pm\dfrac{\sqrt{41}}{4}$

15. $\dfrac{1}{x-3}-\dfrac{2}{x^2-9}=4$

$x=\dfrac{1}{8}\pm\dfrac{\sqrt{593}}{8}$

16. $\dfrac{5}{x-2}-\dfrac{3}{x^2-4}=-2$

$x=-\dfrac{5}{4}\pm\dfrac{\sqrt{33}}{4}$

17. $\dfrac{2}{x^n}-\dfrac{3}{x^{n+1}}=\dfrac{5}{x^n}$

$x=-1$

18. $\dfrac{3}{25-x^2}-\dfrac{4}{5-x}=1$

$x=2\pm\sqrt{46}$

19. $\dfrac{1}{x^2}=\dfrac{1}{9}$

$x=\pm3$

20. $\dfrac{1}{x^2}=25$

$x=\pm\dfrac{1}{5}$

Radical Equations

1. $\sqrt{3}=\sqrt{x}\quad x=3$
2. $3=\sqrt{x}\quad x=9$
3. $1=\sqrt{-2x}\quad x=-\dfrac{1}{2}$
4. $\dfrac{2}{\sqrt{x}}=1+x\quad x=1$

5. $\sqrt{8x+2}=0$

$x=-\dfrac{1}{4}$

6. $\sqrt{5x-2}=6$

$x=\dfrac{38}{5}$

7. $\sqrt{5x^2-2}=3$

$$x = \pm\sqrt{\frac{11}{5}}$$

8. $\sqrt{x^2 + 1} = -2$

 $x = \pm\sqrt{3}$, Assuming negative root

9. $\sqrt{x^2 - 2} + 4 = -2$

 $x = \pm\sqrt{38}$, Assuming negative root

10. $\sqrt{2x^2 - 2} + 4x = -2$

 No Solution

11. $\sqrt{2x - 2} + 3x + 2 = -2$

 No Solution

12. $\sqrt{x + 1} + \sqrt{x + 3} = 2$

 $x = -\dfrac{3}{4}$

13. $\sqrt{x - 1} + \sqrt{x + 3} = 2$

 $x = 1$

14. $\sqrt{x - 3} + \sqrt{x + 3} = 3$

 $x = \dfrac{13}{4}$

15. $\sqrt{5x + 1} - \sqrt{3x - 3} = 2$

 $x = 6 \pm 2\sqrt{6}$

16. $\sqrt{8x + 2} - \sqrt{3x - 3} = 0$

 $x = -1$

17. $\sqrt{x - 1} + \sqrt{x + 2} = -2$

 $x = \dfrac{17}{16}$, Assuming negative root

18. $\dfrac{12}{\sqrt{x}} = 8 - \sqrt{x}$

 $x = 4, 36$

19. $\sqrt{x + 9} = x - \sqrt{2 + x}$

 $x = 7$

Higher degree simple equations

1. $x^4 - 2x^2 = 0$ $x = 0, \pm\sqrt{2}$

2. $10(2x - 3)(x^2 - 3)(x + 5)(x^3 + 2) = 0$ $x = \dfrac{3}{2}, \pm\sqrt{3}, -5, \sqrt[3]{-2}$

3. $(2x - 3)(x - 3) = 1$ $x = \dfrac{9}{4} \pm \dfrac{\sqrt{17}}{4}$

4. $(6x - 7)(3x^2 - 5)(2x + 7)(2x^5 - 64)(4x^4 + 5) = 0$ $x = \dfrac{7}{26}, \pm\sqrt{\dfrac{5}{3}}, -\dfrac{7}{2}, 2$

5. $3x^5 - x^2 = 0$ $x = 0, \sqrt[3]{\dfrac{1}{3}}$

6. $100(x - 2)^{100}(x^2 - 5)^{10} = 0$

 $x = 2, \pm\sqrt{5}$

7. $x^6 - 32x = 0$ $x = 0, 2$

8. $x^6 - 2x^5 + x^4 = 0$ $x = 0, 1$

9. $x^3 - 4x^2 + 3x = 0$ $x = 0, 1, 3$

10. $2x^3 - 5x = 0$ $x = 0, \pm\dfrac{\sqrt{10}}{2}$

11. $2x^3 - x^2 = 0$ $x = 0, \dfrac{1}{2}$

12. $ax^4 - 3x = 0$ $x = 0, \sqrt[3]{\dfrac{3}{a}}$

13. $ax^5 - x^2 = 0$ $x = 0, \sqrt[3]{\dfrac{1}{a}}$

14. $a(x - a)^{10}(x^2 - a)^{12}(x^3 - a)^{12} = 0$

 $x = a, \pm\sqrt{a}, \sqrt[3]{a}$

15. $x^4 - 5x^2 + 3 = -1$ $x = \pm 1, \pm 2$

16. $x^4 - 10x^2 + 3 = -6$ $x = \pm 1, \pm 3$

17. $x^6 + 3x^3 - 10 = 0$

 $x = \sqrt[3]{2}, \sqrt[3]{-5}$

18. $x^8 = -2x^4 - 1$

 No Solution

19. $x^4 - 13x^2 + 36 = 0$
    $x = \pm 2, \pm 3$

20. $x^5 - 15x^3 + 54x = 0$
    $x = 0, \pm 3, \pm\sqrt{6}$

21. $x^5 + x^3 - 6x = 0$

    $x = 0, \pm\sqrt{2}$

22. $x^4 = 6x^2 - 5$
    $x = \pm 1, \pm\sqrt{5}$

Rational exponent equations

1. $x^{\frac{1}{2}} = 2$ $x = 4$

2. $x^{-1} = a$ $x = \dfrac{1}{a}$

3. $x^{-2} = 0$ *No Solution*

4. $2x^{\frac{2}{3}} = 3$ $x = \sqrt{\dfrac{27}{8}}$

5. $3x^{-\frac{1}{2}} = 2$ $x = \sqrt{\dfrac{9}{4}}$

6. $x + x^{\frac{1}{2}} = 0$
    $x = 0, 1,$ Assuming negative root

7. $2x - x^{\frac{2}{5}} = 0$ $x = 0, \dfrac{\sqrt[3]{2}}{4}$

8. $3x^{-\frac{1}{2}} = 0$ *No Solution*

9. $ax^{-\frac{3}{7}} = 0$ *No Solution*

10. $3x^{-\frac{6}{7}} = -2$ *No Solution*

11. $x^{\frac{1}{3}} + 1 = 0$
    $x = -1$

12. $3x^{\frac{1}{2}} - x^2 = 0$ $x = 0, 3^{\frac{3}{5}}$

13. $8x^{-2} = 2$ $x = 2$

14. $5x^{\frac{4}{3}} = -1$ *No Solution*

15. $3x^{-\frac{3}{4}} = -2$ *No Solution*

16. $x - 2x^{\frac{2}{3}} = 0$ $x = 0, 8$

17. $2x^2 - x^{-\frac{3}{2}} = 0$ $x = 2^{-\frac{3}{8}}$

18. $3x^{-2} = -5$ *No Solution*

19. $x^{\frac{1}{2}} - 2x^{\frac{1}{6}} = 0$ $x = 0, 8$

20. $4x^{\frac{1}{4}} - 2x^{\frac{1}{2}} = 0$ $x = 0, 16$

Exponential equations

1. $2^x = 2$
    $x = 1$

2. $2^{x+2} = 2^2$
    $x = 0$

3. $\left(\dfrac{1}{32}\right)2^{3x+4} = 4$
    $x = 1$

4. $2^{-4x+1} = 8$
    $x = -\dfrac{1}{2}$

5. $3^{-5x+3} = 9$

    $x = \dfrac{1}{5}$

6. $\left(\dfrac{1}{4}\right)^{x+2} = \dfrac{1}{16}$
    $x = 0$

7. $2^{x+2} = \dfrac{-1}{16}$
    No Solution

8. $2^{-2x+1} = 8^x$
    $x = \dfrac{1}{5}$

9. $\left(\dfrac{1}{3}\right)^{4x^2-1} = 9^{2x}$

    $x = -\dfrac{1}{2} \pm \dfrac{\sqrt{2}}{2}$

10. $\left(\dfrac{1}{125}\right)5^{x-1} = 1$
    $x = 4$

11. $3^{2x-5} = \dfrac{1}{3}$
    $x = 2$

12. $3^{2x^2-5} = \dfrac{1}{27}$

$$x = \pm 1$$

13. $\left(\dfrac{1}{5}\right)^{x-1} = -1$

    No Solution

14. $5^{x-1} = 5^{x(x-1)}$

    $x = 1$

15. $6^{x^2-8} = 6$

    $x = \pm 3$

16. $5^{x-1} = \dfrac{1}{125}$

    $x = -2$

17. $\left(\dfrac{1}{36}\right)^{2x-3} = \dfrac{1}{6}$

    $x = \dfrac{7}{4}$

18. $6^{2x-3} = -\dfrac{3}{4}$

    No Solution

19. $2^x = 3$

    $x \in (1,2)$

20. $5^x = 3$

    $x \in (0,1)$

21. $1^x = 2$

    No Solution

22. $2^x = -2$

    No Solution

$$4^x = (0.5)^{x-2}$$

23. $2^{2x} = 2^{2-x}$

    $x = \dfrac{2}{3}$

$$1000^{2x-1} = (0.01)^{3x-2}$$

24. $10^{6x-3} = 10^{-6x+4}$

    $x = \dfrac{7}{12}$

25. $\dfrac{1}{5^x - 4} = 1$

    $x = 1$

26. $\dfrac{1}{5^x - 24} = 1$

    $x = 2$

27. $\dfrac{1}{5^{3x} - 24} = 1$

    $x = \dfrac{2}{3}$

28. $\dfrac{2}{2^x - 7} = 2$

    $x = 3$

29. $\dfrac{125}{2^{\frac{x}{3}} - 7} = 5$

    $x = 15$

30. $6^x + 6^{x+1} = \dfrac{7}{6}$

    $x = -1$

31. $5^x + 5^{x+1} + 5^{x-1} = \dfrac{31}{5}$

    $x = 0$

32. $7^{x-1} + 7^{x-2} = \dfrac{8}{49}$

    $x = 0$

33. $7^{x-1} + 7^{x-2} = \dfrac{8}{7}$

    $x = 1$

34. $2^x + 2^{x-1} + 2^{x+2} = 11$

    $x = -1$

35. $2^x + 2^{x-1} + 2^{x+2} = 22$

    $x = 2$

36. $5^{2x} - 6 \times 5^x = -5$

    $x = 0,1$

37. $3^{2x} - 4 \times 3^x - 2 = -5$

    $x = 0,1$

38. $5^{2x} + 4 \times 5^x - 10 = -5$

    $x = 0$

39. $8^{2x} - 9 \times 8^x + 8 = 0$

    $x = 0,1$

40. $2 \times 8^{2x} - 18 \times 8^x + 10 = -6$

    $x = 0,1$

41. $3^{2x+1} - 3^{x+2} + 81 = 0$

    No Solution

42. $5^{2x-1} - 6 \times 5^{x-1} = -1$

    $x = 0,1$

43. $3^{2x+2} - 4 \times 3^{x+2} + 27 = 0$

    $x = 0,1$

Systems of equations

1. One equation with 1 variable may have <u>0</u> or 1 or <u>infinite</u> solutions. Examples:
   2x + 5 = 7 (1 solution) , x + 3 = x – 4 (0 solutions), x + 1 = x + 1 (infinite solutions)

2. One equation with 2 two variable may have <u>0</u> or <u>1</u> or <u>infinite</u> solutions. Examples:
   2x + y = 7 + y (1 solution), x + y = x + y + 5 (0 solutions) 2x + y = 1 (infinite solutions)

3. Equations of the first degree are equations in which <u>the variables are all</u> to the power of <u>1</u>. Examples:
   1 variable: 3x + 1 = 5
   2 variables: 3x + 7y = 15
   3 variables: 3x + y – 3z = 2

4. Equations of the 2nd degree are equations <u>in which the highest power of at least one of the variables is 2</u>. Give examples with 1 and 2 variables:

1 variable: $3x^2 + 1 = 5$

2 variables: $3x^2 + 7y = 15$

5. The solution to one equation of the first degree with 2 two variable, graphically speaking, <u>is a point</u> The collection of points will form a <u>straight line.</u>

6. A system of equations whose only solution is x = 1, y = 2.

$$x + y = 3$$
$$x - y = -1$$

7. A system of equations whose only solution is x = 0, y = $-\dfrac{1}{2}$.

$$x - 2y = 1$$
$$2x + 10y = -5$$

8. A system of equations whose only solution is x = –3, y = $-\dfrac{3}{2}$.

$$-x - 2y = 6$$
$$2x + 4y = -12$$

9. A system of equations whose only solution is x = 15, y = –6.

$$10x + y = 144$$
$$x + 10y = -45$$

10. Given the equations I) 2x + y = 3, II) 2y – x = 4
    a. Write a few solutions to the equations
       I) <u>(0, 3), (1, 1), (2, -1), (-1, 5)</u>
       II) <u>(0, 2), (-4, 0), (-2, 1), (2, 3)</u>
    b. Show the solutions on the graph.
    c. Draw a conclusion:
    In each one of the cases the points lie on a straight line. The lines intersect.

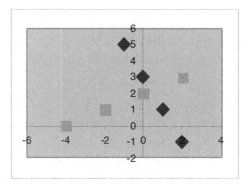

11. Given the equations I) 4x + 2y = 3, II) y + 2x = 8
    a. Write a few solutions to the equations
       I) <u>(0, 3/2), (3/4, 0), (1, -1/2), (-1, 7/2)</u>
       II) <u>(0, 8), (4, 0), (1, 6), (2, 4)</u>
    b. Show the solutions on the graph.
    c. Draw a conclusion:

    In each one of the cases the points lie on a straight line. The lines are parallel.

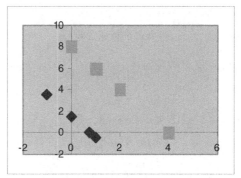

12. Given the equations I)6x – 2y = 2, II) y – 3x= –1
    a. Write a few solutions to the equations
       I) <u>(0, -1), (1/3, 0), (1, 2), (2, 5)</u>
       II) <u>(0, -1), (1/3, 0), (1, 2), (2, 5)</u>
    b. Show the solutions on the graph.
    c. Draw a conclusion: <u>The 2 lines are identical</u>

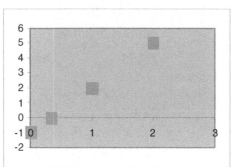

47

13.
$$5x + 1 = 2y$$
$$4y + x - 3 = 0$$
$$x = \frac{1}{11}, y = \frac{8}{11}$$

14.
$$5x + 3y = 2 - 2y$$
$$-y + 2x - 5 = 0$$
$$x = \frac{9}{5}, y = -\frac{7}{5}$$

15.
$$5x = 2y$$
$$-y + 2x = 0$$
$$x = 0, y = 0$$

16.
$$x = 2y - 7$$
$$4y - 2x = 0$$
No Solution

17.
$$-5x + 1 = 2y$$
$$-4y + x - 3 = x$$
$$x = \frac{1}{2}, y = -\frac{3}{4}$$

18.
$$5x + 1 = 2y$$
$$10y - 25x = 10$$
No Solution

19.
$$2x + 1 = 2y$$
$$-4y + 4x + 2 = 0$$
$$x = 0, y = \frac{1}{2}$$

20.
$$x + 1 = 2y$$
$$4y - 2x - 3 = 0$$
No Solution

21.
$$4x = y$$
$$3y - 12x = 0$$
Infinite Solutions
$$y = 4x$$

22.
$$2x + 7y = 4$$
$$3y - 5x - 3 = 0$$
$$x = -\frac{9}{41}, y = \frac{26}{41}$$

23.
$$\frac{x}{2} - 1 = 5y$$
$$3y + x - 2 = 0$$
$$x = 2, y = 0$$

24.
$$\frac{x}{5} + 1 = 2y$$
$$\frac{y}{3} + \frac{x}{2} - 3 = 0$$
$$x = \frac{85}{16}, y = \frac{33}{32}$$

25.
$$\frac{x}{5} + 2 = 6y$$
$$-3y + \frac{x}{10} + 1 = 0$$
$$x = -40, y = -1$$

26.
$$x = 2y$$
$$-y + x^2 - 5 = 0$$
$$x = -2, y = -1$$
$$x = \frac{5}{2}, y = \frac{5}{4}$$

27.
$$x = 1 - y$$
$$-y + x^2 - 5 = 0$$
$$x = 2, y = -1$$
$$x = -3, y = 4$$

28.
$$x = 1 - y^2$$
$$-y^2 + x^2 - 5 = 0$$
$$x = -3, y = 2$$
$$x = -3, y = -2$$

1.10. – EXPANDING AND FACTORING

Expand:

1. $(x+1)^2 = x^2 + 2x + 1$

2. $(x-1)^2 = x^2 - 2x + 1$

3. $(x+2)^2 = x^2 + 4x + 4$

4. $(x-2)^2 = x^2 - 4x + 4$

5. $(a+b)^2 = a^2 + 2ab + b^2$

6. $(a-b)^2 = a^2 - 2ab + b^2$

7. $(2a+b)^2 = 4a^2 + 4ab + b^2$

8. $(a-3b)^2 = a^2 - 6ab + 9b^2$

9. $(2x+3)^2 = 4x^2 + 6x + 9$

10. $(4-x)^2 = 16 - 8x + x^2$

11. $(x+2)(x-3) = x^2 - x - 6$

12. $(x-2)(x+2) = x^2 - 4$

13. $(3+x)(x-7) = x^2 - 4x - 21$

14. $(2x+2)(x-5) = 2x^2 - 8x - 10$

15. $(3x-1)(x+2) = 3x^2 + 5x - 2$

16. $(x+4)(x-4) = x^2 - 16$

17. $(x+6)(x-6) = x^2 - 36$

18. $(x-a)(x+a) = x^2 - a^2$

19. $(a-b)(a+b) = a^2 - b^2$

20. $(2x-3c)(2x+3c) = 4x^2 - 9c^2$

21. $x(x+8)^2 = x^3 + 16x^2 + 64x$

22. $(x-6)^2 3x = 3x^3 - 36x^2 + 108x$

23. $2 - (x+1)^2 = -x^2 - 2x + 1$

24. $(x+3)^2 - (x+2)^2 = 2x + 5$

25. $(x-2)^2 + (x+2)^2 = 2x^2 + 8$

26. $(x-\sqrt{2})^2 = x^2 - 2\sqrt{2}x + 2$

27. $(x-\sqrt{2})(x+\sqrt{2}) = x^2 - 2$

28. $5(x-\sqrt{a})(x+\sqrt{a}) = 5x^2 - 5a$

29. $(\sqrt{a}-\sqrt{b})^2 = a - 2\sqrt{ab} + b$

30. $2(x-\sqrt{10})(x+\sqrt{10}) = 2x^2 - 10$

31. $(x-\dfrac{2}{x})^2 = x^2 - 4 + 4x^{-2}$

32. $(x-\dfrac{2}{\sqrt{x}})^2 = x^2 - 4\sqrt{x} + 4x^{-1}$

33. $(3x-\dfrac{2}{3\sqrt{x}})^2 = 9x^2 - 4\sqrt{x} + \dfrac{4}{9x}$

34. $2(\sqrt{a}-\dfrac{1}{\sqrt{a}})^2 = 2a - 4 + 2a^{-1}$

35. $(\sqrt{a}-\dfrac{1}{\sqrt{a}})(-\sqrt{a}-\dfrac{1}{\sqrt{a}}) = -a + a^{-1}$

36. $(2^x + 2^{-x})^2 = 2^{2x} + 2 + 2^{-2x}$

37. $(4^{2x} + 2^{-x})^2 = 2^{8x} + 2^{3x+1} + 2^{-2x}$

38. $(3^{2x} + 3^{-2x})^2 = 3^{4x} + 2 + 3^{-4x}$

39. $(7^x - 7)^2 = 7^{2x} - 2 \cdot 7^{x+1} + 49$

40. $(a^{nx} - b^{nx})^2 = a^{2nx} - 2a^{nx}b^{nx} + b^{2nx}$

41. $(x^2 - y^2)(x^2 + y^2) = x^4 - y^4$

42. $(x^3 - y^3)(x^3 + y^3) = x^6 - y^6$

43. $(x^n - y^n)(x^n + y^n) = x^{2n} - y^{2n}$

44. $(a^x - b^x)^2 = a^{2x} - 2a^x b^x + b^{2x}$

45. $(a^{mx} - a^{-mx})^2 = a^{2mx} - 2 + b^{-2mx}$

46. $(a^{mx} - a^{-mx})(a^{mx} + a^{-mx}) = a^{2mx} - a^{-2mx}$

Given the following polynomials, obtain the maximum possible common factor:

1. $x - ax = x(1 - a)$

2. $3x - x - ax = x(2 - a)$

3. $-x + ax = x(a - 1)$

4. $xy + 2x = x(y + 2)$

5. $8xy - 2y = 2x(4y - 1)$

6. $-6x + 12xy = 6x(2y - 1)$

7. $12xyz + 2xy = 2xy(6z - 1)$

8. $14xy - 2yz = 2y(7x - z)$

9. $12xz + 14xyz = 2xz(6 + 7y)$

10. $xy + 4y^2 + 5y = y(x + 4y + 5)$

11. $z - 4z^2 + 8zy = z(1 - 4z + 8y)$

12. $-8x^3 - 4xyz = -4x(x^2 + yz)$

13. $-6x^4 + x^2y^2 + x^2 = x^2(-6x^2 + y^2 + 1)$

14. $-9x^7y^3 + 3x^3y = 3yx^2(-3y^2x^5 + x)$

15. $-90x^{10}y^5 - 3x^3y^4 = -3x^3y^4(-30x^7y + 1)$

16. $-80x^4y^6z^8 + 8x^{12}y^4z^6 = 8x^4y^4z^6(-10x^8y^2z^2 + x^8)$

17. $xyz + 2x^2y^2z^2 + 3x^3y^3z^3 = xyz(1 + 2xyz + x^2y^2z^2)$

18. $10x^3y^2z^4 + 2x^2y^6z^4 - 5x^2y^4z^2 = x^2y^2z^2(10xz^2 + 2z^2y^4 + 5y^2)$

19. $20x^{30}y^{20}z^{40} - 2x^{20}y^{60}z^{40} - 2x^{20}y^{40}z^{20} = 2x^{20}y^{20}z^{20}(10x2z20 - z^{20}y^{40} - y^{20})$

49

20. $ax^m + x^m = x^m(a + 1)$

21. $ax^{m+1} + x^m = x^m(ax + 1)$

22. $ax^m + x^{m-1} = x^m(a + x^{-1})$

23. $ax^m - x = x(ax^{m-1} - 1)$

24. $-ax^m - x^{2m} = -x^m(a + x^m)$

25. $z^{n+1} - z^{n+2} = z^n(z - z^2)$

26. $ax^{m+2} + x^{m-1} = x^{m-1}(ax^3 + 1)$

Given the following polynomials, if possible factor, otherwise complete the square:

1. $x^2 - 6x + 9 = (x - 3)^2$

2. $x^2 - 5x + 6 = (x - 3)(x - 2)$

3. $x^2 + 4x + 10 = Not\ \ possible$

4. $-x^2 - x + 6 = -(x + 3)(x - 2)$

5. $x^2 + x - 6 = (x + 3)(x - 2)$

6. $x^2 + 5x + 6 = (x + 3)(x + 2)$

7. $-x^2 + 7x - 10 = -(x - 2)(x - 5)$

8. $x^2 - 6x + 12 = Not\ \ possible$

9. $x^2 + 3x + 2 = (x + 2)(x + 1)$

10. $x^2 - x - 2 = (x - 2)(x + 1)$

11. $-x^2 + 4x = -x(x - 4)$

12. $-x^2 + 4x - 10 = Not\ \ possible$

13. $x^2 + x - 2 = (x + 2)(x - 1)$

14. $x^2 + 3x + 7 = Not\ \ possible$

15. $x^2 - 3x + 2 = (x - 2)(x - 1)$

16. $x^2 - x + 7 = Not\ \ possible$

17. $x^2 + 5x + 9 = Not\ \ possible$

18. $-x^2 - 5x + 6 = Not\ \ possible$

19. $x^2 - 2xa + a^2 = (x - a)^2$

20. $x^2 - a^2 = (x - a)(x + a)$

21. $c^2 - a^2 = (c - a)(c + a)$

22. $x^2 - x = x(x - 1)$

23. $2x^2 - x = x(2x - 1)$

24. $2x^2 + 3x = x(2x + 3)$

25. $x^2 + 5x = x(x + 5)$

26. $x^2 - 7x + 12 = (x - 3)(x - 4)$

27. $2x^2 - 4x = 2x(x - 2)$

28. $x^2 - 7x + 10 = (x - 2)(x - 5)$

29. $x^2 - 7x + 6 = (x - 1)(x - 6)$

30. $x^2 - x - 12 = (x - 4)(x + 3)$

31. $x^2 + x - 12 = (x + 4)(x - 3)$

32. $x^2 - 3x - 10 = (x - 5)(x + 2)$

33. $x^2 - 8x - 9 = (x - 9)(x + 1)$

34. $x^2 - 1 = (x - 1)(x + 1)$

35. $x^2 + 1 = Not\ \ possible$

36. $x^2 - 2 = (x - \sqrt{2})(x + \sqrt{2})$

37. $x^2 - 3 = (x - \sqrt{3})(x + \sqrt{3})$

38. $x^2 - 4 = (x - 2)(x + 2)$

39. $-x^2 + 1 = -(x + 1)(x - 1)$

40. $-x^2 + 2 = -(x + \sqrt{2})(x - \sqrt{2})$

41. $-x^2 + 3 = -(x + \sqrt{3})(x - \sqrt{3})$

42. $-x^2 + 4 = -(x + 2)(x - 2)$

43. $-x^2 + 13 = -(x + \sqrt{13})(x - \sqrt{13})$

44. $-x^2 + 49 = -(x + 7)(x - 7)$

45. $2x^2 - 72 = 2(x + 6)(x - 6)$

46. $-x^2 - 2 = Not\ \ possible$

47. $5x^2 - 125 = 5(x - 5)(x + 5)$

48. $-x^2 + 81 = -(x + 9)(x - 9)$

49. $-3x^2 + 27 = -3(x + 3)(x - 3)$

50. $2x^2 - 6 = 2(x + \sqrt{3})(x - \sqrt{3})$

51. $3x^2 - 1 = 3(x + \sqrt{\frac{1}{3}})(x - \sqrt{\frac{1}{3}})$

52. $-2x^2 - 3 = -2(x^2 + \frac{3}{2})$

53. $5x^2 - 6 = 5(x - \sqrt{\frac{6}{5}})(x + \sqrt{\frac{6}{5}})$

54. $4x^2 - 2 = 4(x - \sqrt{\frac{1}{2}})(x + \sqrt{\frac{1}{2}})$

55. $-8x^2 - 1 = -8(x^2 + \frac{1}{8})$

56. $x^2 - b = (x + \sqrt{b})(x - \sqrt{b})$

57. $ax^2 - b = a(x + \sqrt{\frac{b}{a}})(x - \sqrt{\frac{b}{a}})$

58. $-ax^2 + b = -a(x + \sqrt{\frac{b}{a}})(x - \sqrt{\frac{b}{a}})$

59. $2x^2 - 4x + 2 = 2(x - 1)^2$

60. $3x^2 - 3x - 18 = 3(x - 3)(x + 2)$

61. $-4x^2 + 20x + 24 = -4(x - 6)(x + 1)$

62. $7x^2 + 7x - 630 = 7(x + 10)(x - 9)$

63. $-5x^2+10x+75=-5(x-5)(x+3)$

64. $3x^2-12x-63=3(x-7)(x+3)$

65. $2x^2+2x-112=2(x+8)(x-7)$

66. $2x^2-12x-14=2(x-7)(x+1)$

67. $-5x^2+15x+90=-5(x-6)(x+3)$

68. $-3x^2-12x-12=-3(x+2)^2$

69. $-2x^2-26x-84=-2(x+6)(x+7)$

70. $6x^2+48x+72=6(x+6)(x+2)$

Given the following polynomials, complete the square.

1. $x^2-6x+9=(x-3)^2$

2. $x^2-5x+6=(x-\dfrac{5}{2})^2-\dfrac{1}{4}$

3. $x^2+4x+10=(x+2)^2+6$

4. $-x^2-x+6=-(x+\dfrac{1}{2})^2+\dfrac{25}{4}$

5. $x^2+x-6=(x+\dfrac{1}{2})^2-\dfrac{25}{4}$

6. $x^2+5x+6=(x+\dfrac{5}{2})^2-\dfrac{1}{4}$

7. $-x^2+7x-10=-(x-\dfrac{7}{2})^2+\dfrac{9}{4}$

8. $x^2-6x+12=(x-3)^2+3$

9. $x^2+3x+2=(x+\dfrac{3}{2})^2-\dfrac{1}{4}$

10. $x^2-x-2=(x-\dfrac{1}{2})^2-\dfrac{9}{4}$

11. $-x^2+4x=-(x-2)^2+4$

12. $-x^2+4x-10=-(x-2)^2-6$

13. $x^2+x-2=(x+\dfrac{1}{2})^2-\dfrac{9}{4}$

14. $x^2+3x+7=(x+\dfrac{3}{2})^2+\dfrac{19}{4}$

15. $2x^2-4x+2=2(x-1)^2$

16. $3x^2-3x-6=3(x-\dfrac{1}{2})^2-\dfrac{27}{4}$

17. $-4x^2+20x-24=-4(x-\dfrac{5}{2})^2+1$

18. $7x^2-7x-630=7(x-\dfrac{1}{2})^2+\dfrac{2513}{4}$

19. $-5x^2+10x+75=-5(x-1)^2+70$

20. $3x^2-12x-63=3(x-2)^2-75$

21. $2x^2+2x-112=2(x+\dfrac{1}{2})^2-\dfrac{225}{2}$

22. $2x^2-12x-14=2(x-3)^2-32$

23. $-5x^2+15x+90=-5(x-\dfrac{3}{2})^2+\dfrac{405}{4}$

24. $-3x^2-12x-12=-3(x+2)^2$

25. $-2x^2-26x-84=-2(x+\dfrac{13}{2})^2+\dfrac{1}{2}$

26. $6x^2+48x+72=6(x+4)^2-12$

Factor and simplify:

1. $\dfrac{x^2-6x+9}{x^2-7x+12}=\dfrac{(x-3)}{(x-4)}$

2. $\dfrac{x^2-5x+6}{x^2+x-6}=\dfrac{(x-3)}{(x+3)}$

3. $\dfrac{x^2-9}{x^2-7x+12}=\dfrac{(x+3)}{(x-4)}$

4. $\dfrac{x^2-1}{x^2-2x+1}=\dfrac{(x+1)}{(x-1)}$

5. $\dfrac{x^2-6x+8}{x^2-4x+4}=\dfrac{(x-4)}{(x-2)}$

6. $\dfrac{x^2-16}{x^2+5x+4}=\dfrac{(x-4)}{(x+1)}$

7. $\dfrac{x^2-x-2}{x^2+6x+5}=\dfrac{(x-2)}{(x+5)}$

8. $\dfrac{3x+9}{x^2-9}=\dfrac{3}{(x-3)}$

9. $\dfrac{x^2-6x}{x^2-7x+6}=\dfrac{x}{(x-1)}$

10. $\dfrac{x^2-x}{x^2+x-2}=\dfrac{x}{(x+2)}$

11. $\dfrac{x^2-4}{x^2+x-2}=\dfrac{(x-2)}{(x-1)}$

12. $\dfrac{4-x}{x-4}=-1$

13. $\dfrac{x^2 - x}{1 - x} = -x$

14. $\dfrac{2x - 1}{4x^2 - 4x + 1} = \dfrac{1}{(2x - 1)}$

15. $\dfrac{x^2 - 2x}{x^2 - 4} = \dfrac{x}{(x + 2)}$

16. $\dfrac{4x^2 + 4x + 1}{2x^2 + 5x + 2} = \dfrac{(2x + 1)}{(x + 2)}$

17. $\dfrac{3x^2 + 4x + 1}{9x^2 - 1} = \dfrac{(3x + 1)}{(3x - 1)}$

18. $\dfrac{4x^2 + 4x - 3}{2x^2 - 13x + 15} = \dfrac{(2x - 1)(2x + 3)}{(x - 5)(2x - 3)}$

19. $\dfrac{4x^2 + 4x - 3}{2x^2 + 13x + 15} = \dfrac{(2x - 1)}{(x + 5)}$

20. $\dfrac{5x^2 - 12x + 4}{10x^2 + 16x - 8} = \dfrac{(x - 2)}{(2x + 4)}$

1.11. – EVALUATING EXPRESSIONS

Evaluate the expression given the value of x:

1. $x = 3$, $x^2 + x = 12$

2. $x = -3$, $x^2 + x = 6$

3. $x = -2$, $2x^2 + 3x = 2$

4. $x = -2$, $x^{-1} = -\dfrac{1}{2}$

5. $x = -2$, $x^3 = -8$

6. $x = -3$, $x^{-3} = -\dfrac{1}{27}$

7. $x = -9$, $2x^{-2} = \dfrac{2}{81}$

8. $x = 4$, $x^{-2} + x = \dfrac{65}{16}$

9. $x = -2$, $2x^2 + \dfrac{x}{2} = 7$

10. $x = -2$, $\dfrac{1}{x} + \dfrac{x}{2} = -\dfrac{3}{2}$

11. $x = 4$, $\dfrac{1}{x-3} + \dfrac{x}{2} = 3$

12. $x = 10$, $\dfrac{10}{x-5} + \dfrac{x-2}{2} = 6$

13. $x = -1$, $5x^{-3} + 2x^{-1} + 1 = -6$

14. $x = 3$, $x^{-2} + x + x^2 = \dfrac{91}{9}$

15. $x = 2$, $x^{-3} + x^{-2} + x^{-1} + x^0 = \dfrac{7}{4}$

16. $x = 2$, $2x^{-2} \cdot x^{-1} = \dfrac{1}{4}$

17. $x = -1$, $x^{-200} - 2x^{501} = 3$

18. $x = -5$, $5x^{-2} - x^2 = -\dfrac{124}{5}$

19. $x = -2$, $2^x = \dfrac{1}{4}$

20. $x = -2$, $3^x = \dfrac{1}{9}$

21. $x = -2$, $2^{2x+1} = \dfrac{1}{8}$

22. $x = -1$, $2^{3x-1} = \dfrac{1}{16}$

23. $x = 2$, $2^{\frac{3}{x}} = \sqrt{8}$

24. $x = -\dfrac{1}{2}$, $4^x = \dfrac{1}{2}$

25. $x = -\dfrac{2}{3}$, $8^x = \dfrac{1}{4}$

1.12. – ABSOLUTE VALUE

1. $|-3| = \underline{3}$ $\qquad$ $|3| = \underline{3}$ $\qquad$ $|-3+3| = \underline{0}$ $\qquad$ $|-3-3| = \underline{6}$

2. $|-3| + 3 = \underline{6}$ $\qquad$ $|3| - 4 = \underline{-1}$ $\qquad$ $|-3+5| + 2 = \underline{4}$ $\qquad$ $|-3-3| - 3 = \underline{3}$

3. $\left|1 - 3 + |-2|\right| = \underline{0}$

4. $|-2-3| + |-2| = \underline{7}$

5. $|-2-23| - |-12| = \underline{13}$

6. $2\left|1 - 3 + |-2| + 1\right| - 2 = \underline{0}$

7. $|-2-3||-2| = \underline{10}$

8. $-|-12-3| - |-2-1| = \underline{-18}$

9. $5 - \left|12 - 3 + |1-2|\right| - |-12-10| + 1 = \underline{-26}$

10. $\left|2 - |-12-3| - |-2-1|\right| = \underline{16}$

11. $|x| - 2|x| = \underline{-|x|}$

12. $|x||x| = |x^2| = \underline{x^2}$

13. An absolute value of a number represents <u>its distance from the origin</u>

14. $|x| = |-x|$ $\qquad$ **True** / False, if false write down an example to show it

15. $|x+y| = |x| + |y|$ $\qquad$ True / **False**, if false write down an example to show it

    $|2 + (-3)| \neq |2| + |-3|$

    $1 \neq 5$

16. $-|x|$ is <u>always a negative</u> number

17. If $x = |x|$ it means x is <u>positive</u>

18. If $x = -|x|$ it means x is <u>negative</u>

19. If x is a negative number than $-x = |x|$ $\qquad$ **True** / False

20. If x is a positive number than $x = |x|$ $\qquad$ **True** / False

1. $|2x| = 5$ $\qquad$ $x = \pm\dfrac{5}{2}$

2. $|x| = 7$ $\qquad$ $x = \pm 7$

3. $|4x| = 8$ $\qquad$ $x = \pm 2$

4. $|x| = -5$ $\qquad$ *No Solution*

5. $|2x| = 0$ $\qquad$ $x = 0$

6. $|2x| = -1$ $\qquad$ *No Solution*

7. $|2x| = 15$ $\qquad$ $x = \pm\dfrac{15}{2}$

8. $|2x| < 5$ $\qquad$ $x \in (-5, 5)$

9. $|x| > 7$ $\qquad$ $x \in (-\infty, -7) \cup (7, \infty)$

10. $|4x| < 8$ $\qquad$ $x \in (-2, 2)$

11. $|x| < -5$ $\qquad$ *No Solution*

12. $|3x| < 0$ $\qquad$ *No Solution*

13. $|6x| > -1$ $\qquad$ $x \in \Re$

14. $|5x| > 0$ $\qquad$ $x \in \Re, x \neq 0$

15. $|3x| < 6$ $\qquad$ $x \in (-2, 2)$

16. $|x| \geq 7$ $\qquad$ $x \in (-\infty, -7] \cup [7, \infty)$

17. $|4x| < 2$ $\qquad$ $x \in (-\dfrac{1}{2}, \dfrac{1}{2})$

18. $|x| \leq -5$ $\qquad$ *No Solution*

19. $|2x| \leq 0$ $\qquad$ $x = 0$

20. $|2x| > -1$ $\qquad$ $x \in \Re$

21. $|x| \geq 0$ $\qquad$ $x \in \Re$

22. $|2 + x| = 5$ $\qquad$ $x = 3, -7$

23. $|-x| = 7$ $\qquad$ $x = 7, -7$

24. $|4 - x| = 8$ $x = -4, 12$

25. $|3 - 2x| = -5$ *No Solution*

26. $|2 - 3x| = 0$ $x = \dfrac{3}{2}$

27. $|2 + x| = -1$ *No Solution*

28. $|2x + 3| = 15$ $x = 6, -9$

29. $|4 - 2x| < 5$ $x \in (-\dfrac{1}{2}, \dfrac{9}{2})$

30. $|-x| > 7$ $x \in (-\infty, -7) \cup (7, \infty)$

31. $|4 + 2x| < 8$ $x \in (-6, 2)$

32. $|x| < -5$ *No Solution*

33. $|3 + x| < 0$ *No Solution*

34. $|6 - 2x| > -1$ $x \in \Re$

35. $|5 + x| > 0$ $x \in \Re, x \neq -5$

36. $|1 - 3x| \leq 6$ $x \in [-\dfrac{5}{3}, \dfrac{7}{3}]$

37. $|1 + x| \geq 7$ $x \in (-\infty, -8] \cup [6, \infty)$

38. $|4 + x| \leq 2$ $x \in [-6, -2]$

39. $|3 + 2x| \leq -5$ *No Solution*

40. $|2 + 3x| < 0$ *No Solution*

41. $|7 - 6x| \geq -1$ $x \in \Re$

42. $|1 - x| \geq 0$ $x \in \Re$

43. $|2x + 1| + 3 = 5$ $x = \dfrac{1}{2}, -\dfrac{3}{2}$

44. $|7x + 21| - 5 = -5$ $x = -3$

45. $2 - |5 - 8x| = 15$ *No Solution*

46. $|4x + 2| = -5$ *No Solution*

47. $|8x + 12| = 100$ $x = 11, -14$

48. $|2x + 1| < 2$ $x \in (-\dfrac{13}{2}, -\dfrac{9}{2})$

49. $|8 - 2x + 1| > 6$

     $x \in (-\infty, \dfrac{3}{2}) \cup (\dfrac{15}{2}, \infty)$

50. $|5x - 21| > 0$ $x \in \Re, x \neq \dfrac{21}{5}$

51. $|5x - 21| \geq 0$ $x \in \Re$

52. $|8x + 11| > -2$ $x \in \Re$

53. $|91x + 61| < -2$ *No Solution*

54. $|8 - 3x| > 8$

     $x \in (-\infty, 0) \cup (\dfrac{16}{3}, \infty)$

55. $|18 - 6x| > 3$

     $x \in (-\infty, \dfrac{5}{2}) \cup (\dfrac{7}{2}, \infty)$

56. $|1 - 6x| < 7$ $x \in (-1, \dfrac{4}{3})$

57. $|8 - 5x| \leq 0$ $x = \dfrac{8}{5}$

58. $|5x - 21| > 1$

     $x \in (-\infty, 4) \cup (\dfrac{22}{5}, \infty)$

59. $|x + 11| = 5$ $x = -6, -16$

60. $|x + 3| \leq 5$ $x \in [-8, 2]$

61. $|x + 11| = -15$ *No Solution*

62. $|2x + 11| + 2 < 15$ $x \in (-12, 1)$

63. $|3x + 11| = x$ *No Solution*

64. $|x + 2| = 5 - x$ $x = \dfrac{3}{2}$

65. $|3x + 1| < 5x$ $x = \dfrac{1}{2}$

66. $|x - 4| = 3x$ $x = 1$

67. $|2x - 6| \leq 5 + 2x$ $x \in [\dfrac{1}{4}, \infty)$

68. $|2x + 4| < 2 - 3x$ $x \in (-\infty, -\dfrac{2}{5})$

69. $|2x - 2| > 11 - 2x$ $x \in (-\infty, \dfrac{13}{4})$

70. $|7x - 16| = 5 + 12x$ $x = \dfrac{11}{19}$

71. $|2x - 6| = 21$ $x = \dfrac{27}{2}, -\dfrac{15}{2}$

72. $|2x - 6| \geq 4$

     $x \in (-\infty, 1] \cup [5, \infty)$

73. $|3x - 6| + 1 > -4$ $x \in \Re$

74. $|4x - 6| - 4 < -4x$ *No Solution*

75. $|\dfrac{1}{2}x - 4| \leq 1 + x$ $x \in [2, \infty)$

76. $|2x + \dfrac{1}{2}| > 2 - 3x$ $x \in (\dfrac{3}{10}, \infty)$

77. $|2x - \dfrac{1}{2}| = 1 - 2x$ $x \in (\dfrac{3}{8}, \infty)$

78. $|\dfrac{1}{2}x - 7| \leq 3 + 2x$ $x \in [\dfrac{8}{5}, \infty)$

79. $|\dfrac{x}{2} + 2| = 1 - x$ $x = -\dfrac{2}{3}$

1.13. – LOGARITHMS AND LOGARITHMIC EQUATIONS

1.

Exponential Form	Logarithmic Form
$5^3 = 125$	$\log_5 125 = 3$
$6^2 = 36$	$\log_6 36 = 2$
$x^2 = 64; x = 8$	$\log_x 64 = 2$
$x^3 = 27; x = 3$	$\log_x 27 = 3$
$3^2 = x + 1; x = 8$	$\log_3(x+1) = 2$
$e^x = 9$	$\log_e 9 = x$
$e^2 = x$	$\ln x = \log_e x = 2$
$e^{2x-1} = 17; x = \dfrac{\ln 17 + 1}{2}$	$\ln 17 = \log_e 17 = 2x - 1$
$e^2 = 3x + 2; x = \dfrac{e^2 - 2}{3}$	$\ln(3x+2) = \log_e(3x+2) = 2$
$4^x = 9$	$\log_4 9 = x$
$6^2 = x$	$\log_6 x = 2$
$2^x = e$	$\log_2 e = x$
$e^4 = x^2; x = e^2$	$\ln(x^2) = \log_e(x^2) = 4$
$e^x = 0.001$	$\log 0.001 = x$
$10^x = 200$	$\log 200 = x$
$3^{-2} = \dfrac{1}{9}$	$\log_3 \dfrac{1}{9} = -2$
$2^x = \dfrac{1}{2} : x = -1$	$\log_2 0.5 = x$

Logarithms were "invented" in order to solve equations in which: the variable is the exponent

Evaluate

1. $Log_2(2) = 1$

2. $Log_2(4) = 2$

3. $Log_2(8) = 3$

4. $Log_2(16) = 4$

5. $Log_2(32) = 5$

6. $Log_2(2^n) = n$

7. $Log_5(25) = 2$

8. $Log_5(125) = 3$

9. $Log_5(625) = 4$

10. $Log_3(3) = 1$

11. $Log_5(0) = undefined$

12. $Log_5(1) = 0$

13. $Log_a(1) = 0$

14. $Log_2(-3) = undefined$

15. $Log_2(\frac{1}{8}) = -3$

16. $Log_7(\frac{1}{49}) = -2$

17. $Log_4(32) = \frac{5}{2}$

18. $Log_8(32) = \frac{5}{3}$

19. $Log_{\frac{1}{2}}(4) = -2$

20. $Log_{\frac{1}{2}}(16) = -4$

21. $Log_{\frac{1}{3}}(81) = -4$

22. $Log_{\frac{1}{2}}(8) = -3$

23. $Log_{\frac{1}{2}}(-8) = undefined$

24. $Log_{\frac{1}{3}}(\frac{1}{9}) = 2$

25. $Log_{\frac{1}{5}}(\frac{1}{125}) = 3$

26. $Log_1(8) = undefined, 1 \neq b \geq 0$

27. $Log_2(\frac{1}{\sqrt{8}}) = -\frac{3}{2}$

28. $Log_2(\sqrt[3]{32}) = \frac{5}{3}$

29. $Log_3(\sqrt[3]{81}) = \frac{4}{3}$

30. $Log_{\sqrt[5]{8}}(\sqrt[5]{8}) = 1$

31. $Log_{\frac{1}{2}}(\sqrt[5]{16}) = -\frac{4}{5}$

32. $Log_{17}(\frac{17}{17^{\frac{1}{3}}}\sqrt[5]{17}) = \frac{13}{15}$

33. $Log(\sqrt{10}) = \frac{1}{2}$

34. $Log(\sqrt[3]{10}) = \frac{1}{3}$

35. $Log(\sqrt[7]{100}) = \frac{2}{7}$

36. $Log(\sqrt[3]{10000}) = \frac{4}{3}$

37. $Log(10^{-19}) = -19$

38. $Log(50) - Log(5) = Log(10) = 1$

39. $Log(25) + Log(4) = Log(100) = 2$

40. $Log_3(45) - Log_3(5) = Log_3(9) = 2$

41. $Log_6(18) + Log_6(2) = Log_6(36) = 2$

42. $Log_a(a) + Log_a(a^2) = 3$

43. $Log_a(a) + Log_a(\frac{1}{a}) = 0$

44. $Log_a(\frac{1}{a}) - Log_a(a) = -2$

45. $\frac{Log_a(a)}{Log_a(2a)} = \frac{1}{Log_a(2)+1}$

46. $Log_a(a^x) = x$

47. $Log_a(a^{2x-3}) = 2x - 3$

48. $Log_e(e) = 1$

49. $Ln(e) = 1$

50. $Ln(e^2) = 2$

51. $Ln(e^{\frac{1}{2}}) = \frac{1}{2}$

52. $Ln(e^{\frac{2}{5}}) = \frac{2}{5}$

53. $Ln(e\sqrt[3]{e^4}) = \frac{7}{3}$

54. $Ln(1) = 0$

55. $Ln(0) = undefined$

56. $Ln(e^0) = 0$

57. $Ln(e^n) = n$

58. $Ln(\frac{1}{\sqrt{e}}) = -\frac{1}{2}$

59. $Ln(\frac{1}{\sqrt[3]{e^2}}) = -\frac{2}{3}$

60. $Log_\pi(\frac{1}{\pi^4}) = -4$

61. $Log_\pi(\frac{1}{\sqrt{\pi^5}}) = -\frac{5}{2}$

62. $Log_a(\frac{1}{\sqrt[3]{a^2}}) = -\frac{2}{3}$

63. $\dfrac{Ln(e^{-1})}{Log_{12}(\sqrt{12})} = \dfrac{-1}{\left(\frac{1}{2}\right)} = -2$

64. $\dfrac{Ln(\sqrt{e})}{Log_2(40) - Log_2(5)} = \dfrac{\left(\frac{1}{2}\right)}{3} = \dfrac{1}{6}$

65. $\dfrac{Log(500) - Log(5)}{Log_7(98) - Log_7(2)} = \dfrac{Log(100)}{Log_7(49)} = 1$

66. $\dfrac{Ln(a) + Ln(\frac{e}{a})}{Log_{12}(288) - Log_{12}(2)} = \dfrac{Ln(e)}{Log_{12}(144)} = \dfrac{1}{2}$

67. $\dfrac{\left(\frac{1}{\log(100)}\right)}{Log_a(2a) - Log_a(2a^2)} = \dfrac{\left(\frac{1}{2}\right)}{-1} = -\dfrac{1}{2}$

68. $Log_2(3b) - Log_2(3b^2) - Log_2(\frac{1}{8b}) =$
$-Log_2(8) = -3$

69. $Log_b(b-1) - Log_b(1-b^2) + Log_b(b+1) =$
$Log_b\left(\dfrac{(b-1)(b+1)}{1-b^2}\right) = Log_b(-1) = D.E.$

70. $10^{Log(100)} = 100$

71. $10^{Log(100)} = 10$

72. $3^{Log_3(9)} = 9$

73. $3^{Log_3(\frac{1}{27})} = \dfrac{1}{27}$

74. $9^{Log_3(\frac{1}{81})} = 3^{-8}$

75. $32^{Log_2(\sqrt{2})} = 2^{\frac{5}{2}} = \sqrt{32}$

True or False

1. $Log(2x) - Log(3) = Log(2x+3)$ F

2. $Log(x) - Log(9) = 2 \Leftrightarrow \dfrac{x}{9} = 100$ T

3. $Log(12) + Log(x) = 1 \Leftrightarrow 12x = 10$ T

4. $Log(2) + Log(5) = Log(7)$ F

5. $Log(10) - Log(5) = Log(2)$ T

6. $Log(20) + Log(2) = Log(22)$ F

7. $Log(15) - Log(3) = Log(5)$ T

8. $Log(A+B) = Log(A) + Log(B)$ F

Simplify

1. $Log_2(2^x 2^{x+y}) = 2x + y$

2. $5^{Log_5(x+y)} = x + y$

3. $Log_7(49^{xy}) = 2xy$

4. $Log_2(xy) - \dfrac{1}{3}Log_2(x^2) = Log_2(x^{\frac{1}{3}}y)$

5. $Log_2(\dfrac{8x^2}{y}) - 2Log_2(2x^2 y) = Log_2(2x^{-2}y^{-3})$

6. $\dfrac{1}{2}Log_3(\dfrac{9xy^2}{y}) - Log_3(27xy) = Log_3(3^{-2}x^{-\frac{1}{2}}y^{-\frac{1}{2}})$

7. $3Log_4((xy)^3) - Log_4(xy) = Log_4((xy)^8)$

8. $Log(x) - Log(y) - Log(z) = Log(\dfrac{x}{yz})$

9. $Log(x) - Log(y^2) - Log(\sqrt{z}) = Log(\dfrac{x}{y^2\sqrt{z}})$

10. $Log(\sqrt{x}) - Log(y^2) - Log(\sqrt{z}) - Log(\sqrt[3]{t}) = Log(\dfrac{\sqrt{x}}{y^2\sqrt{z}\sqrt[3]{t}})$

11. $Log(\sqrt{x}) - Log(y^2z) + Log(t) - Log(\sqrt[3]{t}) = Log(\dfrac{t^{\frac{2}{3}}\sqrt{x}}{y^2z})$

12. $Log(2A) + Log(B) - 2Log(AB) = Log(\dfrac{2}{AB})$

13. $Ln(ab) - Ln((ab)^t) - 2Ln(a) = Ln(a^{-t-1})$

14. If $Log_{10}(8) = x$ and $Log_{10}(3) = y$ express the following in terms of x and y only:

    a. $Log_{10}(24) = x + y$

    b. $Log_{10}(\dfrac{8}{3}) = x - y$

    c. $Log_{10}(72) = x + 2y$

    d. $Log_{10}(\dfrac{9}{8}) = 2x - y$

    e. $Log_{10}(720) = 1 + x + 2y$

    $Log_{10}(\dfrac{4}{2700}) =$

    f. $Log_{10}(8^{\frac{2}{3}}) - Log_{10}(3^3 \cdot 100) =$
    $\dfrac{2}{3}x - 3y - 2$

15. If $Log_3(2) = a$ and $Log_3(7) = b$ express the following in terms of x and y only:

    a. $Log_3(14) = a + b =$

    b. $Log_3(196) =$
    $Log_3(2^2 7^2) = 2a + 2b$

    c. $Log_3(42) =$
    $Log_3(2 \cdot 3 \cdot 7) = 1 + a + b$

    d. $Log_3(\dfrac{7}{2}) = b - a$

    $Log_3(\dfrac{21}{2}) =$

    e. $Log_3(3 \cdot 7) - Log_3(2) =$
    $1 + b - a$

    $Log_3(\dfrac{72}{63}) =$

    f. $Log_3(2^3 3^2) - Log_3(3^2 7^2) =$
    $2 + 2a - 2 - 2b = 2a - 2b$

    $Log_3(\dfrac{48}{49}) =$

    g. $Log_3(2^4 \cdot 3) - Log_3(7^2) =$
    $1 + 4a - 2b$

Change of base

1. $Log_2(5) = \dfrac{Log_7(5)}{Log_7(2)}$

2. $Log_3(-12) = Undefined$

3. $Log_{22}(51) = \dfrac{Log_{70}(51)}{Log_{70}(22)}$

4. $Log_{2.3}(1) = \dfrac{Log_3(1)}{Log_3(2.3)} = 0$

5. $Log_{2.9}(2.9) = \dfrac{Log_4(2.9)}{Log_4(2.9)} = 1$

6. $Log_3(-5) = undefined$

7. $Log_a(5) = \dfrac{Log_b(5)}{Log_b(a)}$

8. $Log_{12}(5y) = \dfrac{Ln(5y)}{Ln(12)}$

9. $Log_e(2) = \dfrac{Log_7(2)}{Log_7(e)}$

10. $Log(5) = \dfrac{Log_8(5)}{Log_8(10)}$

11. $Ln(15) = \dfrac{Log_3(15)}{Log_3(e)}$

12. $Log_{\sqrt{2}}(5) = \dfrac{Log_{12}(5)}{Log_{12}(\sqrt{2})}$

13. $Log_3(\dfrac{2}{3}) = \dfrac{Log_7(\dfrac{2}{3})}{Log_7(3)}$

14. $Log_5(\dfrac{2}{\sqrt{5}}) = \dfrac{Ln(\dfrac{2}{\sqrt{5}})}{Ln(5)}$

15. Simplify:

a. $\log_x b \cdot \log_b x = \dfrac{Ln(b)}{Ln(x)} \dfrac{Ln(x)}{Ln(b)} = 1$

b. $\log_x q \cdot \log_q r \cdot \log_r x = \dfrac{Ln(q)}{Ln(x)} \dfrac{Ln(r)}{Ln(q)} \dfrac{Ln(x)}{Ln(r)} = 1$

Logarithmic Equations (In this section student is encouraged to check the validity of the solutions by him/herself)

1. $Log_4(x) = 2$
   $x = 16$

2. $Log_{\frac{1}{3}}(x) = 4$
   $x = \sqrt[3]{4}$

3. $Log_4(x) = 4$
   $x = 256$

4. $Log_4(x) + Log_4(x) = 4$
   $Log_4(x^2) = 4$
   $x = 16$

5. $Log_{10}(2x+1) = 2$
   $x = \dfrac{99}{2}$

6. $Log_6(4x^2 - 6) = 2$
   $4x^2 - 6 = 36; x = \sqrt{\dfrac{21}{2}}$

7. $Log_2(64) = x$
   $x = 6$

8.
$$Log_2(x+2) + Log_2(x) = 0$$
$$(x+2)x = 1$$
$$x^2 + 2x - 1 = 0$$
$$x = \sqrt{2} - 1$$

9.
$$Log_5(5x+5) - Log_5(x+1) = 1$$
$$Log_5(5) = 1; x \in \Re$$

10.
$$Log_2(x-1) - Log_2(x) = -1$$
$$\frac{x-1}{x} = \frac{1}{2}; x = 2$$

11. $3^x = 81; 3^x = 3^4; x = 4$

12. $3^{2x} = \sqrt{27}; 3^{2x} = 3^{\frac{3}{2}}; x = \frac{3}{4}$

13. $2^{5x+2} = \dfrac{1}{\sqrt[3]{\sqrt{32}}}; 2^{5x+2} = 2^{-\frac{5}{6}}; x = -\dfrac{17}{30}$

14.
$$Ln(x) = 2.7$$
$$x = e^{2.7}$$

15.
$$Ln(x+1) = 1.86$$
$$x = e^{1.86} - 1$$

16.
$$e^x = 3$$
$$x = Ln(3)$$

17.
$$e^x = \sqrt{e}$$
$$x = \frac{1}{2}$$

18.
$$Log_b(81) = 4$$
$$b = 3$$

19.
$$e^{-2x} = 4.12$$
$$x = \frac{Ln(4.12)}{-2}$$

20.
$$Log_3(x) = Log_3(7) + Log_3(3)$$
$$x = 21$$

21.
$$Log_3(x^2 - 5) = Log_3(12) - Log_3(3)$$
$$Log_3(x^2 - 5) = Log_3(4)$$
$$x^2 - 5 = 4$$
$$x = \pm 3$$

22.
$$5 \cdot 9^x = 10$$
$$x = \frac{Ln(2)}{Ln(9)}$$

23.
$$10e^{4x+1} = 20$$
$$x = \frac{Ln(2) - 1}{4}$$

24.
$$3^t = 2 \cdot 5^{2t}$$
$$t = \frac{Ln(2)}{Ln(3) - 2Ln(5)}$$

25.
$$3^{t+1} = 4 \cdot 6^{2t-3}$$
$$x = \frac{Ln(3) + 3Ln(6) - 2Ln(2)}{2Ln(6) - Ln(3)}$$

26.
$$3 \cdot 2^t = 5 \cdot 6^{2t-3}$$
$$t = \frac{3Ln(3) + Ln(3) - Ln(5)}{2Ln(6) - Ln(2)}$$

27.
$$2 \cdot e^t = 8 \cdot 7^{2t-3}$$
$$t = \frac{2Ln(2) - 3Ln(7)}{2Ln(7) - 1}$$

28.
$$b^t = c \cdot d^{2t}$$
$$t = \frac{Ln(c)}{Ln(b) - 2Ln(d)}$$

29.
$$a \cdot b^t = c \cdot d^{2t}$$
$$t = \frac{Ln(a) - Ln(c)}{2Ln(d) - Ln(b)}$$

30.
$$e^t + e^t = 2$$
$$t = 1$$

31.
$$e^{2t} + e^{2t} = 3$$
$$x = \frac{Ln(3) - Ln(2)}{2}$$

32.
$$Ln(x) = 2$$
$$x = e^2$$

33.
$$Ln(x^2) = 2$$
$$x = \pm e$$

34.
$$Ln(x^2 - 1) = 2$$
$$x = \pm\sqrt{e^2 + 1}$$

35.
$$Ln(x+1) - Ln(2x) = -1$$
$$x = \frac{e}{2-e}$$

36.
$$Ln(x^2 + 1) = 1$$
$$x = \pm\sqrt{e-1}$$

37.
$$Log_{10}(x^2 + 19) = 2$$
$$x = \pm 9$$

38.
$$Ln(x-2) + Ln(2x-5) = 0$$
$$(x-2)(2x-5) = 1$$
$$x = 3, \left(\frac{3}{2} : No\right)$$

39.
$$Log(x+9) + Log(x) = 1$$
$$x = 1$$

40.
$$Log_2\left(\frac{1}{x}\right) - Log_2(4x+2) = -1$$
$$x = \frac{1}{2}, -1$$

41.
$$Log_5\left(1 + \frac{1}{x}\right) + Log_5\left(\frac{5}{4x}\right) = 2$$
$$x = -\frac{3}{4}$$

42.
$$Log_3\left(\frac{x}{2}\right) - Log_9(x+9) = \frac{1}{2}$$
$$Log_3\left(\frac{x}{2}\right) - \frac{Log_3(x+9)}{Log_3(9)} = \frac{1}{2}$$
$$Log_3\left(\frac{x}{2}\right) - \frac{Log_3(x+9)}{2} = \frac{1}{2}$$
$$Log_3\left(\frac{x}{2}\right) - \frac{Log_3(x+9)}{2} = \frac{1}{2}$$
$$2Log_3\left(\frac{x}{2}\right) - Log_3(x+9) = 1$$
$$Log_3\left(\left(\frac{x}{2}\right)^2\right) - Log_3(x+9) = 1$$
$$Log_3\left(\frac{\left(\frac{x^2}{4}\right)}{(x+9)}\right) = 1$$
$$Log_3\left(\frac{x^2}{4x+36}\right) = 1$$
$$3 = \frac{x^2}{4x+36}$$
$$12x + 108 = x^2$$
$$0 = x^2 - 12x - 108$$
$$x = \frac{12 \pm \sqrt{144 - 4 \cdot (-108)}}{2} =$$
$$= \frac{12 \pm 24}{2} = 18, -6$$

$$Log_2(\frac{x}{3}) - Log_4(x+2) = -\frac{1}{2}$$

43. $Log_2(\frac{x}{3}) - \dfrac{Log_2(x+2)}{Log_2(4)} = -\dfrac{1}{2}$

$$Log_2(\frac{x}{3}) - \dfrac{Log_2(x+2)}{2} = -\dfrac{1}{2}$$

$$2Log_2(\frac{x}{3}) - Log_2(x+2) = -1$$

$$Log_2(\frac{x^2}{9}) - Log_2(x+2) = -1$$

$$Log_2\left(\dfrac{\left(\dfrac{x^2}{9}\right)}{x+2}\right) = -1; \dfrac{x^2}{9x+18} = \dfrac{1}{2}$$

$$2x^2 - 9x - 18 = 0$$

$$x = \dfrac{9 \pm \sqrt{81 - 8 \cdot (-18)}}{4} =$$

$$x = \dfrac{9 \pm 25}{2} = 8.5, 4$$

44. $Log(\frac{1}{x}) - Log_{0.1}(x+90) = 1$

$$Log(\frac{1}{x}) - \dfrac{Log(x+90)}{-1} = 1$$

$$-Log(\frac{1}{x}) - Log(x+90) = -1$$

$$Log\left(\dfrac{x}{x+90}\right) = -1$$

$$\dfrac{x}{x+90} = \dfrac{1}{10}$$

$$10x = x + 90$$

$$x = 10$$

45. $2Log_9(9x) + Log_3(3x+2) = 2$

$$2\dfrac{Log_3(9x)}{Log_3(9)} + Log_3(3x+2) = 2$$

$$Log_3(9x) + Log_3(3x+2) = 2$$

$$Log_3(27x^2 + 18x) = 2$$

$$27x^2 + 18x = 9$$

$$3x^2 + 2x - 1 = 0$$

$$x = \dfrac{-2 \pm \sqrt{4 - 12 \cdot (-1)}}{6}$$

$$= \dfrac{-2 \pm 4}{6} = -1(No), \dfrac{1}{3}$$

46. $Log_2(\frac{1}{x}) - 2Log_2(x) = 3$

$$Log_2(\frac{1}{x^3}) = 3; \dfrac{1}{x^3} = 8; x = \dfrac{1}{2}$$

47. $Log_2(x) - Log_3(x) = Log_3(x)$

$$Log_2(x) = 2Log_3(x)$$

$$Log_2(x) = Log_3(x^2)$$

$$x = x^2; x^2 - x = 0$$

$$x(x-1) = 0$$

$$x = 0(No), 1$$

48. $Log_2(x) - 2Log_x(2) = 0$

$$Log_2(x) - 2\dfrac{Log_2(2)}{Log_2(x)} = 0$$

$$Log_2(x) - \dfrac{2}{Log_2(x)} = 0$$

$$(Log_2(x))^2 = 2$$

$$Log_2(x) = \sqrt{2}$$

$$x = 2^{\sqrt{2}}$$

49. $Log_2(x) - 2Log_x(2) = 1$

$$Log_2(x) - 2Log_x(2) = 1$$

$$Log_2(x) - 2\dfrac{Log_2(2)}{Log_2(x)} = 1$$

$$t = Log_2(x)$$

$$t - \dfrac{2}{t} = 1; t^2 - t - 2 = 0$$

$$(t-2)(t+1) = 0$$

$$t = 2 = Log_2(x); x = 4$$

$$t = -1 = Log_2(x); x = \dfrac{1}{2}$$

50. $Log_2(x) - 2Log_x(3) = 0$

$$e^{\pm\sqrt{Ln(2)Ln(3)}}$$

1.14. – SEQUENCES AND SERIES

Given The following sequences, write the first 3 terms and the term in the 20th position. If possible identify the pattern using text (follow example):

1. $a_n = 3n$ $a_1 = 3$ $a_2 = 6$ $a_3 = 9$ $a_{20} = 60$ Pattern: __add 3__

2. $a_n = 3n + 1$ $a_1 = 4$ $a_2 = 7$ $a_3 = 10$ $a_{20} = 61$ Pattern: __add 3__

3. $a_n = 3n - 5$ $a_1 = -5$ $a_2 = -2$ $a_3 = 1$ $a_{20} = 55$ Pattern: __add 3__

4. $a_n = 2n + 1$ $a_1 = 3$ $a_2 = 5$ $a_3 = 7$ $a_{20} = 41$ Pattern: __add 2__

5. $a_n = 2n$ $a_1 = 2$ $a_2 = 4$ $a_3 = 6$ $a_{20} = 40$ Pattern: __add 2__

6. $a_n = 2n - 4$ $a_1 = -2$ $a_2 = 0$ $a_3 = 2$ $a_{20} = 36$ Pattern: __add 2__

7. $a_n = -4n$ $a_1 = -4$ $a_2 = -8$ $a_3 = -12$ $a_{20} = -80$ Pattern: __add –4__

8. $a_n = -4n + 10$ $a_1 = 6$ $a_2 = 2$ $a_3 = -2$ $a_{20} = -70$ Pattern: __add –4__

9. $a_n = -4n - 6$ $a_1 = -10$ $a_2 = -14$ $a_3 = -18$ $a_{20} = -86$ Pattern: __add –4__

10. $a_n = \dfrac{n}{3}$ $a_1 = \dfrac{1}{3}$ $a_2 = \dfrac{2}{3}$ $a_3 = 1$ $a_{20} = \dfrac{20}{3}$ Pattern: __add $\dfrac{1}{3}$__

11. $a_n = \dfrac{n}{2}$ $a_1 = \dfrac{1}{2}$ $a_2 = 1$ $a_3 = \dfrac{3}{2}$ $a_{20} = 10$ Pattern: __add $\dfrac{1}{2}$__

12. $a_n = \dfrac{2n}{5} + 1$ $a_1 = \dfrac{7}{5}$ $a_2 = \dfrac{9}{5}$ $a_3 = \dfrac{11}{5}$ $a_{20} = 9$ Pattern: __add $\dfrac{2}{5}$__

13. $a_n = \dfrac{-3n}{7} + 5$ $a_1 = \dfrac{32}{7}$ $a_2 = \dfrac{29}{7}$ $a_3 = \dfrac{26}{7}$ $a_{20} = \dfrac{-25}{7}$ Pattern: __add $-\dfrac{3}{7}$__

14. $a_n = \dfrac{n}{9} - 5$ $a_1 = \dfrac{-44}{9}$ $a_2 = \dfrac{-43}{9}$ $a_3 = \dfrac{-42}{9}$ $a_{20} = \dfrac{-25}{9}$ Pattern: __add $\dfrac{1}{9}$__

15. $a_n = \dfrac{n}{10} - 1$ $a_1 = \dfrac{-9}{10}$ $a_2 = \dfrac{-8}{10}$ $a_3 = \dfrac{-7}{10}$ $a_{20} = 1$ Pattern: __add $\dfrac{1}{10}$__

16. $a_n = \dfrac{3n}{4} + 2$ $a_1 = \dfrac{11}{4}$ $a_2 = \dfrac{14}{4}$ $a_3 = \dfrac{17}{4}$ $a_{20} = \dfrac{68}{4}$ Pattern: __add $\dfrac{3}{4}$__

17. $a_n = n^2$ $a_1 = 1$ $a_2 = 4$ $a_3 = 9$ $a_{20} = 400$ Pattern: __different__

18. $a_n = n^3$ $a_1 = 1$ $a_2 = 8$ $a_3 = 27$ $a_{20} = 8000$ Pattern: __different__

19. $a_n = 2^n$ $a_1 = 2$ $a_2 = 4$ $a_3 = 8$ $a_{20} = 2^{20}$ Pattern: __multiply by 2__

20. $a_n = -2^n$ $a_1 = -2$ $a_2 = -4$ $a_3 = -8$ $a_{20} = -2^{20}$ Pattern: __multiply by 2__

21. $a_n = 2^{-n}$ $a_1 = \dfrac{1}{2}$ $a_2 = \dfrac{1}{4}$ $a_3 = \dfrac{1}{8}$ $a_{20} = \dfrac{1}{2^{20}}$ Pattern: __multiply by $\dfrac{1}{2}$__

22. $a_n = -2^{-n}$ $a_1 = -\dfrac{1}{2}$ $a_2 = -\dfrac{1}{4}$ $a_3 = -\dfrac{1}{8}$ $a_{20} = -\dfrac{1}{2^{20}}$ Pattern: __multiply by $\dfrac{1}{2}$__

23. $a_n = (-2)^n$ $a_1 = -2$ $a_2 = 4$ $a_3 = -8$ $a_{20} = 2^{20}$ Pattern: __multiply by –2__

24. $a_n = 2^{n-1}$ $a_1 = 1$ $a_2 = 2$ $a_3 = 4$ $a_{20} = 2^{19}$ Pattern: __multiply by 2__

25. $a_n = 2^{n+2}$ $a_1 = 8$ $a_2 = 16$ $a_3 = 32$ $a_{20} = 2^{22}$ Pattern: __multiply by 2__

26. $a_n = 3 \times 2^n$ $a_1 = 6$ $a_2 = 12$ $a_3 = 24$ $a_{20} = 3 \cdot 2^{20}$ Pattern: __multiply by 2__

27. $a_n = -5 \times 2^{n-1}$ $a_1 = -5$ $a_2 = -10$ $a_3 = -20$ $a_{20} = -5 \cdot 2^{19}$ Pattern: __multiply by 2__

28. $a_n = 5 \times 2^{1-n}$ $a_1 = 5$ $a_2 = \dfrac{5}{2}$ $a_3 = \dfrac{5}{4}$ $a_{20} = \dfrac{5}{2^{19}}$ Pattern: __multiply by $\dfrac{1}{2}$__

29. $a_n = (-3)^{2-n}$ $a_1 = -3$ $a_2 = 1$ $a_3 = -\dfrac{1}{3}$ $a_{20} = \dfrac{1}{3^{18}}$ Pattern: <u> multiply by $-\dfrac{1}{3}$ </u>

30. $a_n = 2 \times (-3)^n$ $a_1 = -6$ $a_2 = 18$ $a_3 = -54$ $a_{20} = 2 \cdot 3^{20}$ Pattern: <u> multiply by -3 </u>

31. $a_n = 2 \times (-5)^{n-1}$ $a_1 = 2$ $a_2 = -10$ $a_3 = 50$ $a_{20} = 2 \cdot (-5)^{19}$ Pattern: <u> multiply by -5 </u>

32. $a_n = (-3)^{n+1}$ $a_1 = 9$ $a_2 = -27$ $a_3 = 81$ $a_{20} = (-3)^{21}$ Pattern: <u> multiply by -3 </u>

33. $a_n = 1 + 5^{n-2}$ $a_1 = \dfrac{6}{5}$ $a_2 = 2$ $a_3 = 6$ $a_{20} = 1 + 5^{18}$ Pattern: <u> different   </u>

34. $a_n = 3 \times 2^n$ $a_1 = 6$ $a_2 = 12$ $a_3 = 24$ $a_{20} = 3 \cdot 2^{20}$ Pattern: <u> multiply by 2   </u>

35. $a_n = -5 \times 2^{n-1}$ $a_1 = -5$ $a_2 = -10$ $a_3 = -20$ $a_{20} = -5 \cdot 2^{19}$ Pattern: <u> multiply by 2 </u>

36. $a_n = 2 \times 3^n$ $a_1 = 6$ $a_2 = 18$ $a_3 = 54$ $a_{20} = 2 \cdot 3^{20}$ Pattern: <u> multiply by 3   </u>

37. $a_n = 5^{n-2} + 3$ $a_1 = \dfrac{16}{5}$ $a_2 = 4$ $a_3 = 8$ $a_{20} = 3 + 5^{18}$ Pattern: <u> different   </u>

38. $a_n = (-3)^n$ $a_1 = -3$ $a_2 = 9$ $a_3 = -27$ $a_{20} = 3^{20}$ Pattern: <u>   multiply by -3 </u>

39. $a_n = 2 \times (-3)^n$ $a_1 = -6$ $a_2 = 18$ $a_3 = -54$ $a_{20} = 2 \cdot 3^{20}$ Pattern: <u> multiply by -3 </u>

40. $a_n = 2 \times (-5)^{n-1}$ $a_1 = 2$ $a_2 = -10$ $a_3 = 50$ $a_{20} = 2 \cdot (-5)^{19}$ Pattern: <u> multiply by -5 </u>

41. $a_n = (-3)^{n+1}$ $a_1 = 9$ $a_2 = -27$ $a_3 = 81$ $a_{20} = -3^{21}$ Pattern: <u> multiply by -3 </u>

42. $a_n = 1 + 5^{n-2}$ $a_1 = \dfrac{6}{5}$ $a_2 = 2$ $a_3 = 6$ $a_{20} = 1 + 5^{18}$ Pattern: <u> different   </u>

43. The sequences in which the pattern is add/subtract a number are called <u>Arithmetic</u>

44. The sequences in which the pattern is multiply/divide (pay attention that dividing by a is the same as multiplying by <u>the inverse</u>) a number are called <u>Geometric</u>

45. $a_n = 2a_{n-1}$ $a_1 = 1$ $a_2 = 2$ $a_3 = 4$ $a_{20} = 2^{19}$ Pattern: <u>multiply by 2</u>

46. $a_{n+2} = a_n + a_{n+1}$ $a_1 = 1$ $a_2 = 1$ $a_3 = 2$ $a_{20} =$ Pattern: <u>Each term is the sum of the previous 2 (Fibonacci)</u>

47. In the last 2 sequences the terms are given <u>in terms of the previous terms</u>

48. (T/<u>F</u>) Arithmetic and Geometric sequences are most of the sequences that exist.

49. The terms in a convergent geometric sequence tend to <u>a number</u>, in a none–convergent sequence the terms tend to <u>infinity</u> or <u>negative infinity (or alternate)</u>.

50. An example of a convergent geometric sequence: 200, 100, 50, 25…

51. An example of a divergent geometric sequence: 7, 21, 63, 189…

52. An example of a alternating convergent geometric sequence: 80, –40, 20, –10…

53. An example of a none alternating divergent geometric sequence: 2, 10, 50, 250...

54. A convergent geometric sequence is a sequence in which r is <u>between –1 and 1</u>

Given the following sequences:

a. For each one write: arithmetic, geometric convergent, geometric divergent or neither, the <u>next term</u> and their <u>general term</u> (in case they are geometric or arithmetic only).

b. Try to write the general term of the other sequences as well.

55. 1, 2, 3, 4, <u> 5 </u>   56. 1, 2, 4, 8, <u> 16 </u>

    $a_n = 1 + (n-1)1$, Arithmetic $a_n = 2^{n-1}$, Geometric

    $a_n = n$

57. 1, 3, 5, 7, ___

$a_n = 1 + (n-1)2$, Arithmetic

$a_n = -1 + 2n$

58. 1, 3, 9, 27, _81_

$a_n = 3^{n-1}$, Geometric

59. 4, 6, 9, 13,5, _20.25_

$a_n = 4\left(\dfrac{3}{2}\right)^{n-1}$, Geometric

60. 4, 1, –2, –5, _–8_

$a_n = 4 + (n-1)(-3)$, Arithmetic

$a_n = 7 - 3n$

61. 5, 0, –4, –7, ___

Neither

62. 10, 1000, 100000, _10000000_

$a_n = 10 \cdot 100^{n-1}$, Geometric

63. 30, 10, $\dfrac{10}{3}$, $\dfrac{10}{9}$, $\dfrac{10}{27}$

$a_n = 30 \cdot \left(\dfrac{1}{3}\right)^{n-1}$, Geometric

64. 2, 10, 50, 250, _1250_

$a_n = 2 \cdot 5^{n-1}$, Geometric

65. 2, 102, 202, 302, _402_

$a_n = 2 + (n-1)100$, Arithmetic

$a_n = -98 + 100n$

66. 1, –1, 1, –1, _1_

$a_n = (-1)^{n-1}$, Geometric

67. –2, 2, –2, 2, _–2_

$a_n = -2(-1)^{n-1}$, Geometric

68. 3, –6, 12, –24, _48_

$a_n = 3(-2)^{n-1}$, Geometric

69. –8, 4, –2, 1, $\left(-\dfrac{1}{2}\right)$

$a_n = -8\left(-\dfrac{1}{2}\right)^{n-1}$, Geometric

70. 5, 1, $\dfrac{1}{5}$, $\dfrac{1}{25}$, $\dfrac{1}{125}$

$a_n = 5\left(\dfrac{1}{5}\right)^{n-1}$, Geometric

71. 100, 10, 1, $\dfrac{1}{10}$, $\dfrac{1}{100}$

$a_n = 100\left(\dfrac{1}{10}\right)^{n-1}$, Geometric

72. $\dfrac{3}{4}$, $\dfrac{3}{8}$, $\dfrac{3}{16}$, $\dfrac{3}{32}$

$a_n = \dfrac{3}{4}\left(\dfrac{1}{2}\right)^{n-1}$, Geometric

73. 12, 11, 10, 9, _8_

$a_n = 12 + (n-1)(-1)$, Arithmetic

$a_n = 13 - n$

74. $\dfrac{4}{9}$, $\dfrac{5}{9}$, $\dfrac{6}{9}$, $\dfrac{6}{9}$

$a_n = \dfrac{4}{9} + (n-1)\left(\dfrac{1}{9}\right)$, Arithmetic

$a_n = -98 + 100n$

75. 9, 8, 6, 5, 3, 2, ___

Neither

76. 5, 9, 13, _17_

$a_n = 5 + (n-1)4$, Arithmetic

$a_n = 1 + 4n$

77. 1, $\dfrac{3}{2}$, $\dfrac{9}{4}$, $\dfrac{27}{8}$, $\dfrac{81}{16}$

$a_n = \left(\dfrac{3}{2}\right)^{n-1}$, Geometric

78. 5, $-\dfrac{5}{3}$, $\dfrac{5}{9}$, $-\dfrac{5}{27}$, $\dfrac{5}{81}$

$a_n = 5\left(-\dfrac{1}{3}\right)^{n-1}$, Geometric

79. –1, –2, –3, _–4_

$a_n = -1 + (n-1)(-1)$, Arithmetic

$a_n = -n$

80. –2, 4, –8, _16_

$a_n = -2(-2)^{n-1}$, Geometric

81. 70, 20, $\dfrac{40}{7}$, $\dfrac{80}{14}$

$a_n = 70\left(\dfrac{2}{7}\right)^{n-1}$, Geometric

82. 100, 10, 1, $\dfrac{1}{10}$

$a_n = 100\left(\dfrac{1}{10}\right)^{n-1}$, Geometric

83. $100, -10, 1, \dfrac{-1}{10}, \dfrac{1}{100}$

$a_n = 100\left(-\dfrac{1}{10}\right)^{n-1}$, Geometric

84. $3, 24, 192, \underline{1536}$

$a_n = 3 \cdot 8^{n-1}$, Geometric

85. $90, 9, \dfrac{9}{10}, \dfrac{9}{100}$

$a_n = 90 \cdot \left(\dfrac{1}{10}\right)^{n-1}$, Geometric

86. $\dfrac{3}{2}, \dfrac{4}{3}, \dfrac{5}{4}, \dfrac{6}{5}$

Neither, General term:

$a_n = \dfrac{2+n}{1+n}$ Numerator and

denominator are arithmetic.

87. $\dfrac{40}{3}, \dfrac{20}{6}, \dfrac{10}{12}, \dfrac{5}{24}, \dfrac{5}{96}$

$a_n = \dfrac{40}{3}\left(\dfrac{1}{4}\right)^{n-1}$, Geometric

88. $\dfrac{2}{3}, -\dfrac{4}{9}, \dfrac{8}{27}, -\dfrac{16}{81}, \dfrac{32}{243}$

$a_n = \dfrac{2}{3}\left(-\dfrac{2}{3}\right)^{n-1}$, Geometric

89. $-\dfrac{1}{2}, -\dfrac{1}{4}, -\dfrac{1}{8}, -\dfrac{1}{16}, -\dfrac{1}{32}$

$a_n = -\dfrac{1}{2}\left(-\dfrac{1}{2}\right)^{n-1}$, Geometric

90. $\dfrac{1}{7}, -\dfrac{1}{14}, \dfrac{1}{21}, -\dfrac{1}{28}, \dfrac{1}{35}$

Neither, General term:

$a_n = \dfrac{1}{7n}(-1)^{n-1}$

91. $8, 5, 3, 0, \underline{\quad} ...$

Neither

92. $3, \dfrac{3}{4}, \dfrac{3}{16}, \dfrac{3}{64}$

$a_n = 3\left(\dfrac{1}{4}\right)^{n-1}$, Geometric

93. $81, -9, 1, -\dfrac{1}{9}, \dfrac{1}{81}$

$a_n = 81\left(-\dfrac{1}{9}\right)^{n-1}$, Geometric

94. $2, -10, 50, -250$

$a_n = 2(-5)^{n-1}$, Geometric

In each one of the following sequences find the term indicated:

95. $1, 4, 7 ... (a_{31})$ $a_{31} = 1 + 3 \cdot 30 = 91$

96. $-8, -5, -2 ... (a_{37})$ $a_{37} = -8 + 3 \cdot 36 = 100$

97. $4, -8, 16 ... (a_{15})$ $a_{15} = 4(-2)^{14}$

98. $32, -8, 2 ... (a_{11})$ $a_{37} = 32\left(-\dfrac{1}{4}\right)^{10}$

99. $68, -34, 17 ... (a_9)$ $a_9 = 68\left(-\dfrac{1}{2}\right)^8 = \dfrac{68}{256}$

100. $3, 14, 25 ... (a_9)$ $a_9 = 3 + 8 \cdot 11 = 91$

101. $-4000, 1000, -250, ... (a_7)$ $a_7 = -4000\left(-\dfrac{1}{4}\right)^6 = -\dfrac{125}{128}$

102. $\ln(200), \ln(100), \ln(50) ... (a_7)$ $a_7 = \ln(200) + 6 \cdot \ln(\dfrac{1}{2}) = \ln(\dfrac{200}{64})$

103. The 4th term of a geometric sequence is 3, the 6th term is $\dfrac{27}{4}$.

a. The ratio of the sequence.

$$a_6 = a_4 r^2; \dfrac{27}{4} = 3r^2$$

$$r = \pm\dfrac{3}{2}$$

b. Divergent |r| > 1

$$a_4 = a_1 r^3; 3 = \pm\left(\dfrac{3}{2}\right)^3 a_1$$

c.

$$a_1 = \pm\left(\dfrac{8}{9}\right)$$

d. Find a$_{12}$

$$a_{12} = \left(\pm\left(\dfrac{8}{9}\right)\right)\left(\pm\left(\dfrac{3}{2}\right)^{11}\right) = \dfrac{3^9}{2^8}$$

e. Sum the first 15 terms.

$$S_{15} = \dfrac{\left(\pm\left(\dfrac{8}{9}\right)\right)\left(\left(\pm\left(\dfrac{3}{2}\right)\right)^{15} - 1\right)}{\pm\left(\dfrac{3}{2}\right) - 1}$$

104. The 2nd term of a arithmetic sequence is –2, the 6th term is –4.

a. Find the difference of the sequence. $a_6 = a_2 + 4d; -4 = -2 + 4d; d = \dfrac{1}{2}$

b. a$_1$ $a_2 = a_1 + d; -2 = a_1 + \dfrac{1}{2}; a_1 = -\dfrac{5}{2}$

c. a$_{12}$ $a_{12} = a_1 + 11d; a_{12} = -\dfrac{5}{2} + \dfrac{11}{2}; a_{12} = \dfrac{6}{2} = 3$

d. Sum of the first 50 terms. $S_{50} = \dfrac{50}{2}\left(\dfrac{-10}{2} + \dfrac{49}{2}\right) = \dfrac{1950}{4}$

105. The 10th term of a geometric sequence is 5, the 14th term is $\dfrac{80}{81}$

a. The ratio of the sequence. $a_{14} = a_{10} r^4; \dfrac{80}{81} = 5r^4; r = \pm\dfrac{2}{3}$

b. a$_1$ $a_{10} = a_1 r^9; 5 = a_1\left(\pm\dfrac{2}{3}\right)^9; a_1 = 5\left(\pm\dfrac{3}{2}\right)^9$

c. a$_7$ $a_{10} = a_7 r^3; 5 = a_7\left(\pm\dfrac{2}{3}\right)^3; a_1 = 5\left(\pm\dfrac{3}{2}\right)^3 = \pm\dfrac{135}{8}$

d. Sum the first 10 terms. $S_{10} = \dfrac{\left(5\left(\pm\dfrac{3}{2}\right)^9\right)\left(\left(\pm\left(\dfrac{2}{3}\right)\right)^{10} - 1\right)}{\pm\left(\dfrac{2}{3}\right) - 1}$

106. The 7th term of a arithmetic sequence is 120, the 16th term is 201.

a. The difference of the sequence. $a_{16} = a_7 + 9d; 201 = 120 + 9d; d = 9$

b. Find a$_1$ $a_7 = a_1 + 6d$
$a_1 = 66$

c. Find a$_{12}$ $a_{12} = a_1 + 11d = 66 + 99 = 165$

d. Sum the first 50 terms. $S_{50} = \dfrac{50}{2}(132 + 49 \cdot 9) = 14325$

68

107. All the terms in a geometric sequence are positive. The first term is 7 and the 3rd term is 28.

$$a_3 = a_1 r^2$$

a. Find the common ratio. $28 = 7r^2$ Positive since all terms are positive.

$$r = +2$$

b. Find the sum of the first 14 terms. $S_{14} = \dfrac{7\left(2^{14} - 1\right)}{2 - 1} = 114681$

108. The fifth term of an arithmetic sequence is –20 and the twelfth term is –44.

$$a_{12} = a_5 + 7d$$

a. Find the common difference.

$$d = -\dfrac{24}{7}$$

$$a_5 = a_1 + 4d$$

b. Find the first term of the sequence. $-20 = a_1 - \dfrac{24}{7} \cdot 4$

$$a_1 = -\dfrac{44}{7}$$

c. Calculate eighty–seventh term. $a_{87} = a_1 + 86d = -\dfrac{44}{7} - 86 \cdot \dfrac{24}{7} = -\dfrac{2108}{7}$

d. Sum of the first 150 terms. $S_{150} = \dfrac{150}{2}(-\dfrac{88}{7} + 149 \cdot \dfrac{24}{7}) = \dfrac{261600}{7}$

109. Sum the following sequences:

a. $3 + 6 + 9 + 12 + \ldots + 69 =$ First find the number of terms:

$69 = 3 + (n - 1)3; n = 23$ $S_{23} = \dfrac{23}{2}(6 + 22 \cdot 3) = 828$

b. $6 + 14 + 22 + 30 + \ldots + 54 =$ First find the number of terms:

$54 = 6 + (n - 1)8; n = 7$ $S_7 = \dfrac{7}{2}(12 + 6 \cdot 8) = 210$

c. $5 + \dfrac{5}{3} + \dfrac{5}{9} + \ldots = S_\infty = \dfrac{a_1(r^\infty - 1)}{r - 1} = \dfrac{5\left(\left(\dfrac{1}{3}\right)^\infty - 1\right)}{\left(\dfrac{1}{3}\right) - 1} = \dfrac{-5}{\left(-\dfrac{2}{3}\right)} = -\dfrac{15}{2}$

Attention: $\left(\dfrac{1}{3}\right)^\infty \approx 0$

d. $1 + 2 + 3 + 4 + \ldots + 158 =$ First find the number of terms:

$158 = 1 + (n - 1)1; n = 158$ $S_{158} = \dfrac{158}{2}(2 + 157 \cdot 1) = 12561$

e. $9 + 18 + 27 + 36 + \ldots + 900 =$ First find the number of terms:

$900 = 9 + (n - 1)9; n = 100$ $S_{100} = \dfrac{100}{2}(18 + 99 \cdot 9) = 45450$

f. $80 + 20 + 5 + \ldots$ $S_\infty = \dfrac{a_1(r^\infty - 1)}{r-1} = \dfrac{80\left(\left(\dfrac{1}{4}\right)^\infty - 1\right)}{\left(\dfrac{1}{4}\right) - 1} = \dfrac{-80}{\left(-\dfrac{3}{4}\right)} = \dfrac{320}{3}$

Attention that $\left(\dfrac{1}{4}\right)^\infty \approx 0$

g. $100 + 97 + 94 + \ldots + 19 =$ First find the number of terms:

$19 = 100 + (n-1)(-3); n = 28$ $\qquad S_{28} = \dfrac{28}{2}(200 + 27 \cdot (-3)) = 1666$

h. $18 + 6 + 2 + \ldots =$ $\qquad S_\infty = \dfrac{a_1}{r-1} = \dfrac{18}{\left(1 - \dfrac{1}{3}\right)} = \dfrac{54}{2} = 27$

i. $\dfrac{2}{5} + \dfrac{6}{10} + \dfrac{18}{20} + \ldots + \dfrac{243}{80}$ $\qquad$ Find the number of terms:

$\dfrac{243}{80} = \dfrac{2}{5} \cdot \left(\dfrac{3}{2}\right)^{n-1}; n = 5$ $\qquad S_5 = \dfrac{\dfrac{2}{5}\left(\left(\dfrac{3}{2}\right)^5 - 1\right)}{\left(\dfrac{3}{2} - 1\right)} = \dfrac{211}{40}$

j. $\dfrac{1}{3} + \dfrac{2}{9} + \dfrac{4}{27} + \ldots = S_\infty = \dfrac{a_1}{r-1} = \dfrac{\left(\dfrac{1}{3}\right)}{\left(1 - \dfrac{2}{3}\right)} = 1$

k. $12 + 7 + 2 + \ldots - 98 =$ First find the number of terms:

$-98 = 12 + (n-1)(-5); n = 23$ $\qquad S_{23} = \dfrac{23}{2}(24 + 22 \cdot (-5)) = 989$

l. $100 + 150 + 200 + \ldots + 1000 =$ First find the number of terms:

$1000 = 100 + (n-1)(50); n = 19$ $\qquad S_{19} = \dfrac{19}{2}(200 + 18 \cdot (50)) = 10450$

110. $S_n = \dfrac{n}{2}(-12 + (n-1)7) = 10000$ $\qquad$ So 55 terms are needed.

$n \approx 54.8$

111. $\qquad$ 20, 23, 26 … Arithmetic $\qquad S_{40} = \dfrac{40}{2}(40 + 39 \cdot 3) = 3140 \, seats$

112. A ball bounces on the floor. It is released from a height of 160 cm. After the 1st bounce it reaches a height of 120 cm and 90 cm after the 2nd. If the patterns continue find:

   a. The height the ball will reach after the 6th bounce.

   160, 120, 90, … Geometric, $r = \dfrac{120}{160} = \dfrac{90}{120} = \dfrac{3}{4}$

   $a_n = 160 \cdot \left(\dfrac{3}{4}\right)^{n-1}; a_7 = 160 \cdot \left(\dfrac{3}{4}\right)^6 = \dfrac{3645}{128} \approx 28.5 \, cm$

   Attention that a_7 corresponds to height <u>after</u> the 6th bounce.

b. The total distance the ball passed after a <u>long period o time</u>.

$$S_\infty = \frac{a_1(r^\infty - 1)}{r - 1} = \frac{160\left(\left(\frac{3}{4}\right)^\infty - 1\right)}{\left(\frac{3}{4}\right) - 1} = \frac{-160}{\left(-\frac{1}{4}\right)} = 640cm \qquad \left(\frac{3}{4}\right)^\infty \approx 0$$

113. In a certain forest the current population of rabbits is 200 objects. It is know that the population increases by 20% every year.

   a. The population of rabbits after a year. $\quad \frac{120}{100} \cdot 200 = 240rabbits$

   b. The population of rabbits after 2 years. $\quad \frac{120}{100} \cdot 240 = 288rabbits$

   c. What kind of a sequence is it? State the expression for the population after n years. Geometric. $r = \frac{120}{100} = \frac{6}{5} \qquad a_n = 200 \cdot \left(\frac{6}{5}\right)^{n-1}$

   d. Find the total number of rabbits after 10 years (assuming none has died).

   $$a_{11} = 200 \cdot \left(\frac{6}{5}\right)^{10} \approx 1240rabbits$$

114. In a research it was observed that the number of defective products produced by a machine per year decreases by 10% every year (due to technological improvements). In a certain year the machine made 300 products.

   a. Find the number of defective products produced a year later.

   $$\frac{90}{100} \cdot 300 = 270defective$$

   b. Find the number of defective products produced 2 years later.

   $$\frac{90}{100} \cdot 270 = 243defective$$

   c. What kind of a sequence is it? State the expression for the number of errors committed after n years.

   Geometric. $r = \frac{90}{100} = \frac{9}{10} \qquad a_n = 300 \cdot \left(\frac{9}{10}\right)^{n-1}$

   d. The <u>total number</u> produced $\quad S_8 = \frac{300\left(\left(\frac{9}{10}\right)^8 - 1\right)}{\left(\frac{9}{10}\right) - 1} \approx 1710defective$

115. In a certain company the pay scale follows a pattern of an arithmetic sequence (every year). This means:

   a. The salary increases by a certain % every year (True/**False**), explain.
   <u>Since the amount of the increase is fixed, the percentage is not the same</u>
   <u>one every year. An increase by a percentage corresponds to a geometric</u>
   <u>sequence.</u>

   b. The salary increases by a certain amount every year (**True**/False),
   <u>Since the amount of the increase is fixed, the pattern is identical to an</u>
   <u>Arithmetic sequence.</u>

116. Given the sequence: $a, a^2, a^3 \ldots$
   a. This is a <u>geometric</u> sequence.
   b. Its general term: $t_n = a^n$

   c. The infinite sequence adds up to 10, find a. $S_\infty = 10 = \dfrac{a}{1-a}; a = \dfrac{10}{11}$

117. Given the sequence: $a^{-2}, a^{-3}, a^{-4} \ldots$

   a. This is a <u>geometric</u> sequence.
   b. Its general term, simplified. $t_n = a^{-n-1}$

   c. The infinite sequence adds up to $\dfrac{1}{2}$, find a.

   $$S_\infty = \frac{1}{2} = \frac{a^{-2}}{1-a^{-1}}; \frac{1}{2} = \frac{1}{a^2 - a}; a^2 - a - 2 = 0$$
   $$(a-2)(a+1) = 0; a = 2, -1$$

COMPOUND INTEREST
1. 1200$ are put in account that gives 2% per year. Calculate the amount of money in the account after:
   a. 1 year. <u>Amount = 1200(1.02) = 1224 $</u>

   b. 2 years. <u>Amount = $1200(1.02)^2 = 1248.48$ $</u>

2. It should be multiplied by <u>1.05</u>
3. It should be multiplied by <u>1.56</u>
4. It should be multiplied by 0.<u>95</u>

5. It should be multiplied by <u>1.15</u>
6. It should be multiplied by <u>0.88</u>
7. It should be multiplied by <u>3.3</u>

8. 1000$ are put in account that takes 5% commission per year. Calculate the amount of money in the account after:
   a. 1 year. Amount = $1000(0.95) = 950$ $

   b. 2 years. Amount = $1000(0.95)^2 = 902.5$ $

9. 2000$ are being put in a deposit that pays 5% (per year).

   a. Fill the table:

Number of Years	Interest earned at the end of the year	Amount in deposit ($)
0		2000
1	$\dfrac{5}{100} 2000 = 100$	2100
2	$\dfrac{5}{100} 2100 = 105$	2205
3	$\dfrac{5}{100} 2205 = 110.25$	2315.25
4	$\dfrac{5}{100} 2315.25 = 115.7625$	2431.0125
5	$\dfrac{5}{100} 2431.0125 = 121.550625$	2552.563125

b. Observe the numbers in the compound interest column: 2000, 2100, 2205… What kind of a sequence is that? Write its general term. Geometric sequence. $a_n = 2000(1.05)^{n-1}$

c. $a_{21} = 2000(1.05)^{20} \approx 5310$ $ Attention that a_{21} corresponds to "after 20 years" as a_1 corresponds to "after 0 years".

d. $a_n = 2000(1.05)^{n-1}$ means a_1 corresponds to "after 0 years" while writing $a_n = 2000(1.05)^n$ means a_1 corresponds to "after 1 year"

10. A loan of 1200$ is made at 12% per year compounded semiannually, over 5 years the debt will grow to:
    a. $\$1200(1 + 0.12)^5$
    b. **$\$1200(1 + 0.06)^{10}$**
    c. $\$1200(1 + 0.6)^{10}$
    d. $\$1200(1 + 0.06)^5$
    e. $\$1200(1 + 0.12)^{10}$

11. A loan of 23200$ is made at 8% per year compounded quarterly, over 6 years the debt will grow to:
    a. $\$23200(1 + 0.2)^{24}$
    b. $\$23200(1 + 0.08)^6$
    c. **$\$23200(1 + 0.02)^{24}$**
    d. $\$23200(1 + 0.08)^{24}$
    e. $\$23200(1 + 0.02)^6$

12. A loan of 20$ is made at 12% per year compounded monthly, over 8 years the debt will grow to:
    a. $\$20(1 + 0.12)^{80}$
    b. $\$20(1 + 0.01)^8$
    c. $\$20(1 + 0.012)^{96}$
    d. **$\$20(1 + 0.01)^{96}$**
    e. $\$20(1 + 0.06)^{12}$

13. A loan of X$ is made at 12% per year compounded every 4 months, over 5 years the debt will grow to:
    a. $\$X(1 + 0.12)^4$
    b. $\$X(1 + 0.3)^5$
    c. $\$X(1 + 0.12)^{15}$
    d. **$\$X(1 + 0.03)^{15}$**
    e. $\$X(1 + 0.3)^{15}$

14. A loan of X$ is made at i% per year compounded every m months, over n years the debt will grow to:

$$Debt = X(1 + \frac{i}{100})^{\frac{12n}{m}}$$

15. Calculate the total amount owing after two years on a loan of 1500$ if the interest rate is 11% compounded

    a. Annually $Amount = 1500(1+\dfrac{11}{100})^2 \approx 1848\$$

    b. Semiannually $Amount = 1500(1+\dfrac{11}{200})^4 \approx 1858\$$

    c. Quarterly $Amount = 1500(1+\dfrac{11}{400})^8 \approx 1864\$$

    d. Monthly $Amount = 1500(1+\dfrac{11}{1200})^{24} \approx 1867\$$

16. How much will a client have to repay on a loan of 800$ after 2 years, if the 12% interest is compounded annually. $Amount = 800(1+\dfrac{12}{100})^2 = 1003.52\$$

17. Find the compound interest **earned** by the deposit. Round to the nearest cent. $3000 at 12% compounded semiannually for 10 years

$$AmountObtained = 3000(1+\dfrac{12}{200})^{20} \approx 9620\$$$

$$AmountEarned = 9620 - 3000 = 6620\$$$

18. How many years will it take to a 100$ to double assuming interest rate is 6%. Compounded semiannually. $200 = 100(1+\dfrac{6}{200})^{2n}$ So it will take 12 years.

$$n \approx 11.7$$

19. How many years will it take to a X$ to triple assuming interest rate is 7%. Compounded quarterly $3X = X(1+\dfrac{7}{400})^{4n}$ So it will take 16 years.

$$n \approx 15.8$$

20. Find the interest rate given to a certain person in case he made a deposit of 1000$ and obtained 1200$ after 3 years, compounded monthly.

$$1200 = 1000(1+\dfrac{i}{1200})^{36}$$

$$i \approx 6.09$$

21. Find the interest rate given to a certain person in case he made a deposit of 2500$ and obtained 3000$ after 10 years, compounded yearly.

$$3000 = 2500(1+\dfrac{i}{100})^{10}$$

$$i \approx 1.84$$

SIGMA NOTATION

1. The sum $\displaystyle\sum_{k=2}^{4} 2^k$ is equal to:

   a. $2^1 + 2^2 + 2^3 + 2^4$
   b. $2^2 + 2^4$
   c. $2^2 + 3^3 + 4^4$
   d. **$2^2 + 2^3 + 2^4$**

2. The sum $\displaystyle\frac{1}{4}\sum_{m=2}^{4} x_m$ is equal to:

   a. $\dfrac{\dfrac{1}{4}x_2 + \dfrac{1}{4}x_3 + \dfrac{1}{4}x_4}{\dfrac{1}{4}}$

   b. $\dfrac{1}{4}x_2 + x_3 + x_4$

   c. $\dfrac{1}{2}x_2 + \dfrac{1}{3}x_3 + \dfrac{1}{4}x_4$

   d. $\dfrac{1}{4}(2+3+4)$

3. The sum $\displaystyle\sum_{j=4}^{n} \frac{j}{j+1}$ is equal to:

   a. $\dfrac{1}{2} + \dfrac{3}{4} + \dfrac{5}{6} + ... + \dfrac{n}{n+1}$

   b. $\dfrac{1}{2} + \dfrac{2}{3} + \dfrac{3}{4} + ... + \dfrac{n}{n+1}$

   c. $\dfrac{4}{5} + \dfrac{5}{6} + \dfrac{6}{7} + ... + \dfrac{n}{n+1}$

   d. $\dfrac{4}{5} + \dfrac{5}{6} + \dfrac{6}{7} + ... + \dfrac{n+4}{n+5}$

4. Write out fully what is meant by

   a. $\displaystyle\sum_{i=4}^{i=6} 2i - 1 = 7 + 9 + 11$

   b. $\displaystyle\sum_{i=2}^{i=5} \frac{i}{i^2+1} = \frac{2}{5} + \frac{3}{10} + \frac{4}{17} + \frac{6}{26}$

   c. $\displaystyle\sum_{i=4}^{i=6} (2i-3)^2 = 25 + 49 + 81$

   d. $\displaystyle\sum_{k=3}^{i=7} (2^k + \sqrt{k}) = 8 + \sqrt{3} + 16 + \sqrt{4} + 32 + \sqrt{5} + 64 + \sqrt{6} + 128 + \sqrt{7}$

   e. $\displaystyle\sum_{i=1}^{i=4} (-1)^i \times 3^{2i} = -9 + 81 - 729 + 6561$

5. Write each series using sigma notation:

   a. $4 + 9 + 16 + 25 + 36 + 49 + 64 + 81 = \displaystyle\sum_{i=2}^{i=9} i^2$

   b. $5 + 9 + 13 + 17 + 21 + 25 + 29 + 33... = \displaystyle\sum_{i=1}^{i=\infty} 5 + (i-1)4$

   c. $1 - \dfrac{1}{3} + \dfrac{1}{9} - \dfrac{1}{27} + \dfrac{1}{81} - \dfrac{1}{243} = \displaystyle\sum_{i=1}^{i=6} 1 \cdot \left(-\dfrac{1}{3}\right)^{i-1}$

6. $3 + 6 + 9 + 12 + \dots$ for 28 terms $= \sum_{i=1}^{i=28} 3 + (i-1)3 = \frac{28}{2}(6 + 27 \cdot 3) = 1218$

7. $-3 + 6 - 12 + 24 - 48 + \dots$ for 35 terms $= \sum_{i=1}^{i=35} -3 \cdot (-2)^{i-1} = \frac{-3(2^{35} - 1)}{-2-1}$

8. $8.3 + 8.1 + 7.9 + 7.7 + \dots + 0.9$, sum the terms, first find n, (n =38)

$$\sum_{i=1}^{i=38} 8.3 + (i-1)(-0.2) = \frac{100}{2}(16.6 + 37 \cdot (-0.2)) = 1200$$

9. Use sigma notation to represent: $12 + 9 + 3 + \dots -120$. Sum the terms, first find n, (n =45)

$$\sum_{i=1}^{i=45} 12 + (i-1)(-3) = \frac{45}{2}(24 + 44 \cdot (-3)) = -2430$$

10. An infinite geometric series is given by $\sum_{i=1}^{\infty} 2(1-x)^i$

    a. The value of x: $\qquad -1 < (1-x) < 1; \quad 2 > x > 0$

    b. x = 0.5, the minimum number of terms

    $$\sum_{i=1}^{n} 2(0.5)^i = \frac{1(0.5^n - 1)}{0.5 - 1} = 1.9 \quad n \approx 4.32 \qquad \text{So 5 terms are needed}$$

11. Given the sequence $x, x^2, x^3 \dots$

    a. Use sigma notation to represent the sum of its first 10 terms. $\sum_{i=1}^{i=10} x^n$

    b. Assuming its infinite and that its sum is 5 find x and write down the first three terms of the sequence.

    $$S_{\infty} = \frac{x}{1-x} = 5; x = \frac{5}{6}, a_1 = \frac{5}{6}, a_2 = \frac{25}{36}, a_3 = \frac{125}{216}$$

1.15. – SIGNIFICANT FIGURES

Determine the number of significant digits in each of the following:

1. 273.20 cm	5	9. 101	3
2. 4513.01 L	6	10. 10	1
3. 2.00011 km	6	11. 1.0 ml	2
4. 0.0001010450 sec	7	12. 9.401°C	4
5. 4.75 kg	3	13. 0.2 mm	1
6. 1.0	2	14. 310 kg	2
7. 10.0	3	15. 200.103 mm	6
8. 300	1	16. 704000 h	3

Answer using proper number of significant figures:

11. $3.414 \text{ s} + 10.02 \text{ s} + 58.325 \text{ s} + 0.00098 \text{ s} =$ 71.76s
12. $2.326 \text{ h} - 0.10408 \text{ h} =$ 2.222h
13. $10.19 \text{ m} \times 0.013 \text{ m} =$ 0.13m^2
14. $140.01 \text{ cm} \times 26.042 \text{ cm} \times 0.0159 \text{ cm} =$ 58.0cm^3
15. $80.23 \text{ m} / 2.4 \text{ s} =$ 33m/s
16. $4.301 \text{ kg} / 1.9 \text{ cm}^3 =$ _____ 2.3kg/cm^3 _____
17. A Chemical experiment involves the following substances:
    85.238 g of Iron, 32.1 g of Water, 0.0026 g of Oil, 7.13 g of Glass
    a. How many significant digits are there in each measurement?
       5.238 g of Iron (4)
       32.1 g of Water (3)
       0.0026 g of Oil (2)
       7.13 g of Glass (3)
    b. What is the total mass of substances in this experiment?
       124.5 (one decimal place)
    c. How many significant digits are there in the answer to part b? 4

18. A certain living room was measured to be 12.412m long and 5.212m wide. Determine:
    a. The area of the living room to the correct number of decimal places. 64.69 m^2
    b. The area of the living room to 3 significant figures. 65.0 m^2
    c. The area of the living room to 4 significant figures. 64.69 m^2
    d. The area of the living room to 1 decimal place. 65.0 m^2
    e. The perimeter of the living room to the correct number of decimal places.
       17.624 m
    f. The perimeter of the living room to 3 significant figures. 17.6 m
    g. The perimeter of the living room to 4 significant figures. 17.62 m
    h. The perimeter of the living room to 1 decimal place. 17.6 m

19. You measured 17.40 ml of water in a certain recipient. After a certain experiment 9.0 ml of water was left.
    a. Which measurement is more precise, before or after the experiment? Explain.
       Before, it was accurate to 2 decimal places.
    b. How much water was consumed during the experiment? 8.4 ml

1.16. – SCIENTIFIC NOTATION

1. How many significant figures does the measurement of 200 mm have? __1__, what if whoever performed the measurement was accurate to within 1 mm?
2. Reporting the value as 200.0 suddenly turns the term having one significant digit into a term having <u>4</u>
3. The solution to this problem is called "scientific notation". In this case the solution to the problem would be: <u>$2.00 \cdot 10^{-1} m$</u>. With this notation, it is clear that three significant digits are intended.
4. Typically a <u>number between 1 and 10 is placed to the left of the decimal</u>, and this number is then <u>multiplied by the appropriate power of 10</u>. Our experimenter could report the measured quantity as 10.0×10^1 mm, but the first version is more common.

Write the following numbers in scientific notation and indicate the number of significant figures, later write with 3 significant figures:

1. $1026.90 = \underline{1.02690 \cdot 10^3}$ ___ 3S.F. $\underline{1.03 \cdot 10^3}$
2. $0.03045 = \underline{3.045 \cdot 10^{-2}}$ ___ 3S.F. $\underline{3.05 \cdot 10^{-2}}$
3. $12,000 = \underline{1.2 \cdot 10^4}$ ___ 3S.F. $\underline{1.20 \cdot 10^4}$
4. $0.00690 = \underline{6.90 \cdot 10^{-3}}$ ___ 3S.F. $\underline{6.90 \cdot 10^{-3}}$

Write In scientific notation (use appropriate number of significant figures):

5. $0,11 = \underline{1.1 \cdot 10^{-1}}$
6. $0,015 = \underline{1.5 \cdot 10^{-2}}$
7. $0,0071 = \underline{7.1 \cdot 10^{-3}}$
8. $0,0000001 = \underline{1 \cdot 10^{-7}}$
9. $1.2 = \underline{1.2 \cdot 10^0}$
10. $1.02 = \underline{1.02 \cdot 10^0}$
11. $0.3 = \underline{3 \cdot 10^{-1}}$
12. $0.00004 = \underline{4 \cdot 10^{-5}}$
13. $0.06023 = \underline{6.023 \cdot 10^{-2}}$
14. $0.000345 = \underline{3.45 \cdot 10^{-4}}$
15. $0.00155 = \underline{1.55 \cdot 10^{-3}}$
16. $0.0000204 = \underline{2.04 \cdot 10^{-5}}$
17. $100 = \underline{1 \cdot 10^2}$

18. $10100 = \underline{1.01 \cdot 10^4}$
19. $11.0 = \underline{1.10 \cdot 10^1}$
20. $200 = \underline{2 \cdot 10^2}$
21. $201 = \underline{2.01 \cdot 10^2}$
22. $10.00 = \underline{1.000 \cdot 10^1}$
23. $101.0 = \underline{1.010 \cdot 10^2}$
24. $1.200 = \underline{1.200 \cdot 10^0}$
25. $1500 = \underline{1.5 \cdot 10^3}$
26. $2000 = \underline{2 \cdot 10^3}$
27. $51223 = \underline{5.1223 \cdot 10^4}$
28. $100.80 = \underline{1.0080 \cdot 10^2}$
29. $209.1 = \underline{2.091 \cdot 10^2}$
30. $24.18 = \underline{2.418 \cdot 10^2}$

31. $5500 = \underline{5.5 \cdot 10^3}$
32. $766600 = \underline{7.666 \cdot 10^5}$
33. $54000 = \underline{5.4 \cdot 10^4}$
34. $44500 = \underline{4.45 \cdot 10^4}$
35. $65000 = \underline{6.5 \cdot 10^4}$
36. $0.00545 = \underline{5.45 \cdot 10^{-3}}$
37. $0.001545 = \underline{1.545 \cdot 10^{-3}}$
38. $0.00020545 = \underline{2.0545 \cdot 10^{-4}}$
39. $0.050425 = \underline{5.0425 \cdot 10^{-2}}$
40. $0.0050545 = \underline{5.0545 \cdot 10^{-3}}$
41. $70000 = \underline{7 \cdot 10^4}$

Calculate giving your answers in scientific notation with the proper number of significant figures.

42. $(6.6 \cdot 10^{-8}) / (3.30 \cdot 10^{-4}) = \underline{2.0 \cdot 10^{-4}}$
43. $(1.56 \cdot 10^{-7}) + (2.43 \cdot 10^{-8}) = \underline{1.80 \cdot 10^{-7}}$
44. $(7.4 \cdot 10^{10}) / (3.7 \cdot 10^3) = \underline{2.0 \cdot 10^7}$
45. $(2.5 \cdot 10^{-8}) \cdot (3.0 \cdot 10^{-7}) = \underline{7.5 \cdot 10^{-15}}$
46. $(2.67 \cdot 10^{-3}) - (9.5 \cdot 10^{-4}) = \underline{1.72 \cdot 10^{-3}}$
47. $(2.3 \cdot 10^{-4}) \cdot (2.0 \cdot 10^{-3}) = \underline{4.6 \cdot 10^{-7}}$

CHAPTER 2

2.1. – GEOMETRY

ANGLES

1. An angle is the figure formed by <u>two</u> lines that start at a common point.

   We say that the following angle has a size of <u>90</u> degrees or <u>90</u>º

2. Use the following square to sketch an angle of 45º degrees:

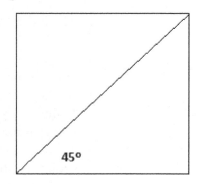

POINTS

3. Indicate the following points on the plane:
   A(1,5), B(–1, 4), C(–3, –7), D(6,–5), E(–1, –1), F(2, 0),G(0,–4), H(–4, 0)

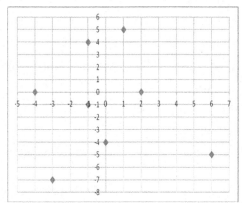

LINES

4. Indicate the following points on the plane: A(0,0), B(1, 1), C(–2, –2), D(6,6)

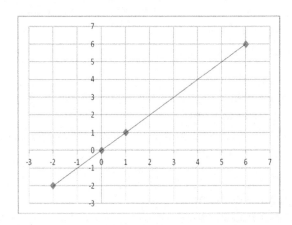

   a. What do these points have in common? <u>y = x in all of them</u>
   b. Could you describe all the points that satisfy this property? How? <u>y = x</u>

5. The points on the plane: A(0,0), B(1, 2), C(–2, –4), D(4,8)

   a. What do these points have in common?
   <u>y = 2x in all of them</u>
   b. Could you describe all the points that satisfy this property? How
   <u>y = 2x in all of them</u>
   c. The following points E(0,1), F(1, 3), G(–2, –3), H(4,9)
   d. What do these points have in common? What is the relation between this line and the previous line?
   <u>In this line y = 2x +1. It is identical to the previous line only shifted 1 unit up.</u>

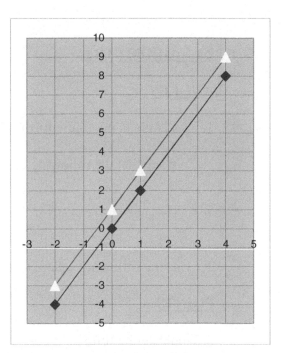

6. The points on the plane: A(0, –2), B(1, 1), C(2, 4), D(–2,–8)
   a. What do these points have in common? <u>y = 3x – 2 in all of them</u>
   b. Could you describe all the points that satisfy this property? How? <u>y = 3x – 2 in all of them</u>

   c. On the same graph sketch the following points E(0,1), F(1, 4), G(–2, –5), H(2, 7)
   d. What do these points have in common? What is the relation between this line and the previous line? <u>y = 3x + 1 in all of them, this line is the same as the other, shifted 3 units up.</u>

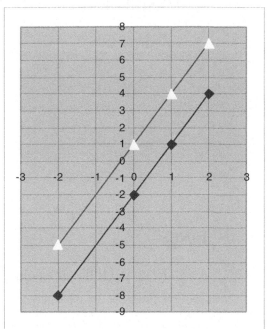

SQUARES, RECTANGLES AND TRIANGLES

7. The following points on the plane: A(0, 6), B(6, 0), C(0, 0)
   b. Find all the angles of the triangles you can
   <u>45°, 45°, 90°.</u>
   c. This kind of triangle is called <u>right angled</u>

   <u>and isosceles</u>
   d. Write down the lengths of the 2 equal sides: <u>6</u>
   e. Write down the Pythagorean Theorem:
   $\underline{H^2 = a^2 + b^2}$ This theorem is only true in <u>right</u> triangles.
   f. Use P. Theorem to find the length of the third side of the triangle. $H = \sqrt{72}$

   g. Add the point D(6, 6) to the graph. The form ABCD is a <u>Rectangle</u>. The area of this shape is <u>A = 36</u>
   h. Use the area of the square to find the area of the triangle. <u>Half of it so 18.</u>

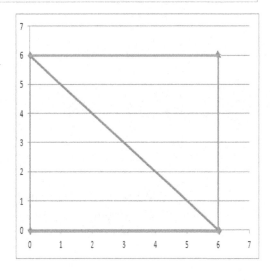

80

8. Indicate the following points on the plane: A(–4, 0), B(2, 6), C(8, 0)

b. This kind of triangle is called <u>isosceles</u>

c. Write down the Pythagorean Theorem: $\underline{H^2 = a^2 + b^2}$ This theorem is only true in <u>right angled</u> triangles.

d. Add the point D (2, 0) to the graph. The triangle ABD is <u>right angled</u>

e. The length of AD is <u>6</u> The Length of BD is <u>6</u> Use P. Theorem to find the length of AB. $AB = \sqrt{72}$

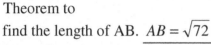

f. In consequence state the length of BC: $BC = \sqrt{72}$

g. The perimeter of the triangle ABC is $\underline{12 + 2\sqrt{72}}$

h. Add the point E (–4, 6) to the graph. The shape AEBD is <u>square</u>. The area of this shape is <u>36</u>. Use this area to find the area of the triangle ABD and ABC. <u>Area ABD is half so 18, ABC is twice ABD so 36</u>

9. Indicate the following points on the plane: A(–6, 0), B(3, 6), C(5, 0)

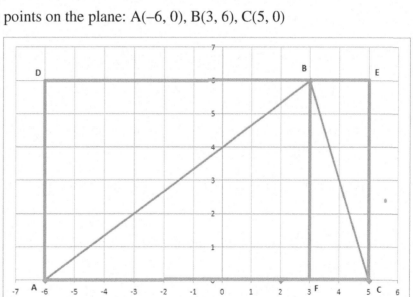

b. Is this triangle isosceles or right angled? <u>No</u>

c. The shape ADEC is a <u>rectangle.</u> The area of this shape is <u>66</u>.

d. The llength of AB:

$AB = \sqrt{36 + 81} = \sqrt{117}$ and BC $BC = \sqrt{4 + 36} = \sqrt{40}$

e. The perimeter of the triangle ABC is $Perimeter = \sqrt{40} + \sqrt{117} + 11$

f. The line BF is called the <u>Height</u> of the triangle.

a. Every triangle has <u>3</u> heights. . A height is a lines that starts at a <u>vertex</u> and ends at <u>the opposite side</u> forming an angle of <u>90°</u> with it.

g. Find the area of the triangles ABF, FBC and ABC.

$$Area_{ABF} = \frac{54}{2} = 27 \qquad Area_{FBC} = \frac{12}{2} = 6 \qquad Area_{ABC} = \frac{66}{2} = 33$$

81

10. Indicate the following points on the plane: A (–5, 0), B (5, 0), C (0, $\sqrt{75}$)

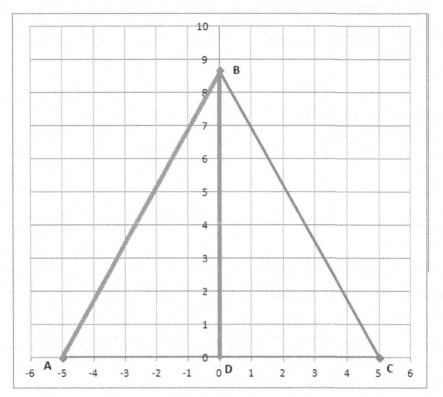

b. Length of AB: $AB = 10$ BC $BC = \sqrt{25+75} = 10$

c. What kind of triangle is this? <u>Equilateral, all sides are equal and have a length of</u>

   <u>10</u>

d. What can you say about the angles of this triangle<u>? All angles are equal and all</u>
   <u>are 60°</u>

e. The perimeter of the triangle ABC is <u>*Perimeter* = 30</u>

f. Find the area of the triangle ABC. $Area_{ABF} = \dfrac{base \cdot height}{2} = \dfrac{10 \cdot \sqrt{75}}{2} = 5\sqrt{75}$

   The area of the triangle is half of the rectangle that can be built around it as seen
   in previous exercises. That is the origin of the formula provided for the area.

11. Define and sketch an example, include all the angles and lengths of sides in your example.

    a. Equilateral triangle:
       <u>3 equal sides, 3 equal angles of</u> 60°

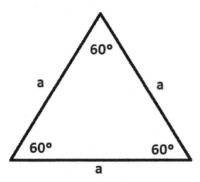

    c. Right angled triangle: <u>One 90°</u> <u>angle</u>

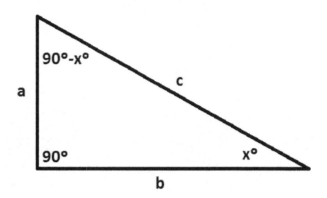

    b. Isosceles triangle:
       <u>2 equal sides with corresponding</u> <u>2 equal angles.</u>

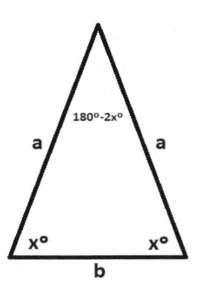

    d. Right angled and isosceles triangle:

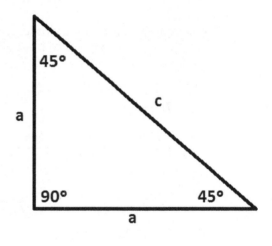

12. Given the following triangle, sketch all the altitudes in the triangle.
An altitude is: a <u>line form a vertex to the opposite side to which is perpendicular.</u>
The point where the altitudes meet is called "orthocenter". (It may be outside of the triangle) Observe here: <u>http://www.mathopenref.com/triangleorthocenter.html</u>

13. Given the following triangle, Sketch all the perpendicular bisectors in the triangle.
The point where they meet is called circumcenter, <u>it is the centre of the circle in</u> <u>which the triangle is circumscribed.</u> Observe here:
http://www.mathopenref.com/trianglecircumcircle.html

14. Given the following triangle, Sketch all the angle bisectors in the triangle. The point where they meet is called incenter, it is the centre <u>of the circumscribed circle</u>. Observe here: <u>http://www.mathopenref.com/triangleincircle.html</u>

15. Given the following triangle, Sketch all the medians in the triangle. The point where they meet is called centroid. If the centroid is M then the following relations are satisfied (complete):

$$AM = \frac{2}{3}AD \qquad\qquad BM = \frac{2}{3}BG \qquad\qquad CM = \frac{2}{3}MF$$

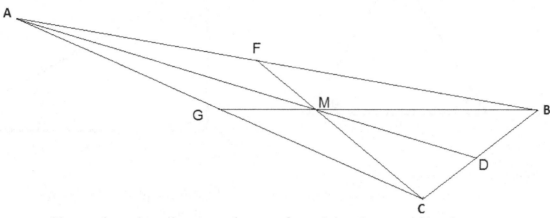

Observe here: <u>http://www.mathopenref.com/trianglecentroid.html</u>

16. Given the following triangle, it is known that AB = 10cm, AD = 7cm and DC = 4cm. Angle CDB = 90°. Find:

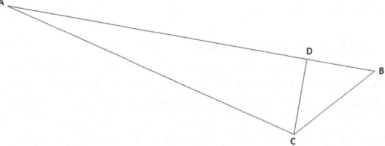

a. DB = 3cm,
$$BC = \sqrt{9+16} = 5cm,$$
$$AC = \sqrt{16+49} = \sqrt{65}cm$$

b. $A_{ABC} = \dfrac{10 \cdot 4}{2} = 20cm^2$

c. $Perimeter_{ABC} = 15 + \sqrt{65} = cm$

17. Given the following triangle, it is known that AC = 13cm, DB = 4cm and DC = 5cm. Angle CDB = 90°. Find:

a. $AD = \sqrt{169-25} = 12cm$ $BC = \sqrt{16+25} = \sqrt{41}cm$

b. $A_{DCB} = \dfrac{4 \cdot 5}{2} = 10cm^2$

c. $Perimeter_{ABC} = 13 + 12 + 4 + \sqrt{41} = 29 + \sqrt{41}cm$

18. Given the following triangle, it is known that AC = 20cm, DB = 10cm and DC = 11 cm. Angle CDB = 90° and angle CEA = 90°. Find:

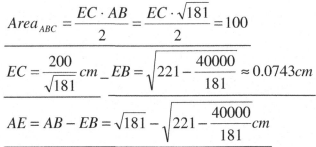

a. $BC = \sqrt{100 + 121} = \sqrt{221}cm$

$AB = \sqrt{81 + 100} = \sqrt{181}cm$

b. $A_{ABC} = \dfrac{20 \cdot 10}{2} = 100cm^2$

c. $Perimeter_{ABC} = 20 + \sqrt{181} + \sqrt{221}cm$

d. What do EC and BD have in common? <u>Both are heights of the triangle ABC.</u>

e. The lengths of EC, EB and

$Area_{ABC} = \dfrac{EC \cdot AB}{2} = \dfrac{EC \cdot \sqrt{181}}{2} = 100$

$EC = \dfrac{200}{\sqrt{181}} cm \quad EB = \sqrt{221 - \dfrac{40000}{181}} \approx 0.0743cm$

$AE = AB - EB = \sqrt{181} - \sqrt{221 - \dfrac{40000}{181}}cm$

19. Given a right angled isosceles triangle whose longest side is 10 cm long.

a. Sketch the triangle.
b. Find the perimeter of the triangle.

$x^2 + x^2 = 100$

$x = \sqrt{50}$

$Perimeter = 10 + 2\sqrt{50}$

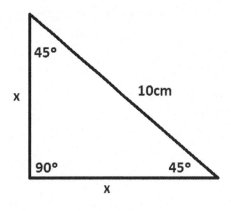

c. Find the area of the triangle.

$Area = \dfrac{\sqrt{50} \cdot \sqrt{50}}{2} = 25cm^2$

20. Given a right angled isosceles triangle whose smallest side is X cm long.

a. Sketch the triangle.
b. Find the perimeter of the triangle in terms of X.

$X^2 + X^2 = c^2$

$c = \sqrt{2}X$

$Perimeter = X(2 + \sqrt{2})$

c. Find the area of the triangle in terms of X.

$Area = \dfrac{X^2}{2} cm^2$

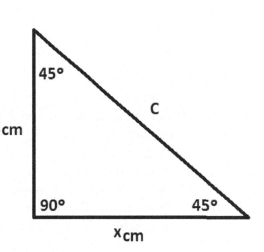

SIMILAR TRIANGLES

21. 2 triangles are similar if all of their angles are <u>equal.</u>

22. 2 triangles are similar if <u>any</u> of the following is satisfied:

    a. 2 of their angles are <u>equal (AAA)</u>. Sketch an example:

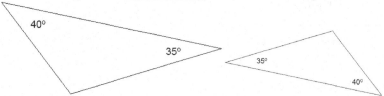

    b. 2 of their sides are <u>proportional</u> and the angles between them are <u>equal (ASA)</u>. Sketch an example:

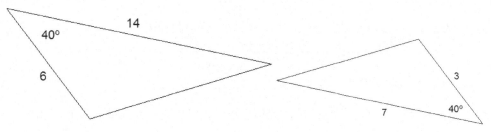

    c. All the sides are <u>proportional (SSS)</u>. Sketch an example:

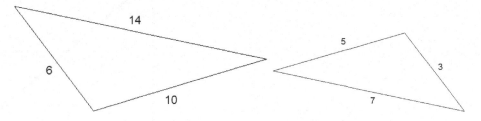

23. All right angled triangles are similar True / **False**. Sketch an example to show answer:

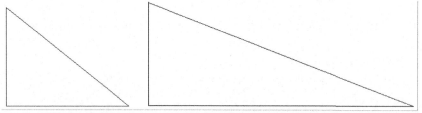

24. Determine if the following pair of triangles are similar, give a reason: <u>Similar, all angles are identical (AAA)</u>

25. Determine if the following pair of triangles are similar, give a reason: <u>Not similar, no condition is satisfied</u>

26. Determine if the following pair of triangles are similar, give a reason: <u>Not similar, no condition is satisfied</u>

27. Determine if the following pair of triangles are similar, give a reason: <u>Similar (SSS)</u>

28. Determine if the following pair of triangles are similar, give a reason: <u>Not similar, no condition is satisfied (in general for any x,y)</u>

29. Determine if the following pair of triangles are similar, give a reason: <u>Similar, AAA (angles are 180°/7, 360°/7, 720°/7 in both)</u>

30. Given that $AB \parallel CD$, determine if the triangles ABE and CED are similar, give a reason: <u>Similar, AAA</u>

31. Given that $BC \parallel DE$, determine if the triangles ABC and ADE are similar, give a reason: <u>Similar, AAA</u>

32. The shadow of a man formed by a street light on the ground is equal to twice its height. If the man is 10m away from the street light and his height is 1.80m, how high is the street light?

$$\frac{3.60}{3.60+10} = \frac{1.80}{h}$$
$$h = 6.8m$$
<u>   </u>

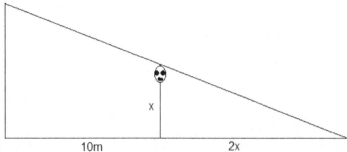

33. Given that $AB \parallel CD$, find ED:

$$\frac{8}{5} = \frac{3}{ED}$$
$$ED = \frac{15}{8}$$
<u>   </u>

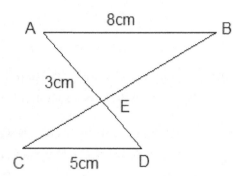

34. In the following triangle the tangle BAC is a right angle. AD is a height from A to BC. Show that triangles ABC, ADB and ADC are all similar. If BC = 10cm and AD = 2DC find the perimeter and area of ABD.

$DC = a$

$AD = 2a$ $Perimeter_{ABD} = 12 + 4\sqrt{5}$

$AC = \sqrt{5}a$ $Area_{ABD} = 16$

$$\frac{10}{\sqrt{5}a} = \frac{\sqrt{5}a}{a}$$

$a = 2 = DC$

$AD = 4$

$AC = 2\sqrt{5}$

<u>$AB = 2AC = 4\sqrt{5}$</u>

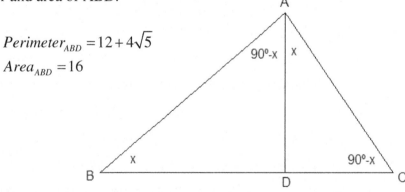

35. The following triangle AB = AC. AD is a height from A to the BC. Show that triangles ABD and ACD are similar. If BD = x and 2AB = 3AD, find the perimeter and area of ABC in terms of x.

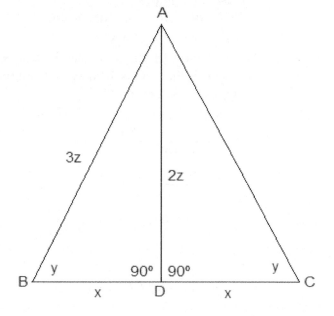

$$9z^2 = 4z^2 + x^2$$

$$z = \frac{x}{\sqrt{5}}$$

$$AD = \frac{2x}{\sqrt{5}}; AB = \frac{3x}{\sqrt{5}}$$

$$Perimeter_{ABC} = x(2 + \frac{6}{\sqrt{5}})$$

$$Area_{ABC} = \frac{2x^2}{\sqrt{5}}$$

36. Given the facade of a certain house, it is known that AC = 4m, CD = 2AC, CE = 7m DE = 3m. ABCD is a rectangle. Find:

a. The height of the house above ground (help: lower a height from E).
   $$CD = 8; CF = x; FD = 8 - x; EF = y$$

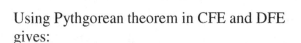

Using Pythgorean theorem in CFE and DFE gives:

If we subtract the equations we
$$x^2 + y^2 = 49$$
$$(8 - x)^2 + y^2 = 9$$

Subtracting the equations we obtain:
$$x^2 - (8 - x)^2 = 40$$
$$16x - 64 = 40$$

$$x = \frac{104}{16} = \frac{13}{2} = 6.5cm = CF \quad\_ y = \sqrt{49 - \frac{169}{4}} = \sqrt{\frac{27}{4}}cm = EF$$

Height of façade = $4 + \sqrt{\frac{27}{4}}cm$

b. The area of the entire facade. $Area = 4 \cdot 8 + \dfrac{8 \cdot \sqrt{\frac{27}{4}}}{2} = 32 + 2\sqrt{27}cm^2$

DISTANCE AND MIDPOINT

37. Indicate the following points on the plane: A(2,3), B(6, 9), C(–3, –7), D(6,–5)

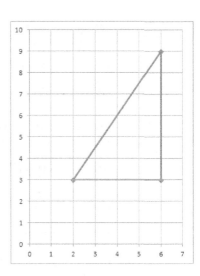

   a. Add the point (6, 3) and use Pythagorean theorem to find the distance between the points A and B.

   $$AB = \sqrt{16+36} = \sqrt{52}$$

   b. The distance between the points C and D.

   $$CD = \sqrt{81+4} = \sqrt{85}$$

   c. Distance AC

   $$AC = \sqrt{25+100} = \sqrt{125}$$

   d. Midpoint between AB

   $$Mid_{AB} = \left(\frac{2+6}{2}, \frac{3+9}{2}\right) = (4,6)$$

   e. Find the midpoint between CD

   $$Mid_{CD} = \left(\frac{-3+6}{2}, \frac{-7-5}{2}\right) = \left(\frac{3}{2}, -6\right)$$

   f. Find the midpoint between AC

   $$Mid_{AC} = \left(\frac{2-3}{2}, \frac{3-7}{2}\right) = \left(-\frac{1}{2}, -2\right)$$

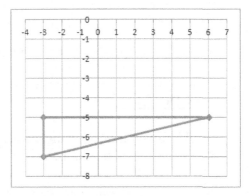

38. Find the distance between (1, 3) and (7, –3), find the mid point.

$$Midpoint = \left(\frac{1+7}{2}, \frac{3-3}{2}\right) = (4,0) \qquad Dis\tan ce = \sqrt{(7-1)^2 + (-3-3)^2} = \sqrt{72}$$

39. Find the distance between (–5, –4) and (2, –9), find the mid point.

$$Midpoint = \left(\frac{-5+2}{2}, \frac{-4-9}{2}\right) = \left(\frac{-3}{2}, \frac{-13}{2}\right) \quad Dis\tan ce = \sqrt{(-5-2)^2 + (-4+9)^2} = \sqrt{74}$$

40. Find a point whose distance to the point (2, 1) is 7. There are infinite, many solutions, for example: (a, b) is the point.

$$Dis\tan ce = \sqrt{(a-2)^2 + (b-1)^2} = 7, \text{ if we choose b = 1, we obtain a = 9 so the}$$

point is (9, 1)

41. Find a point whose distance to the point (–4, 2) is 3, can you draw a conclusion about such points in general? There are infinite, the equation that describes them must be the equation of a circle. For example: (a, b) is the point.

$$Dis\tan ce = \sqrt{(a+4)^2 + (b-2)^2} = 3, \text{ if we choose b = 2, we obtain a = –1 so the}$$

point is (–1, 2)

42. The midpoint between the points (a, 5) and (–2, b) is (0, 0) find a and b.

$$Midpoint = \left(\frac{a-2}{2}, \frac{5+b}{2}\right) = (0,0); a = 2; b = -5$$

43. Given that AB = BC = CD and A, B, C and D are aligned. Point A is (2, 4) and point D is (10, 10). Find points B and C.

In the horizontal the distance 2 to 10 is 8, divide by 3, in the vertical the distance from 4 to 10 is 6, divide by 3. Therefore: $B = (\frac{14}{3}, 6)$, $C = (\frac{22}{3}, 8)$. Can also be obtained using Pythagorean Theorem:

$AD = \sqrt{100} = 10; B = (a, b);$

$AB^2 = (a-2)^2 + (b-4)^2 = \left(\frac{10}{3}\right)^2; BD^2 = (10-a)^2 + (10-b)^2 = \left(\frac{20}{3}\right)^2; a = \frac{14}{3}; b = 6$

---

44. Given that the distance AB = BC = CD. Point A is (–4, 8) and point B is (–2, 1). Find points C and D.

In the horizontal the distance -2 to -4 is 2, divide by 3, in the vertical the distance from 1 to 8 is 7, divide by 3. Therefore: $B = (-\frac{10}{3}, \frac{10}{3})$, $C = (-\frac{8}{3}, \frac{17}{3})$. Can also be

CIRCLES

45. Given the following circle:
   a. Sketch a diameter.
   b. Sketch a radius.
   c. The diameter is <u>twice</u> the radius
   d. Sketch a chord smaller than the diameter
   e. Sketch a chord smaller than the radius

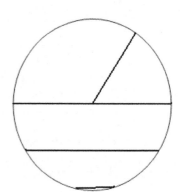

46. Given the following circle:
   a. Sketch a 60° angle.
   b. Show the corresponding minor arc/major arc
   c. Choose 3 points on the circle, connect them with chords. The triangle formed is inscribed in the circle. The circle is circumscribed about the triangle.
   d. Chords that are at the same distance from the centre are <u>equal</u>

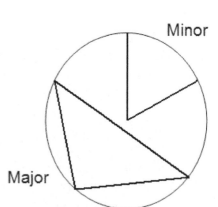

47. Given the following circle:
   a. Choose 3 points on the circle, name them A, B and C. Sketch AB and BC. The angle ABC is inscribed in the circle.
   b. Choose a 4th point on the circle, name it D. Sketch AD and CD. The angle ADC is inscribed in the circle.
   c. What is your conclusion? <u>The angles are identical</u>

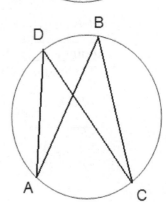

48. Given the following circle:
    a. Choose 3 points on the circle, name them A, B and C. Sketch AB and BC. The angle ABC is inscribed in the circle.
    b. Sketch the center of the circle; name it O. Sketch AO and CO. The angle AOC is inscribed in the circle.
    c. What is your conclusion? <u>AOC = 2ABC</u>
       Observe here:
       http://www.mathopenref.com/arccentralangletheorem.html

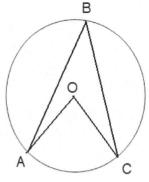

49. Given the following circle:
    a. Sketch the diameter of the circle; name it AC. Sketch a 3rd point B. Connect AB, AC and BC. The angle ABC is inscribed in the circle. Its size is: <u>90°</u>
    b. Choose a 4th point on the circle; name it D. Connect AD, DC. The angle ADC is inscribed in the circle. Its size is: <u>90°</u>
    c. What is your conclusion? <u>All angles supporting diameter are 90°</u>

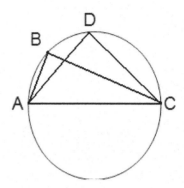

50. $BC = \sqrt{4-1} = \sqrt{3} cm$

$Perimeter_{ABC} = 3 + \sqrt{3} cm$

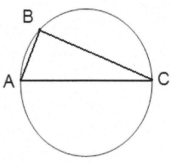

51. Sketch a chord whose length is half of the diameter. In case the radius is 2cm find the area and perimeter of the triangle formed by connecting the center of the circle with the ends of the chord.

$OAB \quad equilateral$

$Perimeter_{OAB} = 3cm$

$Area_{OAB} = \dfrac{3 \cdot \left(\dfrac{\sqrt{3}}{2}\right)}{2} = \dfrac{3\sqrt{3}}{4} cm^2$

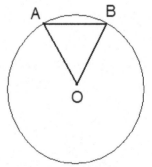

52. Given a circle with radius R, find
    The Perimeter of the circle: $Perimeter = 2\pi r$
    The Area of the circle: $Area = \pi r^2$

53. Given a circle with radius 5cm, find
    The Perimeter of the circle: $Perimeter = 10\pi \quad cm$
    The Area of the circle: $Area = 25\pi \quad cm^2$

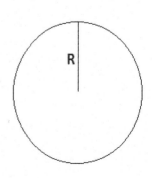

54. Given a circle with perimeter 20π cm, find

The radius of the circle: $Perimeter = 20\pi = 2\pi r; \quad r = 10cm$

The Area of the circle: $Area = 100\pi \quad cm^2$

55. Given a circle with area 16π cm^2, find

The radius of the circle: $Area = 16\pi = \pi r^2; \quad r = 4cm$

The perimeter of the circle: $Perimeter = 8\pi \quad cm$

56. Shade 10% of the figure, find the corresponding angle:

Angle: 10% of 360° is 36°

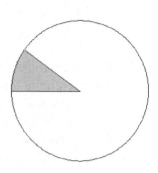

57. Given that R = 5 cm. Shade 20% of the figure, find the corresponding angle and the area shaded.

Angle: 20% of 360° is 72°

Area shaded:

$20\% \quad of \quad \pi r^2 = 25\pi \quad is \quad \dfrac{20}{100}25\pi = 5\pi \quad cm^2$

58. Given that R = 15 cm. Shade 30% of the figure, write the corresponding angle and find the area shaded.

Angle: 30% of 360° is 108°

Area shaded:

$30\% \quad of \quad \pi r^2 = 225\pi \quad is \quad \dfrac{30}{100}225\pi = 67.5\pi \quad cm^2$

59. Given a circle with radius 10cm:

a. The <u>percentage</u> of the area shaded:
$\dfrac{20°}{360°} = 0.0555... \approx 5.55\%$

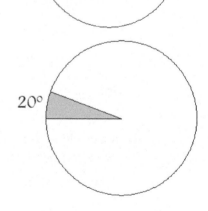

20°

b. Find the <u>size</u> of the shaded area.
$\dfrac{20}{360} \quad of \quad \pi r^2 = 100\pi \quad is \quad \dfrac{30}{360}100\pi = \dfrac{5\pi}{6} \quad cm^2$

c. Find the <u>perimeter</u> of the shaded area.
$Arc = \dfrac{20}{360} \quad of \quad 2\pi r = 20\pi \quad is \quad \dfrac{30}{360}20\pi = \dfrac{5\pi}{3} \quad cm$

$Perimeter \quad area \quad shaded = Arc + 2R = \dfrac{5\pi}{3} + 20 \quad cm$

60.   Given a circle with radius 10cm:

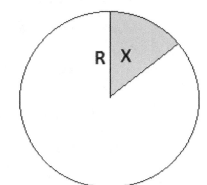

   a. The <u>percentage</u> of the shaded area of the total area of the circle in terms of the angle x. $\dfrac{x^o}{360^o}$

   b.   Find the <u>size</u> of the shaded area in terms of x.

$$\dfrac{x^o}{360^o}\cdot 100\pi = \dfrac{5\pi x}{18}\ cm^2$$

   c. Find the <u>perimeter</u> of the shaded area in terms of x.

$$Arc = \dfrac{x^o}{360^o}\cdot 20\pi = \dfrac{\pi x}{18}\ cm$$

$$Perimeter = Arc + 2R = \dfrac{\pi x}{18} + 20\ cm$$

61. The length of the perimeter of a circle with radius r is <u>$2\pi r$</u> The length of the arc that corresponds an angle x° is <u>$\dfrac{x^o}{360^o}2\pi r$</u> In case the angle x is measured in radians it would be <u>$\dfrac{x}{2\pi}2\pi r = xr$</u> .The area of a circle with radius r is <u>πr^2</u> The area of the sector that corresponds an angle x° is <u>$\dfrac{x^o}{360}\pi r^2$</u> .In case the angle x is measured in radians it would be <u>$\dfrac{x}{2\pi}\pi r^2 = \dfrac{xr^2}{2}$</u>

62. Given the circle with r = 2cm :

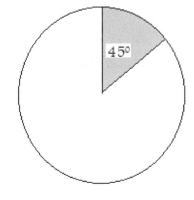

   a. Show the arc corresponding an angle of 45°.

   b. Calculate its length. $\dfrac{45^o}{360^o}2\pi 2 = \dfrac{\pi}{2}\ cm$

   c. Shade the corresponding sector area.

   d. Calculate it. $\dfrac{45^o}{360^o}\pi 4 = \dfrac{\pi}{2}\ cm^2$

63. Given the circle with r = 3.2m:

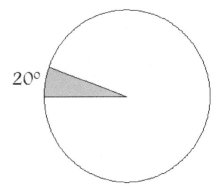

   a. Show the arc corresponding an angle of 20°.

   b. Calculate its length. $\dfrac{20^o}{360^o}2\pi(3.2) = \dfrac{6.4\pi}{18}\ cm$

   c. Shade the corresponding sector area.

   d. Calculate it. $\dfrac{20^o}{360^o}\pi(3.2)^2 = \dfrac{10.24\pi}{18}\ cm^2$

64. Given the circle with r = 3m:

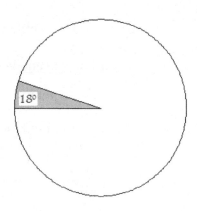

a. The arc corresponding an angle of $\frac{\pi}{10}$ rad . $\frac{\pi}{10}$ rad $= 18°$

b. Calculate its length. $\frac{3\pi}{10}$ cm

c. Calculate its perimeter. $\frac{3\pi}{10} + 6cm$

d. Shade the corresponding sector area.

e. Calculate it. $-\frac{9\pi}{20}$

65. Given the circle with r = 6m:

a. Shade the arc corresponding an angle of 1 radian.

b. Calculate its length. $xr = 6m$

c. Shade the corresponding sector area.

d. Calculate it. $= 158m^2$

66. The shaded area. $A_{shaded} = \pi(25-9) = 16\pi \ \ cm^2$

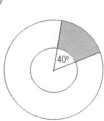

67. The shaded area. $A_{shaded} = \frac{40°}{360°}\pi(196-100) = \frac{96}{9}\pi \ \ cm^2$

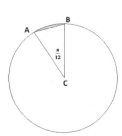

68. The shaded area.

$$A_{shaded} = A_{sector} - A_{triangle} = \frac{100\pi}{24} - 50\sin\left(\frac{\pi}{12}\right) \ \ cm^2 \approx 0.149 \ \ cm^2$$

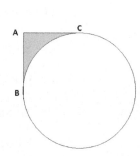

69. The shaded area.

$$A_{shaded} = A_{sector} - A_{shaded} = \frac{A_{square} - A_{circle}}{4} = \frac{256 - 64\pi}{4} \approx 13.7 \ \ cm^2$$

70. Given a circle with radius 10cm in which a square is circumscribed

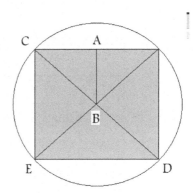

a. Find the length of the side of the square.
   Since CD = 2R = 10cm and EC = ED = x
   Using Pythagorean theorem:
   $$2x^2 = 400; \quad x = \sqrt{200} = EC = ED$$

b. Find the area of the square.
   $$Area_{square} = \sqrt{200}\sqrt{200} = 200cm^2$$

c. Find the area of the circle
   $$Area_{circle} = 100\pi \quad cm^2$$

d. Find the percentage of the area of the circle that the square occupies.
   $$\frac{Area_{square}}{Area_{circle}} = \frac{200}{100\pi} = \frac{2}{\pi} \approx 0.637 \approx 64\%$$

71. Given a circle with radius 10cm circumscribed in a square:

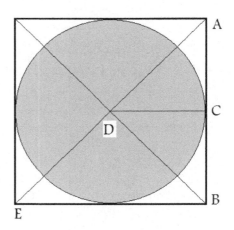

a. Find the length of the side of the square.
   2R = 20 cm
   Find the area of the square.
   Area = 400 cm^2

b. Find the area of the circle
   $$Area_{circle} = 100\pi \quad cm^2$$

c. Find the percentage of the area of the square that the circle occupies.
   $$\frac{Area_{circle}}{Area_{square}} = \frac{100\pi}{400} = \frac{\pi}{4} \approx 0.785 \approx 79\%$$

72. On the following diagram sketch the following directions:

Each direction can be described in more than one way as can be seen

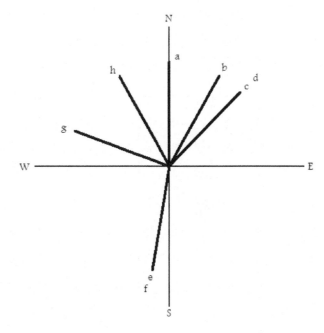

73. Given the following table, fill the blank using a, b, c, d, h, r

	Shape	Area	Perimeter
Square		$A = a^2$	$P = 4a$
Rectangle		$A = ab$	$P = 2(a+b)$
Parallelogram		$A = ah$	$P = 2(a+b)$
Isosceles Trapezoid		$A = \dfrac{h}{2}(a+c)$	$P = a + 2b + c$
Trapezpezoid		$A = \dfrac{h}{2}(a+b)$	$P = a+b+c+d$
Rhombus		$A = \dfrac{dr}{2}$	$P = 4a$
Kite		$A = \dfrac{dr}{2}$	$P = 2(a+b)$

74. Given the following quadrilaterals. Write the name of each one of them:

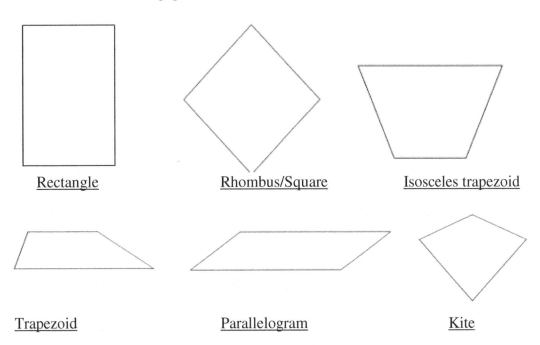

Rectangle   Rhombus/Square   Isosceles trapezoid

Trapezoid   Parallelogram   Kite

75. Given the following table, fill the blanks with yes or no.

	Shape (sketch)	Only 1 pair of parallel sides	2 pairs of parallel sides	1 pair of equal sides	2 pairs of equal sides	4 equal sides
Square		No	Yes	No	No	Yes
Rectangle		No	Yes	No	Yes	No
Parallelogram		No	Yes	No	Yes	No
Isosceles Trapezoid		Yes	No	Yes	No	No
Trapezpezoid		Yes	No	No	No	No
Rhombus		No	Yes	No	No	Yes
Kite		No	No	No	No	No

76. True or False

     a. A square is also a parallelogram   **True** / False

     b. A square is also a rectangle   **True** / False

     c. A square is also a trapezoid   **True** / False

     d. A parallelogram is also a square   True / **False**

     e. A rectangle is also a square   True / **False**

     f. A rhombus is always a parallelogram   **True** / False

     g. A parallelogram is always r rhombus   True / **False**

     h. A parallelogram is sometimes a rhombus   **True** / False

     i. A rhombus is always a kite   **True** / False

     j. All the shapes above mentioned are quadrilaterals   **True** / False

77. Given the following table, fill the blanks with yes or no.

	Shape (Sketch diagonals as well)	Diagonals are perpendicular	Diagonals are equal	Diagonals bisect angle	Diagonals bisect each other
Square		Yes	Yes	Yes	Yes
Rectangle		No	Yes	No	Yes
Paralleogram		No	Yes	No	Yes
Isosceles Trapezoid		No	Yes	No	No
Trapezpezoid		No	No	No	No
Rhombus		Yes	Yes	Yes	Yes
Kite		Yes	No	No	No

78. Given the following table, fill the blanks

	Shape	Surface Area	Volume
Cuboid (Rectangular Prism)		$S = 2(ab + bc + ac)$	$V = abc$
Pyramid (Square based)		$S = a^2 + 4A$ $A = Area\ \ Side$	$V = \dfrac{a^2 h}{3}$
Sphere		$S = 4\pi r^2$	$V = \dfrac{4}{3}\pi r^3$
Cylinder		$S = 2\pi rh$	$V = \pi r^2 h$
Cone		$S = \pi rL + \pi r^2$	$V = \dfrac{\pi r^2 h}{3}$

79. Given the following table, fill the blanks

	Shape	Surface Area	Volume
Triangular prism		$A = 2ac + ab + 2S$	$V = Sa$
Triangle based Pyramid (Tetrahedron)		$S = A_{base} + A_{triangles}$	$S = \dfrac{A_{base} \cdot h}{3}$

80. The volume and surface area of a sphere with radius 10cm.

$$S = 400\pi \ \ cm^2 ; V = \frac{4000\pi}{3} \ \ cm^3$$

81. Find the volume and surface area of a sphere with radius 0.4m.

$$S = 0.64\pi \ \ m^2 ; V = \frac{256\pi}{3000} \ \ cm^3$$

82. Find the volume of a square based pyramid with base length $2x$ cm and height is x cm.

$$V = \frac{4x^3}{3} \ \ cm^3$$

83. Find the volume and surface area of a square based cuboid whose base length is 15 cm and height 0.1m

$$V = 225 \cdot 10 = 2250 \ \ cm^3 \qquad S = 2 \cdot 225 + 4 \cdot 15 \cdot 10 = 450 + 600 = 1050 \ \ cm^2$$

84. Find the volume and surface area of a cone with radius 0.4m and height 2m.

$$V = \frac{2\pi 0.4^2}{3} = \frac{32\pi}{48} \ \ cm^3$$

$$L = \sqrt{0.4^2 + 2^2} = \sqrt{\frac{416}{100}} = \frac{\sqrt{416}}{10}$$

$$S = \frac{4\pi\sqrt{416}}{100} + \frac{16\pi}{100} = \frac{4\pi(\sqrt{416}+4)}{100} \ \ cm^2$$

85. Find the volume and surface area of a cylinder with radius 0.4m and height 2m.

$$V = 2\pi 0.4^2 = \frac{32\pi}{100} \ \ cm^3$$

$$S = 2\pi 0.4^2 + 2\pi \cdot 0.4 \cdot 2 = \frac{32\pi}{100} + \frac{160\pi}{100} = \frac{192\pi}{100} \ \ cm^2$$

2.2. – GEOMETRIC TRANSOFRMATIONS

1. The points on the plane: A(0,0), B(−1,6),C(4,2). Connect them to form a triangle.

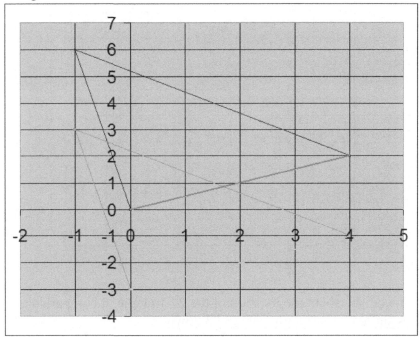

   b. What can you say about the location of the 2nd triangle in comparison to the first one? It is shifted 3 units down
   c. This is a <u>vertical</u> translation.

2. The points on the plane: A(0,0), B(−1,6),C(4,2). Connect them to form a triangle.

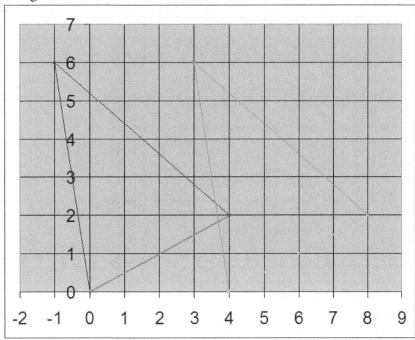

   b. What can you say about the location of the 2nd triangle in comparison to the first one? It is shifted 4 units to the right
   c. This is a <u>horizontal</u> translation.

3. Indicate the following points on the plane: A(0,0), B(–1,6),C(4,2). Connect them to form a triangle.

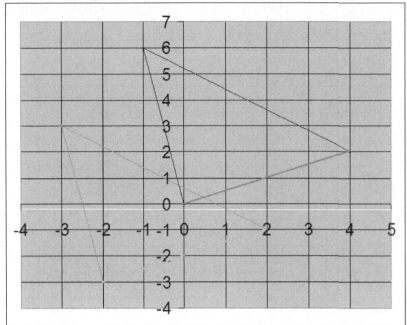

b. What can you say about the location of the 2nd triangle in comparison to the first one? <u>It is shifted 2 units to the left and 3 down</u>

c. This is a <u>horizontal</u> and <u>vertical</u> translations.

4. Indicate the following points on the plane: A(1,0), B(–2,6),C(6,3). Connect them to form a triangle.

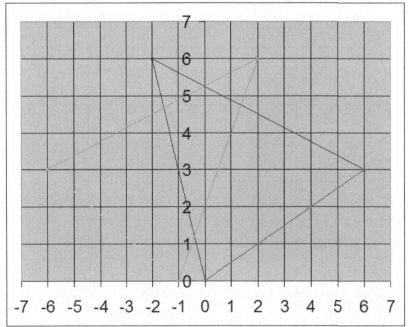

a. What can you say about the location of the 2nd triangle in comparison to the first one? <u>It is reflected.</u>

b. This is a <u>Reflection</u> across the y axis.

c. On changing x into <u>–x</u> we are generating a <u>Reflection</u> across the <u>y axis</u>

5. Indicate the following points on the plane: A(1,1), B(–2,6),C(6,3). Connect them to form a triangle.

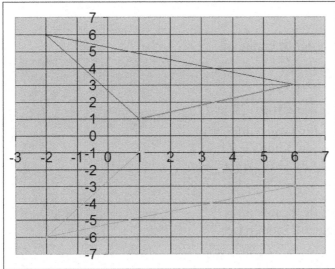

b. What can you say about the location of the 2nd triangle in comparison to the first one?

c. This is a <u>Reflection</u> about the x axis.

d. On changing y into <u>–y</u> we are generating a <u>Reflection</u> across the <u>x axis</u>

6. Indicate the following points on the plane: A(–4,0), B(0,4),C(4,0), D(0, –4). Connect them to form a square.

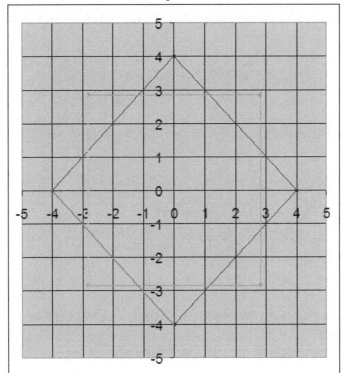

b. What can you say about the location of the 2nd square in comparison to the first one? <u>It is rotated 45° clockwise</u>

c. This is a <u>Rotation</u> of <u>45° clockwise</u> degrees.

d. Write down the coordinates of a square that is a rotation of 90° of the first one:
A'' = (4,0), B'' = (0, –4), C'' = (–4, 0), D'' = (0, 4)
Conclusions? <u>Same coordinates, Squares remain invariant under 90° rotation</u>

7. Indicate the following points on the plane: A(–5,0), B(5,0). Given also the point C(0,*a*)

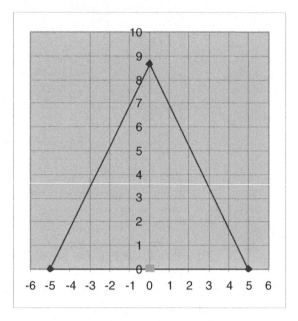

   a. The value of *a* in order to create an equilateral triangle is: $\sqrt{75}$
   Side of triangle is 10. Using Pythagorean T. $a = \sqrt{100 - 25} = \sqrt{75}$

   b. The coordinates of the new points after translating the triangle 3 units left and 1 down. <u>A' = (–8, –1), B' = (2,–1), C' = (–3, $\sqrt{75}$ –1)</u>

   c. The coordinates of the points after rotation the triangle 30° clockwise.
   $$A'' = \left(-5\frac{\sqrt{3}}{2}, \frac{5}{2}\right), B'' = \left(5\frac{\sqrt{3}}{2}, -\frac{5}{2}\right),$$
   $$C'' = \left(\frac{5}{2}, 5\frac{\sqrt{3}}{2}\right)$$

   d. The coordinates of the new points after rotation the triangle 60° clockwise.
   <u>Same coordinates, equilateral triangle remains invariant under 60° rotation</u>

8. Indicate the following points on the plane: A(1,0), B(–2,5),C(4,3). Connect them to form a triangle.

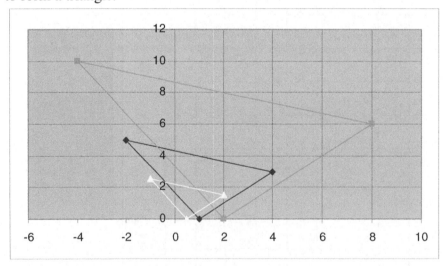

   a. Indicate the following points on the plane: A'(2,0), B'(–4,10),C'(8,6), Connect them to form a triangle.
   b. The 2nd triangle in comparison to the first one? <u>Similar, just bigger</u>
   c. This is a <u>dilation</u> factor <u>2</u>
   d. Indicate the following points on the plane: A'(0.5,0), B'(–1,2.5),C'(2,1.5), Connect them to form a triangle.
   e. The 3rd triangle in comparison to the first one? <u>Similar, just smaller</u>
   f. This is a <u>dilation</u> factor <u>1/2</u>
   g. When making all sides of a shape bigger or smaller using the same factor the shape remains <u>similar</u> to the original one.

9. Indicate the following points on the plane: A(0,0), B(2, 0),C(0,–3). Connect them to form a triangle.

   a. The points are: A' = (0,0), B' = (6, 0), C' = (0, –9)

   b. The relations:
   $$\frac{A'B'}{AB} = 3$$
   $$\frac{A'C'}{AC} = 3$$
   $$\frac{B'C'}{BC} = 3$$

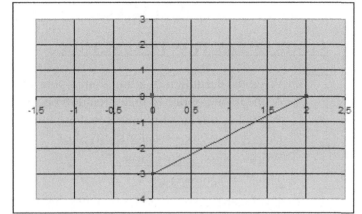

10. Given a triangle ABC whose sides are 3, 4 and 5 cm long.
    a. Is his a right angled triangle? <u>Yes: 25 = 16 + 9</u>
    b. The sides of another triangle whose sides are half the length of the sides of ABC are: <u>2.5, 2, 1.5</u>. Is this triangle right angled? <u>Yes 6.25 = 4 + 2.25</u>

11. Given a triangle ABC whose sides are 2, 4 and x cm long. A similar triangle has sides y, 6 and z correspondingly.

    a. $\dfrac{6}{4} = \dfrac{y}{2}; y = 3$ b. $\dfrac{z}{x} = \dfrac{3}{2}$

    c. A value for x so that ABC will be right angled?
    $$4 + 16 = x^2; x_1 = \sqrt{20}$$
    $$x^2 + 2 = 4; x_2 = \sqrt{2}$$

    d. Find z in that case(s): $z_1 = \dfrac{3}{2}x = \dfrac{3}{2}\sqrt{20}; z_2 = \dfrac{3}{2}x = \dfrac{3}{2}\sqrt{2}$

12. Given a rectangle ABCD whose sides are 8, and x cm long. A similar rectangle has sides y and 16 cm correspondingly. The perimeter of the 2nd rectangle is 3 times as large as the perimeter of the first one.

    a. $\dfrac{8}{y} = \dfrac{x}{16}; xy = 128$ $3(16 + 2x) = 2y + 32; y = 8 + 3x$ $x = \dfrac{16}{3}, y = 24$

    b. The area of the rectangles A$_1$ and A$_2$. $A_1 = \dfrac{128}{3}$ $A_2 = 384$

    c. The quotient $\dfrac{A_2}{A_1} = \dfrac{384}{\left(\dfrac{128}{3}\right)} = 9$, <u>the quotient between the areas is equal to</u>

    <u>the quotient between the sides squared.</u>

13. Given that the area of a square is 16 times as big as the area of a different square. Find the ratio between the sides of the squares.

    $\dfrac{A_2}{A_1} = 16 = \left(\dfrac{a_1}{a_2}\right)^2; \dfrac{a_1}{a_2} = 4$

14. Explain the meaning of the operation "Zooming in/out" frequently used in digital imaging. <u>Zoom means create a similar image by multiplying the distance between any 2 points by a constant. If the constant is great than 1 than we "zoom in", if the constant is between 0 and 1, we "zoom out".</u>

CHAPTER 3 – FUNCTIONS

3.1. – INTRODUCTION TO FUNCTION

1. Write the definition of a function in your own words:
    A one to one or one to many relation between "things" (variables),
2. Write 2 examples of relations that <u>are</u> functions:
    <u>Day of the week</u> → <u>color of my shirt</u>

    <u>Word</u> → <u>First letter of word</u>

    <u>Time</u> → <u>Temperature</u>
3. The independent variable is usually represented in the <u>horizontal axis</u>
4. The dependent variable is usually represented in the <u>vertical axis</u>
5. Draw a sketch of the functions that describe those relations. Can you write the mathematical expression to describe them?
    Only the last example is "mathematical enough" to find an expression:
    f(t) = Asin(kt) + B (this will be discussed later). Approximate sketch can be:

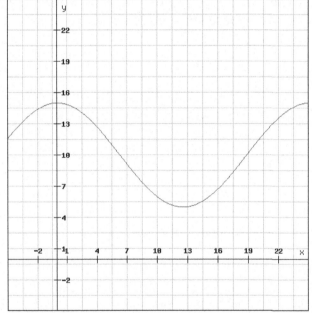

6. Write 2 examples of relations that <u>are not</u> functions:
    <u>Name of person</u> → <u>Personal information</u>   (one to many)
    <u>Name of City</u> → <u>Names of habitants</u>   (one to many)

7. Which one of the following graphs cannot represent function:

Not a function

Not a function

106

8. Draw an example of a curve that is not a function:

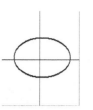

9. Draw an example of a curve that is a function:

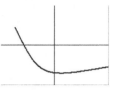

10. The domain of a function is the: <u>The set of allowed values of the independent variable ("what x can be")</u>

11. The Range of a function is the: <u>The set of allowed values of the dependent variable ("what y can be")</u>

12. Out of the following relations circle the ones that are functions:

    a. **Person's name** → **Person's age**
    b. **City** → **Number of habitants**
    c. City → Names of habitants
    d. **Family** → **Home Address**
    e. **Satellite's name** → **Position of satellite**
    f. **Time** → **Position of object**
    g. **One** → **One**
    h. One → Many
    i. **Many** → **One**

13. Given the Height – age curve for a human. Sketch an approximate graph:

    a. Height(0) = <u>50cm</u>, it is the height of <u>a new born baby</u>

    b. Height(t) = 100cm. Then t is: <u>2 years</u>

    c. State its domain: $Age \in [0,80]$

    d. State its range: $Height \in [50,175]$

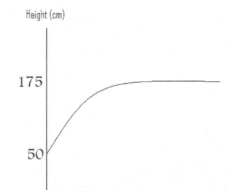

14. Given the following function that describes the temperature in C° as a function of time (t = 0 corresponds to midnight):

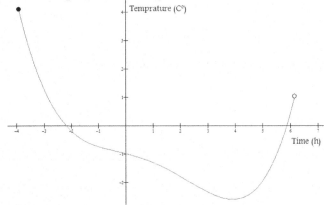

    a. f(0) = <u>–1</u>

    b. f(2) = <u>–1.5</u> = f(<u>5</u>)

    c. f(7) = <u>out of domain</u>

    d. f(x) = 3, x = –3.7

    e. f(x) = 0, <u>x = –2.2, 5.8</u>

    f. f(x) = –2 , <u>x = 2.8, 4.7</u>

    g. State its domain:
       <u>$x \in [-4,6)$</u>

    h. State its range:
       <u>$f(x) \in [-3,4]$</u>

    i. Is this function one to one? One to many? Explain. <u>No, Many to one</u>

15. Given the function the describes the change in the benefit (%) given by a certain stock:

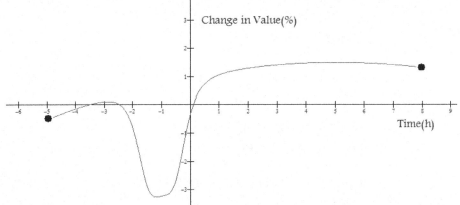

    a. f(x) = 0, <u>x = –2.5, –3.5, 0.2</u>

    b. f(0) = <u>–0.5</u> = f(<u>–2.2</u>)

    c. f(–5) = <u>–0.6</u>

    d. f(1) = <u>1</u>

    e. f(–2) = <u>–1</u> = f(<u>–0.2</u>)

    f. f(3) = <u>1.4</u>

    g. f(x) = –2, <u>x = –0.5, –1.5</u>

    h. Is f(–2) < 0 ? <u>yes</u>

    i. Is f(–2) < f(–1) ? <u>No</u>

    j. Domain: <u>$x \in [-5,8]$</u>

    k. State its range: <u>$f(x) \in [-3.2,1.5]$</u>

    l. Where is the function increasing
       <u>$x \in (-5,-3) \cup (-1.2,5)$</u>

    m. Where is the function decreasing?
       <u>$x \in (-3,-1.2) \cup (5,8)$</u>

    n. Where is the function stationary?
       <u>$x = -3, -1.2$</u>

    o. Is this function one to one? <u>No, it is many to one</u>

16. Given the following function:

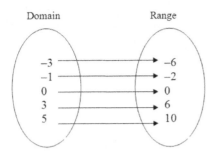

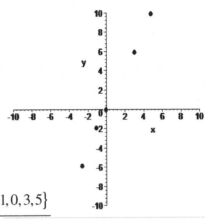

a. Allowed values for independent variable: $\{-3,-1,0,3,5\}$

b. Allowed values for dependent variable: $\{-6,-2,0,6,10\}$

c. Sketch the function on the graph.
d. A mathematical expression to express function:$\underline{f(x) = 2x}$

17. Given the following function:

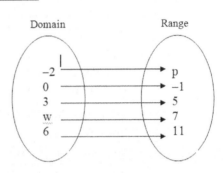

a. A mathematical expression to express this function: $\underline{f(x) = 2x - 1}$
b. Find p. Find w. $\underline{p = -5, w = 4}$

18. Use the graph of the gasoline consumption of a truck to answer:

a. $f(0) = \underline{0}$
b. $f(50) = \underline{12.5}$
c. $f(5) = \underline{2.5}$
d. For what values of x is $f(x) = 12$, $\underline{x = 33, 84, 116}$
e. Is $f(60) > f(70)$? $\underline{\text{Yes}}$
f. For what values of x is $f(x) > 15$? $\underline{,x > 135}$
g. At what positive speed is the consumption of gasoline minimum? $\underline{100}$
h. Where is the function increasing? $\underline{x \in (0,50) \cup (100,145)}$
i. Where is the function decreasing? $\underline{x \in (50,100)}$ $x \in (50,100)$
j. Where is the function stationary? $\underline{x = 100}$

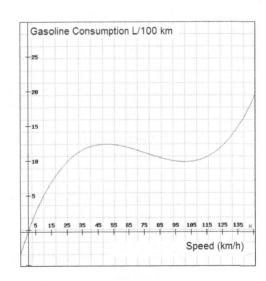

19. Functions can be represented using: <u>Graphs</u> or <u>Expressions</u>

20. The following graph describes the concentration of a drug injected into the blood as a function of the time (in minutes) since the injection. $t = 0$ corresponds to the time of injection.

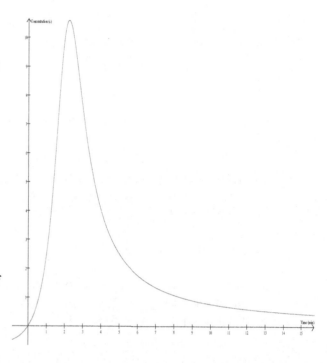

a. What is the concentration of the drug 4 hours after the injection? <u>4c</u>

b. During what period of time is the concentration increasing? <u>$t \in (0, 2.2)$</u>

c. After how long is the concentration maximum? <u>2.2 min</u>

d. When is the concentration greater than 5c? <u>$t \in (1.2, 3.6)$</u>

e. When is the concentration smaller than 2c? <u>$t \in (0,1) \cup (5.5, 16)$</u>

f. State the domain and range of the function.
Domain: <u>$t \in [0, 16]$</u>
Range: <u>$f(t) \in [0, 11]$</u>

21. The graph below shows the temperature in C° on a particular day as a function of time since midnight.

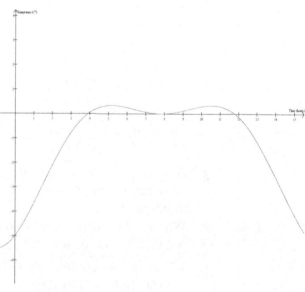

a. What was the temperature at 4:00 a.m.? <u>0.1</u>

b. When was the temperature 0 degrees? <u>3:55 am, 7:55 am, 11:50 am</u>

c. When was the temperature below freezing? (less than 0 degrees) <u>$t \in (11, 3:55) \cup (11:50, 16)$</u>

d. When was the temperature increasing? <u>$t \in (11, 5:05) \cup (7:55, 10:35)$</u>

e. State the domain and range of the function.
Domain: <u>$t \in [11pm, 16pm]$</u>
Range: <u>$f(t) \in [-5.5, 0.5]$</u>

3.2 – LINEAR FUNCTIONS

1. Given the function: f(x) = –5

X	–5	–4	–3	–2	–1	0	1	2	3	4	5
f(x)	–5	–5	–5	–5	–5	–5	–5	–5	–5	–5	–5

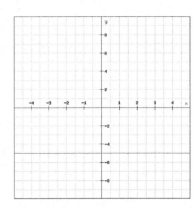

- Sketch the points of the chart on a graph (use a ruler).

- State the domain of the function: $x \in R$

- State the y intercept (sketched on the graph: (0, –5)

- State the x intercept: None

- The function is increasing on the interval: Never

- The function is decreasing on the interval: Never

- Sketch the function of the graph used for the points initially drawn

- State the range of the function: $f(x) \in \{-5\}$

2. Given the function: f(x) = x + 3

x	–5	–4	–3	–2	–1	0	1	2	3	4	5
f(x)	–2	–1	0	1	2	3	4	5	6	7	8

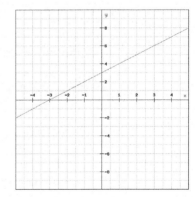

- Sketch the points of the chart on a graph (use a ruler).

- State the domain of the function: $x \in R$

- State the y intercept (sketched on the graph: (0, 3)

- State the x intercept: (–3,0)

- The function is increasing on the interval: $x \in R$

- The function is decreasing on the interval: Never

- Sketch the function of the graph used for the points initially drawn

- State the range of the function: $f(x) \in R$

3. Given the function: f(x) = –2x – 5

x	–5	–4	–3	–2	–1	0	1	2	3	4	5
f(x)	5	3	1	–1	–3	–5	–7	–9	–11	–13	–15

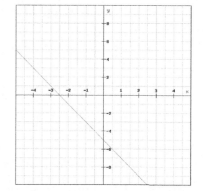

- Sketch the points of the chart on a graph (use a ruler).

- State the domain of the function: $x \in R$

- State the y intercept (sketched on the graph: (0, –5)

- State the x intercept: $\left(\dfrac{5}{2}, 0\right)$

- The function is increasing on the interval: <u>Never</u>

- The function is decreasing on the interval: $x \in R$

- Sketch the function of the graph used for the points initially drawn

- State the range of the function: $f(x) \in R$

4. Given the function: f(x) = 4x – 3

x	–5	–4	–3	–2	–1	0	1	2	3	4	5
f(x)	–23	–19	–15	–11	–7	–3	1	5	9	13	17

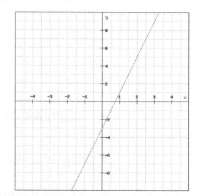

- Sketch the points of the chart on a graph (use a ruler).

- State the domain of the function: $x \in R$

- State the y intercept (sketched on the graph: (0, –3)

- State the x intercept: $\left(\dfrac{3}{4}, 0\right)$

- The function is increasing on the interval: $x \in R$

- The function is decreasing on the interval: <u>Never</u>

- Sketch the function of the graph used for the points initially drawn

- State the range of the function: $f(x) \in R$

5. Given below are the equations for five different lines. Match the function with its graph.

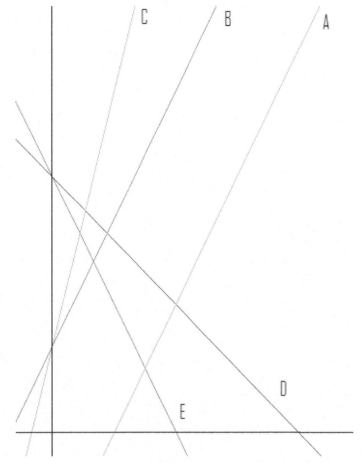

Function	On the graph
f(x) = 20 + 2x	**B**
g(x) = 4x + 20	**C**
s(x) = –30 + 2x	**A**
a(x) = 60 – x	**D**
b(x) = – 2x + 60	**E**

6. The general functions that describes a straight line is <u>f(x) = mx + b</u>

7. We know a function is a straight line because <u>x is to the power of 1 only</u>

8. The y–intercept (also called vertical intercept), tells us where the line crosses the y axis. The corresponding point is of the form <u>(0 , b)</u>.

9. The x–intercept (also called horizontal intercept), tells us where the line crosses the <u>x axis</u>. The corresponding point is of the form (p , 0).

10. If m > 0, the line <u>increases</u> left to right. If <u>m < 0</u> the line decreases left to right.

11. In case the line is horizontal m is <u>zero</u> and the line is of the form <u>f(x) = b</u>

12. The larger the value of m is, the <u>steeper</u> the graph of the line is.

13. Given the graph, write, the slope (m), b and the equation of the line:

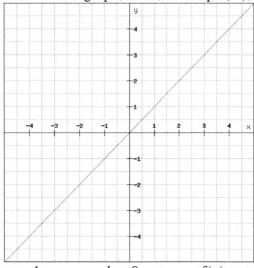

m = 1　　　　　b = 0　　　　　f(x) = x

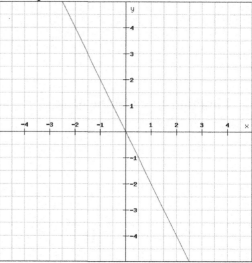

m = 1　　　　　b = 0　　　　　f(x) = x

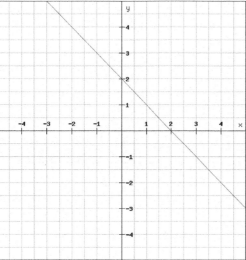

m = −1　　　　b = 2　　　　　f(x) = −x + 2

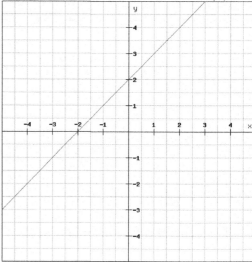

m = 1　　　　　b = 2　　　　　f(x) = x + 2

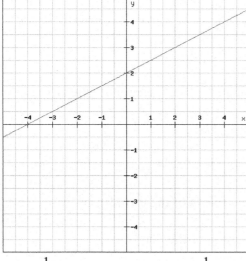

$m = \dfrac{1}{2}$　　　　b = 2　　　$f(x) = \dfrac{1}{2}x + 2$

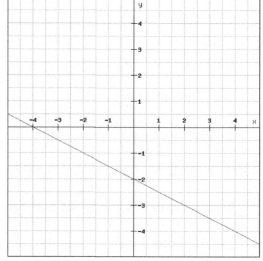

$m = -\dfrac{1}{2}$　　　　b = −2　　　$f(x) = -\dfrac{1}{2}x - 2$

114

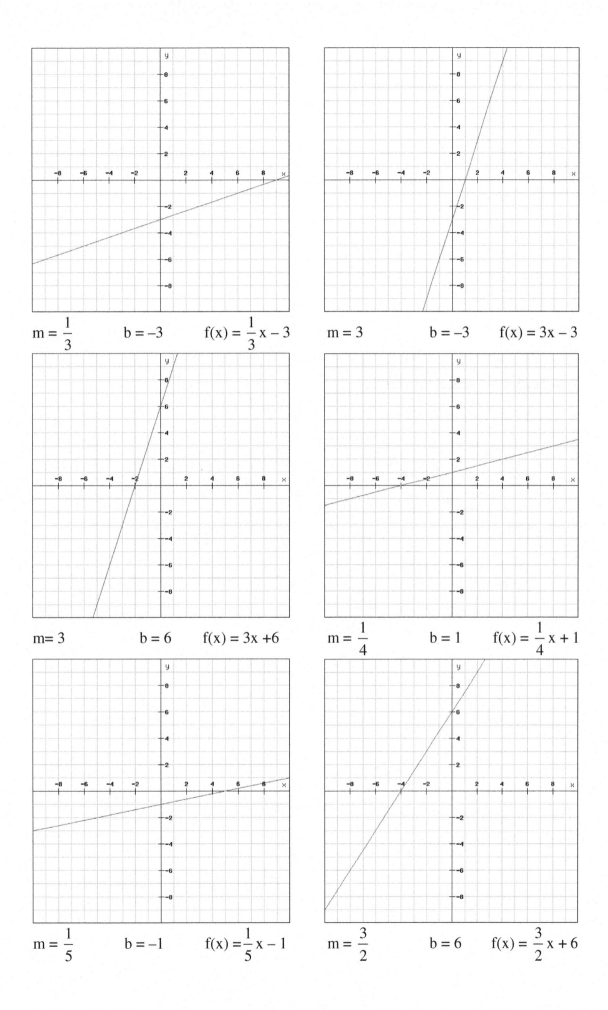

m = $\dfrac{1}{3}$ b = –3   f(x) = $\dfrac{1}{3}$ x – 3

m = 3   b = –3   f(x) = 3x – 3

m= 3   b = 6   f(x) = 3x +6

m = $\dfrac{1}{4}$ b = 1   f(x) = $\dfrac{1}{4}$ x + 1

m = $\dfrac{1}{5}$ b = –1   f(x) = $\dfrac{1}{5}$ x – 1

m = $\dfrac{3}{2}$ b = 6   f(x) = $\dfrac{3}{2}$ x + 6

115

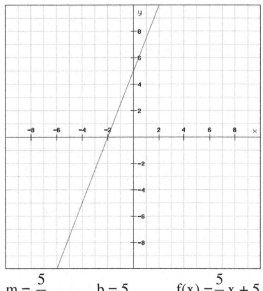

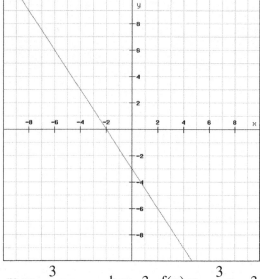

$m = \dfrac{5}{2}$ $b = 5$ $f(x) = \dfrac{5}{2}x + 5$ $m = -\dfrac{3}{2}$ $b = -3$ $f(x) = -\dfrac{3}{2}x - 3$

Analyze the following functions:

1. f(x) = 1

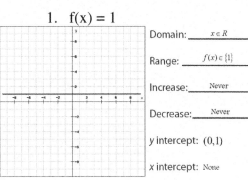

Domain: _____ $x \in R$ _____

Range: _____ $f(x) \in \{1\}$ _____

Increase: _____ Never _____

Decrease: _____ Never _____

y intercept: (0,1)

x intercept: None

2. f(x) = 2

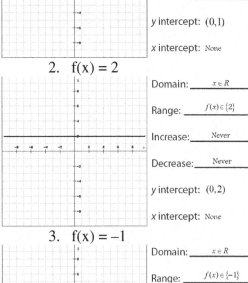

Domain: _____ $x \in R$ _____

Range: _____ $f(x) \in \{2\}$ _____

Increase: _____ Never _____

Decrease: _____ Never _____

y intercept: (0,2)

x intercept: None

3. f(x) = −1

Domain: _____ $x \in R$ _____

Range: _____ $f(x) \in \{-1\}$ _____

Increase: _____ Never _____

Decrease: _____ Never _____

y intercept: (0,−1)

x intercept: None

4. f(x) = 0

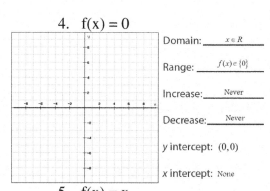

Domain: _____ $x \in R$ _____

Range: _____ $f(x) \in \{0\}$ _____

Increase: _____ Never _____

Decrease: _____ Never _____

y intercept: (0,0)

x intercept: None

5. f(x) = x

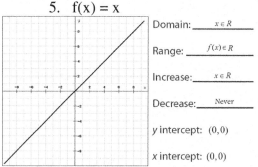

Domain: _____ $x \in R$ _____

Range: _____ $f(x) \in R$ _____

Increase: _____ $x \in R$ _____

Decrease: _____ Never _____

y intercept: (0,0)

x intercept: (0,0)

6. f(x) = x+1

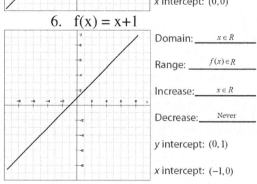

Domain: _____ $x \in R$ _____

Range: _____ $f(x) \in R$ _____

Increase: _____ $x \in R$ _____

Decrease: _____ Never _____

y intercept: (0,1)

x intercept: (−1,0)

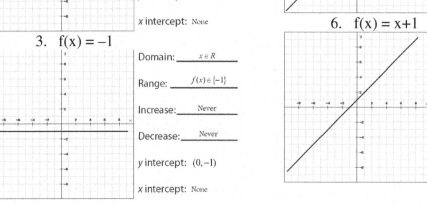

116

7. f(x) = −x

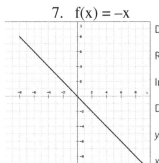

Domain: $x \in R$

Range: $f(x) \in R$

Increase: Never

Decrease: $x \in R$

y intercept: $(0,0)$

x intercept: $(0,0)$

8. f(x) = − x − 2

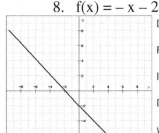

Domain: $x \in R$

Range: $f(x) \in R$

Increase: Never

Decrease: $x \in R$

y intercept: $(0,-2)$

x intercept: $(-2,0)$

9. f(x) = 2x

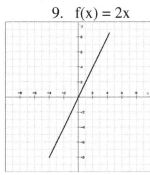

Domain: $x \in R$

Range: $f(x) \in R$

Increase: $x \in R$

Decrease: Never

y intercept: $(0,0)$

x intercept: $(0,0)$

10. f(x) = 3x − 5

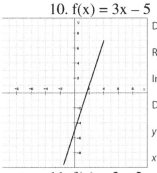

Domain: $x \in R$

Range: $f(x) \in R$

Increase: $x \in R$

Decrease: Never

y intercept: $(0,-5)$

x intercept: $\left(\frac{5}{3},0\right)$

11. f(x) = 3 − 2x

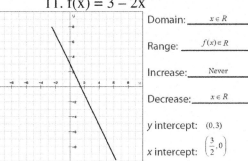

Domain: $x \in R$

Range: $f(x) \in R$

Increase: Never

Decrease: $x \in R$

y intercept: $(0,3)$

x intercept: $\left(\frac{3}{2},0\right)$

12. f(x) = $\frac{x}{3}$

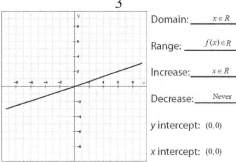

Domain: $x \in R$

Range: $f(x) \in R$

Increase: $x \in R$

Decrease: Never

y intercept: $(0,0)$

x intercept: $(0,0)$

13. f(x) = 2x + 1

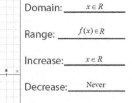

Domain: $x \in R$

Range: $f(x) \in R$

Increase: $x \in R$

Decrease: Never

y intercept: $(0,1)$

x intercept: $\left(-\frac{1}{2},0\right)$

14. f(x) = 2x − 2

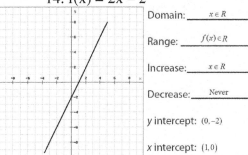

Domain: $x \in R$

Range: $f(x) \in R$

Increase: $x \in R$

Decrease: Never

y intercept: $(0,-2)$

x intercept: $(1,0)$

15. f(x) = 3x + 5

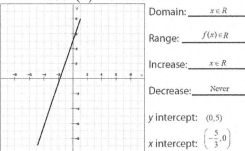

Domain: $x \in R$

Range: $f(x) \in R$

Increase: $x \in R$

Decrease: Never

y intercept: $(0,5)$

x intercept: $\left(-\frac{5}{3},0\right)$

16. f(x) = $\frac{x}{2}$ − 5

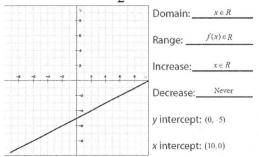

Domain: $x \in R$

Range: $f(x) \in R$

Increase: $x \in R$

Decrease: Never

y intercept: $(0,-5)$

x intercept: $(10,0)$

17. $f(x) = \dfrac{x}{4} + 6$

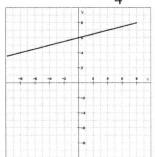

Domain: $x \in R$

Range: $f(x) \in R$

Increase: $x \in R$

Decrease: Never

y intercept: $(0,6)$

x intercept: $(-24,0)$

18. $f(x) \geq \dfrac{3}{2}x - 5$

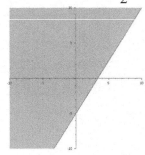

Domain: $x \in R$

Range: $f(x) \in R$

Increase: $x \in R$

Decrease: Never

y intercept: $(0,-5)$

x intercept: $\left(\dfrac{10}{3},0\right)$

19. $f(x) = -\dfrac{3}{2}x - \dfrac{3}{2}$

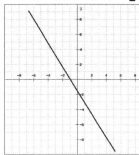

Domain: $x \in R$

Range: $f(x) \in R$

Increase: Never

Decrease: $x \in R$

y intercept: $\left(0,-\dfrac{3}{2}\right)$

x intercept: $(-1,0)$

20. $f(x) = -\dfrac{1}{2}x - \dfrac{3}{2}$

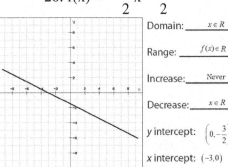

Domain: $x \in R$

Range: $f(x) \in R$

Increase: Never

Decrease: $x \in R$

y intercept: $\left(0,-\dfrac{3}{2}\right)$

x intercept: $(-3,0)$

21. $f(x) = \dfrac{7}{2}x - \dfrac{1}{4}$

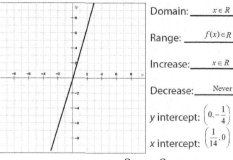

Domain: $x \in R$

Range: $f(x) \in R$

Increase: $x \in R$

Decrease: Never

y intercept: $\left(0,-\dfrac{1}{4}\right)$

x intercept: $\left(\dfrac{1}{14},0\right)$

22. $f(x) = -\dfrac{9}{5}x + \dfrac{8}{3}$

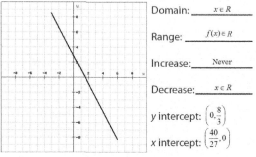

Domain: $x \in R$

Range: $f(x) \in R$

Increase: Never

Decrease: $x \in R$

y intercept: $\left(0,\dfrac{8}{3}\right)$

x intercept: $\left(\dfrac{40}{27},0\right)$

23. $3x + 2y = 2$

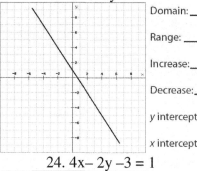

Domain: $x \in R$

Range: $f(x) \in R$

Increase: Never

Decrease: $x \in R$

y intercept: $(0,1)$

x intercept: $\left(\dfrac{2}{3},0\right)$

24. $4x - 2y - 3 = 1$

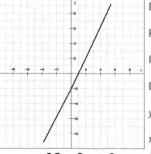

Domain: $x \in R$

Range: $f(x) \in R$

Increase: $x \in R$

Decrease: Never

y intercept: $(0,-2)$

x intercept: $(1,0)$

25. $-2y + 3x = -5$

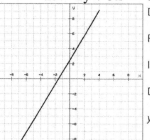

Domain: $x \in R$

Range: $f(x) \in R$

Increase: $x \in R$

Decrease: Never

y intercept: $\left(0,\dfrac{5}{2}\right)$

x intercept: $\left(-\dfrac{5}{3},0\right)$

26. y – x ≤ 2

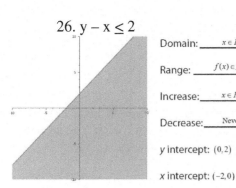

Domain: _____ $x \in R$ _____

Range: _____ $f(x) \in R$ _____

Increase: _____ $x \in R$ _____

Decrease: _____ Never _____

y intercept: $(0,2)$

x intercept: $(-2,0)$

27. y + 2x –3 ≥ 1

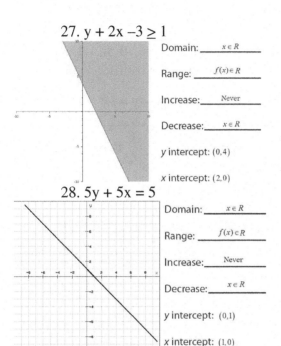

Domain: _____ $x \in R$ _____

Range: _____ $f(x) \in R$ _____

Increase: _____ Never _____

Decrease: _____ $x \in R$ _____

y intercept: $(0,4)$

x intercept: $(2,0)$

28. 5y + 5x = 5

Domain: _____ $x \in R$ _____

Range: _____ $f(x) \in R$ _____

Increase: _____ Never _____

Decrease: _____ $x \in R$ _____

y intercept: $(0,1)$

x intercept: $(1,0)$

29. 2x – 2y –3 = 1

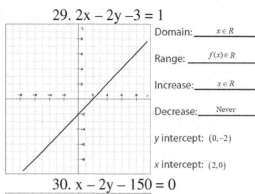

Domain: _____ $x \in R$ _____

Range: _____ $f(x) \in R$ _____

Increase: _____ $x \in R$ _____

Decrease: _____ Never _____

y intercept: $(0,-2)$

x intercept: $(2,0)$

30. x – 2y – 150 = 0

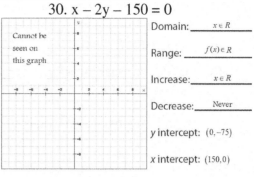

Cannot be seen on this graph

Domain: _____ $x \in R$ _____

Range: _____ $f(x) \in R$ _____

Increase: _____ $x \in R$ _____

Decrease: _____ Never _____

y intercept: $(0,-75)$

x intercept: $(150,0)$

---

31. Write the equation of the line that has a slope of 2 and passes through the point (2, 4) in the forms: y = mx + b and ax + by + c = 0, (a, b ∈ Z)

   $y = 2x; 2x - y = 0$

32. Write the equation of the line that has a slope of $-\dfrac{1}{2}$ and passes through the point (–2, –3) in the forms: y = mx + b and ax + by + c = 0, (a, b ∈ Z)

   $y = \dfrac{1}{2}x - 2; x - 2y - 4 = 0$

33. Write the equation of the line that has a slope of $-\dfrac{5}{2}$ and passes through the point (–1, 2) in the forms: y = mx + b and ax + by + c = 0, (a, b ∈ Z)

   $y = -\dfrac{5}{2}x - \dfrac{1}{2}; 5x + 2y + 1 = 0$

34. Find the equation of the line that passes through the points (1, 1), (2, 4), indicate its y and x intercepts and sketch it. Write its equation in the forms: y = mx + b and ax + by + c = 0, (a, b ∈ Z)

   $y = 3x - 2; 3x - y - 2 = 0$

35. Find the equation of the line that passes through the points (–1, –5), (4, 3), indicate its y and x intercepts and sketch it. Write its equation in the forms: y = mx + b and ax + by + c = 0, (a, b ∈ Z)

$$y = \frac{8}{5}x - \frac{17}{5}; 8x - y - 17 = 0$$

36. Find the equation of the line that passes through the points (–5, 1), (–2, 4), indicate its y and x intercepts, sketch it and write it in both forms y = mx + b and ax + by + c = 0, (a, b ∈ Z) $y = x + 6; -x + y - 6 = 0$

37. Write the equation of the line that is parallel to the line y = 5x – 2 and passes through the point (–2, –1). Write its equation in the forms: y = mx + b and ax + by + c = 0, (a, b ∈ Z) $y = 5x + 9; -5x + y - 9 = 0$

38. Write the equation of the line that is parallel to the line y = –0.5x – 1 and passes through the point (–3, 6). Write its equation in the forms: y = mx +

b and ax + by + c = 0, (a, b ∈ Z) $y = -\frac{1}{2}x + \frac{9}{2}; x + 2y - 9 = 0$

39. Sketch and write the equation of the line with a slope of $-\frac{1}{5}$ that passes

through the point (0,2). $y = -\frac{1}{5}x + 2; x + 5y - 10 = 0$

40. Sketch and write the equation of the lines with a slope: 1, 2, –3, –1, $-\frac{1}{2}, -\frac{1}{3},$

that passes through the point (0,0).

$$y = x; y = 2x; y = -3x; y = -x; y = -\frac{1}{2}x; y = -\frac{1}{3}x$$

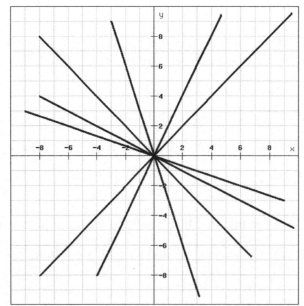

41. Sketch and write the equation of the line with a slope of –3 that passes v through the point (0,–3). $y = -3x - 3$

42. Sketch and write the equation of the line with a slope of 2 that passes through the point (2,0) $y = 2x - 4$

43. Sketch and write the equation of the line with a slope of $-\frac{1}{2}$ that passes

through the point $(-2,0)$ $\quad y=-\frac{1}{2}x-1$

44. Sketch and write the equation of the line with a slope of 2 that passes through the point $(-4,2)$ $\quad y=2x+10$

45. Find the intersection between the lines f(x) = 2x – 3 and f(x) = –5x –2

$$2x-3=-5x-2 \quad x=\frac{1}{7} \quad \left(\frac{1}{7},-\frac{19}{7}\right)$$

46. Find the intersection between the lines f(x) = x – 3 and f(x) = x – 4.
   No intersection, lines are parallel.

47. Find the intersection between the lines f(x) = 2x – 3 and f(x) = –2x + 7 $\left(\frac{7}{2},4\right)$

48. Find the intersection between the lines f(x) = ax – 3 and f(x) = ax + 7
   No intersection, lines are parallel.

49. Find the intersection between the lines f(x) = –12x – 13 and f(x) = 15x +20.

$$-12x-13=15x+20 \quad x=-\frac{33}{27} \quad \left(-\frac{33}{27},\frac{5}{3}\right)$$

50. Given that the lines f(x) = 2ax – 1 and f(x) = 4 – 5x + 20 do not intersect, find a.

$$2a=-5; a=\frac{-5}{2}$$

51. Find the intersection between the lines y = 2x – 3 and 2y – 4x = – 6. The same line, all the points of the line are the intersection.

52. Given that the lines f(x) = mx – 5 and f(x) = 2x + 4 intersect at the point where x = 3, find m. $3m-5=10; m=5$

53. Given that the lines f(x) = 2x – b and f(x) = 3x + 4 intersect at the point where x = 1, find b. $2-b=7; b=-5$

54. Find the intersection between the lines 3y + 2x = 3 and 9y + 6x = 9. The same line, all the points of the line are the intersection.

55. Sketch the line $f(x)=\frac{-x}{2}+3, -4 \le x < 8$

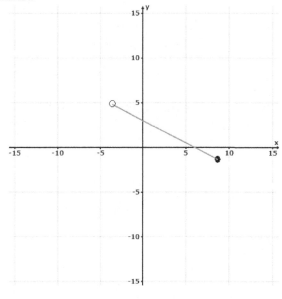

DISTANCE AND MIDPOINT BETWEEN 2 POINTS

56. Given the points (1, 2) and (5, 8). Find the distance between them. Find the midpoint. Sketch to illustrate your answer.

$$\text{Distance} = \sqrt{16+36} = \sqrt{52}$$
$$\text{Midpoint} = (3,5)$$

57. Given the points (–3, 2) and (5, –6). Find the distance between them. Find the midpoint. Sketch to illustrate your answer

$$\text{Distance} = \sqrt{64+64} = \sqrt{128}$$
$$\text{Midpoint} = (1,-4)$$

58. Given the points (–1, –6) and (–5, –1). Find the distance between them. Find the midpoint. Sketch to illustrate your answer.

$$\text{Distance} = \sqrt{16+25} = \sqrt{41}$$
$$\text{Midpoint} = \left(-3,-\frac{7}{2}\right)$$

59. Given that the points $(a, -1)$ and (5, 3) are 5 units away. Find a. Find the midpoint.

$$\text{Distance} = \sqrt{(a-5)^2+16} = 5; a_1 = 2; a_1 = 8$$
$$\text{Midpoint}(1) = \left(\frac{7}{2},1\right); \text{Midpoint}(2) = \left(\frac{13}{2},1\right)$$

60. Given that the points (1, –4) and (5, c) are 10 units away. Find c. Find the midpoint.

$$\text{Distance} = \sqrt{(c+4)^2+16} = 10; a_1 = -4+2\sqrt{21}; a_2 = -4-2\sqrt{21}$$
$$\text{Midpoint}(1) = \left(3,-4+\sqrt{21}\right); \text{Midpoint}(2) = \left(3,-4-\sqrt{21}\right)$$

61. Find the equation of all the points that are 2 units away from the origin. This equation describes a circle $x^2 + y^2 = 4$

62. Find the equation of all the points that are 5 units away from the point (2, –1) . This equation describes a circle $(x-2)^2 + (y+1)^2 = 25$

63. Given that the points (0, 0) and (0, c) are 10 units away. Find c. Find the midpoint. $c^2 = 100; c = \pm 10$ Midpoint $= (0, \pm 5)$

64. Given the points (–8, –7) and (6, 2). Find the distance between them. Find the midpoint. $\text{Distance} = \sqrt{196+49} = \sqrt{245}$ Midpoint $= \left(-1,-\frac{5}{2}\right)$

PERPENDICULAR LINES $(m\, m_\perp = -1)$

65. A slope perpendicular to 1 is <u>-1</u>. A slope perpendicular to 2 is $\underline{-\dfrac{1}{2}}$

  A slope perpendicular to k is $\underline{-\dfrac{1}{k}}$ A slope perpendicular to $\dfrac{a}{b}$ is $\underline{-\dfrac{b}{a}}$

66. Find the equation of a line perpendicular to the line $y = 3x - 2$ that passes

  through the point (3, 12). $\underline{y = -\dfrac{1}{3}x + 13}$

67. Find all the lines perpendicular to the line $y = -3x + 4$. Fin the ones that passes

  through the point (–3, 1). $\underline{y = \dfrac{1}{3}x + 2}$

68. Find a line perpendicular to the line $y = -\dfrac{2}{5}x + 1$ that passes through the point

     (–1, –7). $\underline{y = \dfrac{5}{2}x - \dfrac{9}{2}}$

69. Given the points (–2, 5) and (4, 2).

 a. Find the equation of the line passing through them. $\underline{f(x) = -\dfrac{1}{2}x + 4}$

 b. Is the point (5, 1) on this line? <u>No</u>: $\underline{f(5) = -\dfrac{5}{2} + 4 = \dfrac{3}{2} \neq 1}$

 c. Find a perpendicular line that passes through the mid point between these

  points. $\underline{f(x) = 2x + b}$ $\underline{Midpoint : (1, \dfrac{7}{2})}$ $\underline{f(x) = 2x + \dfrac{3}{2}}$

 d. Find all the points on the line found in c that are 0.5 units away from the
  point (0, 2).

$$\text{Points}: (x, 2x + \tfrac{3}{2}) \quad d = \tfrac{1}{2} = \sqrt{(0-x)^2 + \left(2 - \left(2x + \tfrac{3}{2}\right)\right)^2}$$

$$x_1 = 0 \quad x_2 = \tfrac{5}{2} \quad \text{Points are:} (0, \tfrac{3}{2}), (\tfrac{5}{2}, \tfrac{13}{2})$$

70. Find a point on the x axis that is $\sqrt{5}$ units away from the line $y = 2x + 4$

$$\text{Point}: (a, 0) \quad d = 5 = \sqrt{(a-x)^2 + \left(0 - (2x + 4)\right)^2}$$

$$-\frac{1}{2} = -\frac{2x + 4}{a - x}, \text{ Solving system for } a: (\tfrac{1}{2}, 0), (-\tfrac{9}{2}, 0)$$

71. Find a point on the y axis that is 5 units away from the line $y = 3x + 2$

72. Given that the slope of one of the lines is 3 and that the lines are perpendicular, find the **exact** coordinates of the point of intersection of the two lines.

Increasing line (plug (1,0): $y = 3x - 3$

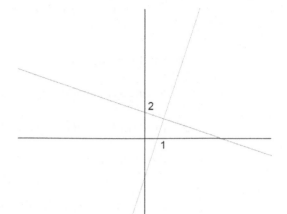

Decreasing line: $y = -\dfrac{1}{3}x + 2$

$$3x - 3 = -\dfrac{1}{3}x + 2$$

Intersection:

$$x = \dfrac{3}{2} \qquad \left(\dfrac{3}{2}, \dfrac{1}{2}\right)$$

SLOPE – INTERCEPT FORM OF A LINE

73. The line $y - 3 = 2(x + 1)$ passes through the point _____ and has a slope of ___
74. The line $y + 5 = -3(x - 51)$ passes through the point _____ and has a slope of ___
75. The line $-y + 1 = (x + 3)$ passes through the point _____ and has a slope of ___
76. The line $2y + 5 = -6(x + 7)$ passes through the point _____ and has a slope of ___
77. The line $y + a = m(x + b)$ passes through the point _____ and has a slope of ___
78. The line $y - a = m(x - b)$ passes through the point _____ and has a slope of ___
79. The line $y - a = m(x + b)$ passes through the point _____ and has a slope of ___
80. Write the equation $y - 3 = 2(x + 1)$ in the explicit form
81. Write the equation $y + 5 = 2(x + 6)$ in the explicit form
82. Write down the equation of a line passing through the point (5, 2) with slope 1.
83. Write down the equation of a line passing through the point (–4, –3) with slope –2.
84. Write down the equation of a line passing through the point (6, 3) with slope $\dfrac{2}{3}$.

85. Write down the equation of a line passing through point (–2, –5) with slope $-\dfrac{2}{5}$.

86. Write down the equation of the line passing through points (–2, –5), (–7, –5),
87. Write down the equation of the line passing through points (–1, –3), (6, 5),
88. Write down the equation of the line passing through points (–1, 5), (7, –2),

124

APPLICATION

1. The price of a new toy (in US$) is C(t) = 20 – 0.5t, t given in days.
   a. Sketch the corresponding graph.
   b. What was the initial price of the toy?   <u>20$</u>
   c. Find the price of the toy after 10 days   <u>15$</u>
   d. What is the domain of the function, argument the answer, $t \in [0, 40]$ <u>Price cannot be negative.</u>
   e. What is the range of the function? $C \in [0, 20]$
   f. What is the meaning of 0.5? Does it have units? What are they? 0.5 <u>$/day</u>, it is the daily reduction of the price.

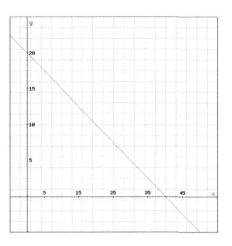

2. On a certain planet the temperature of the soil is 10° on the surface and 0.02° wormer with every meter of depth.

   i. Write a function to describe the temperature as a function of the depth d. State its domain and range. What are the units of the slope?

   $$T(d) = 10 + 0.02 \cdot d ; [d] = \frac{C^o}{m}$$

   $Domain : d \in [0, R], Radius \ Planet$
   $Range : T \in [10, 10 + 0.02R]$

   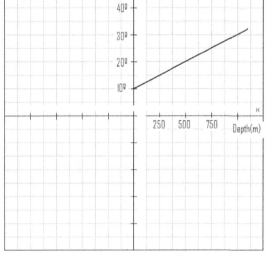

   ii. Find the temperature at depth of 500m
   $T(500) = 10 + 0.02 \cdot 500 = 20°$

   iii. Find the depth at which the temperature is 13°.
   $13 = 10 + 0.02 \cdot d$

   $d = 150m$

   iv. Graph the function, use appropriate scale, variables and units.

3. In a factory there are 2 machines that produce a certain product. The operation cost (electricity, maintenance etc.) of Machine A is 250$ a month and the cost of production per product is 2$. The operation cost of Machine B is 200$ a month and the cost of production per product is 4$. The maximum number of products that both machines can make a month is 200.

    i.   Write the functions to describe the cost C as a function of the number of products n for both machines. Indicate the domain and range of both functions. What are the units of the slope?

$$C_A(n) = 250 + 2 \cdot n; [slope] = \frac{\$}{unit}$$ $$C_B(n) = 200 + 4 \cdot n; [slope] = \frac{\$}{unit}$$

$Domain: n \in [0, 200]$ $Domain: n \in [0, 200]$

$Range: C_A \in [250, 650]$ $Range: C_B \in [200, 1000]$

    ii.   Graph the functions, use appropriate scale, variables and units. Calculate the coordinates of important points on the graph.

Point of intersection:

$$250 + 2n = 200 + 4n$$

$$n = 25$$

$$(25, 300)$$

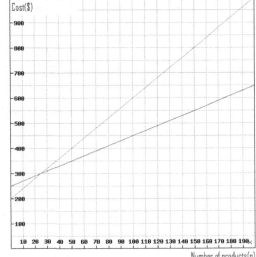

    iii.   Discuss in which case each machine is best.

If $0 \leq n < 25$ Machine B is better.

If $25 < n \leq 200$ Machine A is better.

If $n = 25$ Both machines are as good.

4. A parking lot with 1200 parking spots opens at 6 am. The cars flow in a constant rate. At 10 am the parking is full.

   i. Write the function to describe the number of cars N as function of time t in hours. Indicate the domain and range of the function. What are the units of the slope?

   $$N(t) = \frac{1200}{8} \cdot t = 150t; [slope] = \frac{cars}{hour}$$
   $$Domain: t \in [0,8]$$
   $$Range: N \in [0,1200]$$

   ii. Find the number of free spots at 8:30.

   $$N(2.5) = 150 \cdot 2.5 = 375 cars$$
   $$Free: 1200 - 375 = 825$$

   iii. In case the owner needs 150 free spots at what time should he close the parking?
   $$1050 = 150t$$
   $$t = 7h$$
   Should close at 1pm.

   iv. Graph the function, use appropriate scale, variables and units.

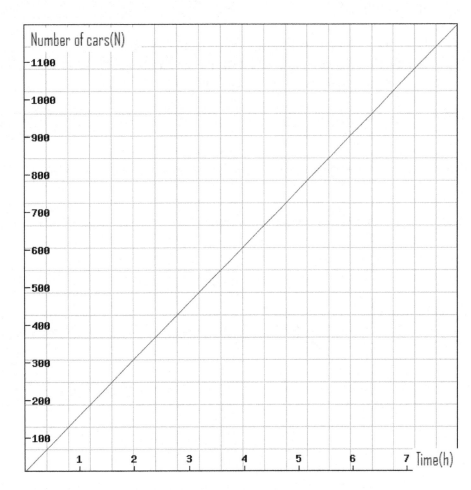

5. You need to rent a car for one day and to compare the charges of 3 different companies. Company I charges 20$ per day with additional cost of 0.20$ per mile. Company II charges 30$ per day with additional cost of 0.10$ per mile. Company III charges 70$ per day with no additional mileage charge.

   a. Write the cost function for each one of the companies.

   $$C_I = 20 + 0.2x$$

   $$C_{II} = 30 + 0.1x$$

   $$C_{III} = 70$$

   b. Sketch all 3 graphs on the same axes system.

   c. Comment on the circumstances in which renting a car from each one of the companies is best. The black line represent the cheapest price:

   It is important to find the intersection points between: lines I, II and lines II, III.
   I, II: (100, 40)
   II, III (400, 70)

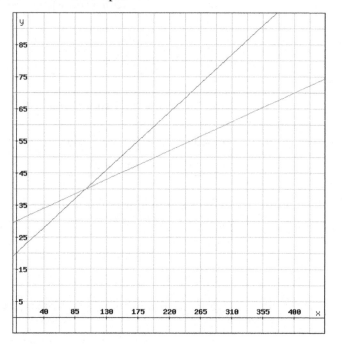

If we travel less than 100 miles Company I is best.
If we travel between 100 and 400 miles Company II is best.
If we travel more than 400 miles Company III is best.

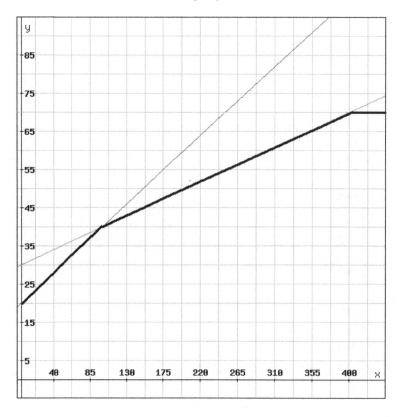

3.3. – QUADRATIC FUNCTIONS

1. Given the functions: $f(x) = x^2$, $g(x) = x^2 - 2$. Complete the following table:

x	−5	−4	−3	−2	−1	0	1	2	3	4	5	6
f(x)	25	16	9	4	1	0	1	4	9	16	25	36
g(x)	23	14	7	2	−1	−2	−1	2	7	14	23	34

- Sketch the points of the table on a graph (use a ruler).

- State the domain of the function: $\underline{x \in R}$

- State the y intercept (sketched on the graph): $\underline{f(x):(0,0); g(x):(0,-2)}$

- State the x intercept(s): $\underline{f(x):(0,0); g(x):(\sqrt{2},0),(-\sqrt{2},0)}$

- Write in all possible forms:

$$\underline{f(x) = x^2} \qquad \underline{g(x) = x^2 - 2 = (x+\sqrt{2})(x-\sqrt{2})}$$

- Find the max/**min** point(s): $\underline{f(x):(0,0); g(x):(0,-2)}$

- The function is increasing on the interval: $\underline{f(x): x \in (0,\infty); g(x): x \in (0,\infty)}$

- The function is decreasing on the interval: $\underline{f(x): x \in (-\infty,0); g(x): x \in (-\infty,0)}$

- State the range of the function: $\underline{f(x) \in [0,\infty); g(x) \in [-2,\infty)}$

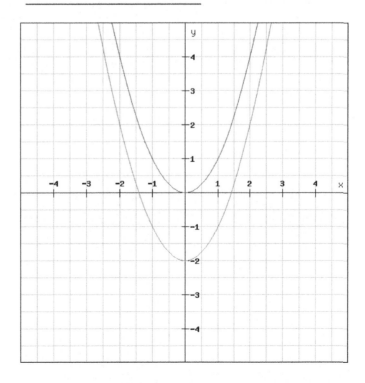

2. Given the functions: f(x) = (x − 2)², g(x) = (x + 3)² − 2. Complete the following table:

x	−5	−4	−3	−2	−1	0	1	2	3	4	5	6
f(x)	49	36	25	16	9	4	1	0	1	4	9	16
g(x)	2	−1	−2	−1	2	7	14	23	34	47	62	79

- State the domain of the function: $x \in R$

- State the y intercept (sketched on the graph): $f(x):(0,4); g(x):(0,7)$

- State the x intercept(s): $f(x):(2,0); g(x):(\sqrt{2}-3,0),(-\sqrt{2}-3,0)$

- Write in all possible forms:

$$f(x) = (x-2)^2 = x^2 - 4x + 4$$

$$g(x) = (x+3)^2 - 2 = (x-(\sqrt{2}-3))(x-(-\sqrt{2}-3)) = x^2 + 6x + 7$$

- Find the max/**min** point(s): $f(x):(2,0); g(x):(-3,-2)$

- The function is increasing on the interval: $f(x): x \in (2,\infty); g(x): x \in (-3,\infty)$

- The function is decreasing on the interval: $f(x): x \in (-\infty,2); g(x): x \in (-\infty,-3)$

- State the range of the function: $f(x) \in [0,\infty); g(x) \in [-2,\infty)$

- State its axes of symmetry: $f(x): x = 2; g(x): x = -3$

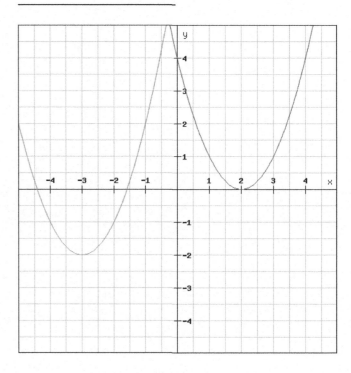

3. Given the function: f(x) = (x + 2)(x − 4), g(x) = 2(x + 2)(x − 4) Complete the following table:

x	−5	−4	−3	−2	−1	0	1	2	3	4	5	6
f(x)	27	16	7	0	−5	−8	−9	−8	−5	0	7	16
g(x)	54	32	14	0	−10	−16	−18	−16	−10	0	14	32

- State the domain of the function: $x \in R$

- State the y intercept (sketched on the graph): $f(x):(0,-8); g(x):(0,-16)$

- State the x intercept(s): $f(x):(-2,0),(4,0); g(x):(-2,0),(4,0)$

- Write in all possible forms:

  $f(x) = (x+2)(x-4) = x^2 - 2x - 8 = (x-1)^2 - 9$

  $g(x) = 2(x+2)(x-4) = 2x^2 - 4x - 16 = 2(x-1)^2 - 18$

- Find the max/**min** point(s): $f(x):(1,-9); g(x):(1,-18)$

- The function is increasing on the interval: $f(x): x \in (1,\infty); g(x): x \in (1,\infty)$

- The function is decreasing on the interval: $f(x): x \in (-\infty,1); g(x): x \in (-\infty,1)$

- State the range of the function: $f(x) \in [-9,\infty); g(x) \in [-18,\infty)$

- State its axes of symmetry: $f(x): x = 1; g(x): x = 1$

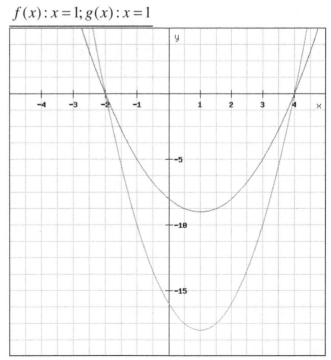

131

In general, a quadratic function f can be written in several different ways:

a. $f(x) = ax^2 + bx + c$ **standard form**, where a, b and c are constants

b. $f(x) = a(x - r)(x - s)$ **factored form**, where a, r and s are constants

c. $f(x) = a(x - h)^2 + k$ **vertex form**, where a, h and k are constants

Example:

Vertex form: $f(x) = 3(x - 2)^2 - 3$

Partial factored form: $f(x) = 3(x - 1)(x - 3)$

Standard form: $f(x) = 3x^2 + 12x + 9$

Complete the sentences:

1. The graph of a quadratic function is called a <u>Parabola</u>

2. In factored form, the numbers r and s represent <u>the x–coordinates of the x intercepts</u> of f.

3. In vertex form, the point (h, k) is called the <u>vertex</u> of the parabola.

   The axis of symmetry of the parabola is the line <u>x = h</u>

4. The graph of the parabola opens upwards if <u>a > 0</u> and downwards if <u>a < 0</u>

5. In case $f(x) = x^2 + 1$, the function can be written in <u>1</u> form(s) only. Why?

   <u>No x intercepts so no factored form. Vertex and standard are identical.</u>

6. In case $f(x) = x^2 - 1$, the function can be written in <u>2</u> form(s) only. Show your answer:

   <u>Vertex and standard are identical.</u>

7. A parabola has its vertex at the point (2, 3) and goes through the point (6, 11). Find the expression of the function.

   $$f(x) = a(x - 2)^2 + 3; 11 = a(6 - 2)^2 + 3; a = \frac{1}{2}$$

   $$f(x) = \frac{1}{2}(x - 2)^2 + 3$$
   _____

8. A parabola has its vertex at the point (– 2, 4) and passes through the point (2, – 6). Find the expression of the function.

   $$f(x) = a(x + 2)^2 + 4; -6 = a(2 + 2)^2 + 4; a = -\frac{10}{16} = -\frac{5}{8}$$

   $$f(x) = -\frac{5}{8}(x + 2)^2 + 4$$
   _____

9. Write the analytical expression that corresponds the following functions in all possible forms, assume $a = 1$ or -1 in both cases:

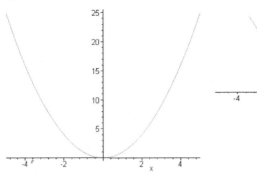

Range: _____ $f(x) \in [0, \infty)$ _____ Range: _____ $f(x) \in [3, \infty)$ _____

Vertex form: _____ $f(x) = x^2$ _____ Vertex form: _____ $f(x) = x^2 + 3$ _____

Factorized form: _____ $f(x) = x^2$ _____ Factorized form: _____ $None$ _____

Standard form: _____ $f(x) = x^2$ _____ Standard form: _____ $f(x) = x^2 + 3$ _____

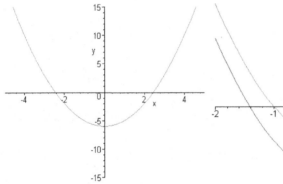

Range: _____ $f(x) \in [-6, \infty)$ _____ Range: _____ $f(x) \in [-1, \infty)$; $f(x) \in [-2, \infty)$ _____

Vertex form: _____ $f(x) = x^2 - 6$ _____ Vertex form: _____ $f(x) = x^2 - 1$; $f(x) = x^2 - 2$ _____

Factorized form: _____ $f(x) = (x - \sqrt{6})(x + \sqrt{6})$ _____ Factorized form: _____ $f(x) = (x-1)(x+1); f(x) = (x - \sqrt{2})(x + \sqrt{2})$ _____

Standard form: _____ $f(x) = x^2 - 6$ _____ Standard form: _____ $f(x) = x^2 - 1$; $f(x) = x^2 - 2$ _____

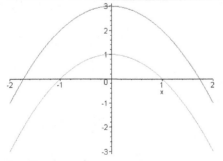

(upper curve) (upper curve)

Range: _____ $f(x) \in [-\infty, 3)$ _____ Range: _____ $f(x) \in [-\infty, -3)$ _____

Vertex form: _____ $f(x) = -x^2 + 3$ _____ Vertex form: _____ $f(x) = -x^2 - 3$ _____

Factorized form: _____ $f(x) = -(x - \sqrt{3})(x + \sqrt{3})$ _____ Factorized form: _____ $None$ _____

Standard form: _____ $f(x) = -x^2 + 3$ _____ Standard form: _____ $f(x) = -x^2 - 3$ _____

10. Complete the tables:

Function	On the graph
$f(x) = x^2$	B
$f(x) = \dfrac{x^2}{2}$	C
$f(x) = \dfrac{x^2}{3}$	D
$f(x) = 2x^2$	A

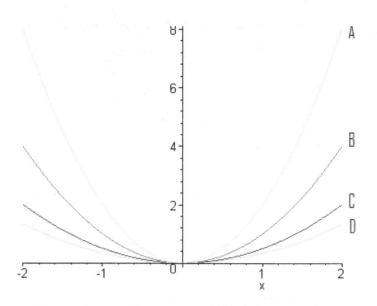

11. Complete the table:

Function	On the graph
$f(x) = x^2 + 2$	B
$f(x) = x^2 - 2$	C
$f(x) = x^2 - 3$	D
$f(x) = 2x^2 + 2$	A

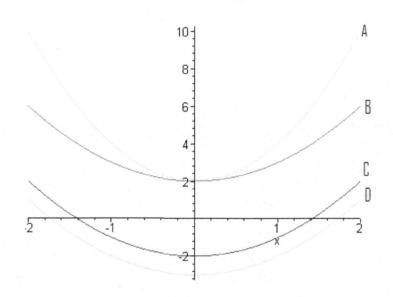

12. Complete the table:

Function	On the graph
$f(x) = -x^2 + 2$	C
$f(x) = x^2 - 4$	D
$f(x) = -x^2 + 3$	B
$f(x) = 2x^2 + 2$	A

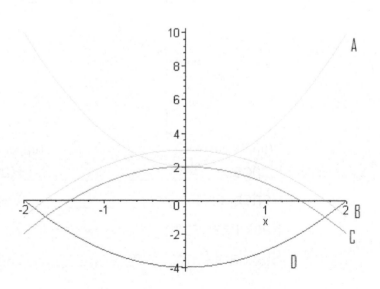

13. Write the expression of the function in all possible forms, indicate the range assume $a = 1$ or -1 in both cases. Use GDC to check your answer.

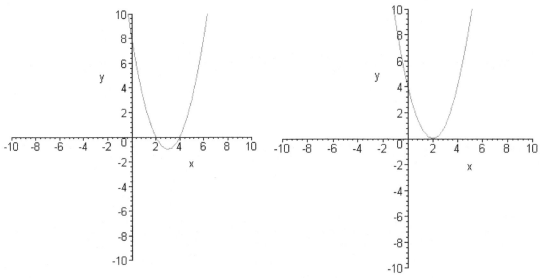

Range: _____ $f(x) \in [-1, \infty)$ _____

Range: _____ $f(x) \in [0, \infty)$ _____

Vertex form: _____ $f(x) = (x-3)^2 - 1$ _____

Vertex form: _____ $f(x) = (x-2)^2$ _____

Factorized form: _____ $f(x) = (x-2)(x-4)$ _____

Factorized form: _____ $f(x) = (x-2)(x-2)$ _____

Standard form: _____ $f(x) = x^2 - 6x + 8$ _____

Standard form: _____ $f(x) = x^2 - 4x + 4$ _____

14. Write the expression of the function in all possible forms, indicate the range assume $a = 1$ or -1 in both cases:

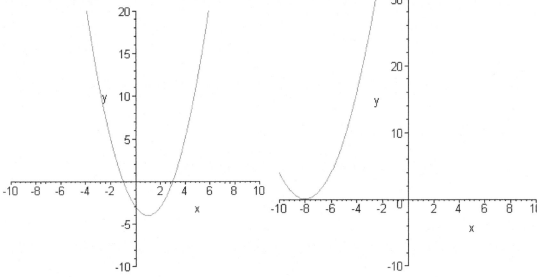

Range: _____ $f(x) \in [-4, \infty)$ _____

Range: _____ $f(x) \in [0, \infty)$ _____

Vertex form: _____ $f(x) = (x-1)^2 - 4$ _____

Vertex form: _____ $f(x) = (x+8)^2$ _____

Factorized form: _____ $f(x) = (x+1)(x-3)$ _____

Factorized form: _____ $f(x) = (x+8)(x+8)$ _____

Standard form: _____ $f(x) = x^2 - 2x - 3$ _____

Standard form: _____ $f(x) = x^2 + 16x + 64$ _____

15. Write the expression of the function in all possible forms, indicate the range assume $a = 1$ or -1 in both cases:

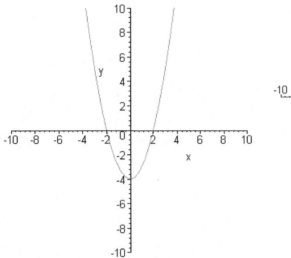 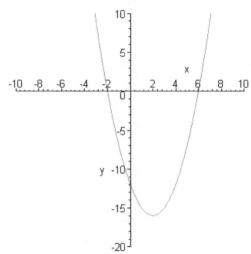

Range: ____$f(x) \in [-4, \infty)$____   Range: ____$f(x) \in [-16, \infty)$____

Vertex form: ____$f(x) = x^2 - 4$____   Vertex form: ____$f(x) = (x-2)^2 - 16$____

Factorized form: ____$f(x) = (x+2)(x-2)$____   Factorized form: ____$f(x) = (x+2)(x-6)$____

Standard form: ____$f(x) = x^2 - 4$____   Standard form: ____$f(x) = x^2 - 4x - 12$____

16. Write the expression of the function in all possible forms, indicate the range assume $a = 1$ or -1 in both cases:

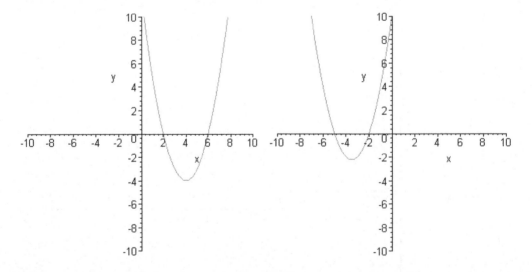

Range: ____$f(x) \in [-4, \infty)$____   Range: ____$f(x) \in [-\frac{9}{4}, \infty)$____

Vertex form: ____$f(x) = (x-4)^2 - 4$____   Vertex form: ____$f(x) = \left(x + \frac{7}{2}\right)^2 - \frac{9}{4}$____

Factorized form: ____$f(x) = (x-2)(x-6)$____   Factorized form: ____$f(x) = (x+2)(x+5)$____

Standard form: ____$f(x) = x^2 - 8x + 12$____   Standard form: ____$f(x) = x^2 + 7x + 10$____

17. Write the expression of the function in all possible forms, indicate the range assume $a = 1$ or -1 in both cases:

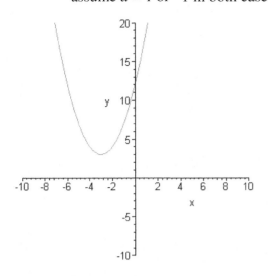 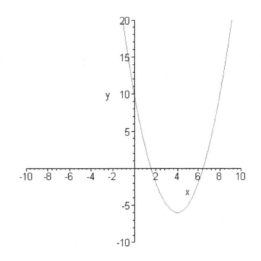

Range: $f(x) \in [3, \infty)$ Range: $f(x) \in [-6, \infty)$

Vertex form: $f(x) = (x+3)^2 + 3$ Vertex form: $f(x) = (x-4)^2 - 6$

Factorized form: $None$ Factorized form: $f(x) = (x-(\sqrt{6}+4))(x-(-\sqrt{6}+4))$

Standard form: $f(x) = x^2 + 6x + 12$ Standard form: $f(x) = x^2 - 8x + 10$

18. Write the expression of the function in all possible forms, indicate the range assume $a = 1$ or -1 in both cases:

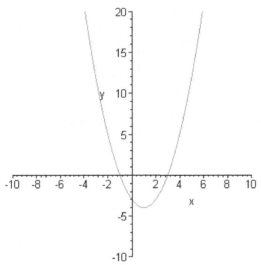 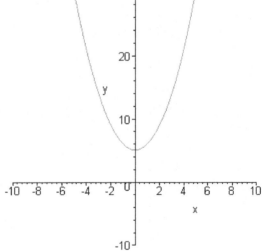

Range: $f(x) \in [-4, \infty)$ Range: $f(x) \in [5, \infty)$

Vertex form: $f(x) = (x-1)^2 - 4$ Vertex form: $f(x) = x^2 + 5$

Factorized form: $f(x) = (x-3)(x+1)$ Factorized form: $None$

Standard form: $f(x) = x^2 - 2x - 3$ Standard form: $f(x) = x^2 + 5$

19. Write the expression of the function in all possible forms, indicate the range assume $a = 1$ or -1 in both cases:

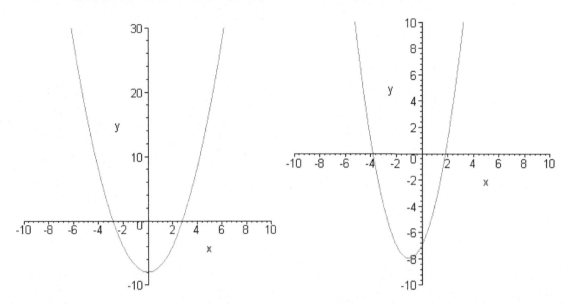

Range: $f(x) \in [-8, \infty)$

Range: $f(x) \in [-9, \infty]$

Vertex form: $f(x) = x^2 - 8$

Vertex form: $f(x) = (x+1)^2 - 9$

Factorized form: $f(x) = (x - \sqrt{8})(x + \sqrt{8})$

Factorized form: $f(x) = (x-2)(x+4)$

Standard form: $f(x) = x^2 - 8$

Standard form: $f(x) = x^2 + 2x - 8$

20. Write the expression of the function in all possible forms, indicate the range assume $a = 1$ or -1 in both cases:

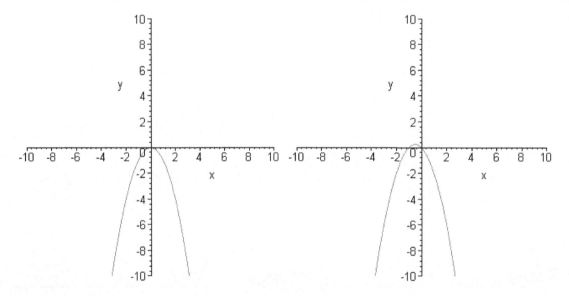

Range: $f(x) \in (-\infty, 0]$

Range: $f(x) \in (-\infty, \frac{1}{4}]$

Vertex form: $f(x) = -x^2$

Vertex form: $f(x) = -\left(x + \frac{1}{2}\right)^2 + \frac{1}{4}$

Factorized form: $f(x) = -x^2$

Factorized form: $f(x) = -x(x+1)$

Standard form: $f(x) = -x^2$

Standard form: $f(x) = -x^2 - x$

21. Write the expression of the function in all possible forms, indicate the range assume $a = 1$ or -1 in both cases:

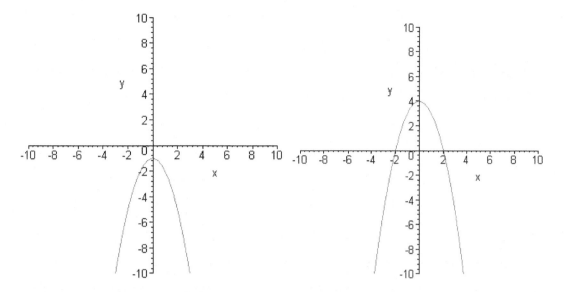

Range: $f(x) \in (-\infty, -1]$ Range: $f(x) \in (-\infty, 4]$

Vertex form: $f(x) = -x^2 - 1$ Vertex form: $f(x) = -x^2 + 4$

Factorized form: $None$ Factorized form: $f(x) = -(x-2)(x+2)$

Standard form: $f(x) = -x^2 - 1$ Standard form: $f(x) = -x^2 + 4$

22. Write the expression of the function in all possible forms, indicate the range assume $a = 1$ or -1 in both cases:

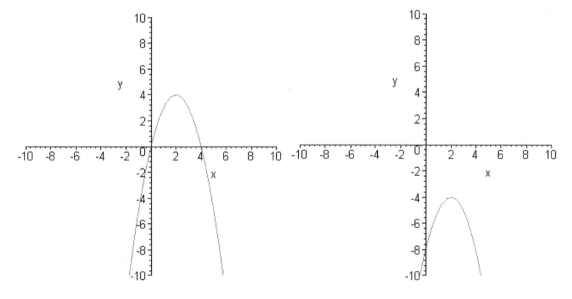

Range: $f(x) \in (-\infty, 4]$ Range: $f(x) \in (-\infty, -4]$

Vertex form: $f(x) = -(x-2)^2 + 4$ Vertex form: $f(x) = -(x-2)^2 - 4$

Factorized form: $f(x) = -x(x-4)$ Factorized form: $None$

Standard form: $f(x) = -x^2 + 4x$ Standard form: $f(x) = -x^2 + 4x - 8$

23. Write the expression of the function in all possible forms, indicate the range assume $a = 1$ or -1 in both cases:

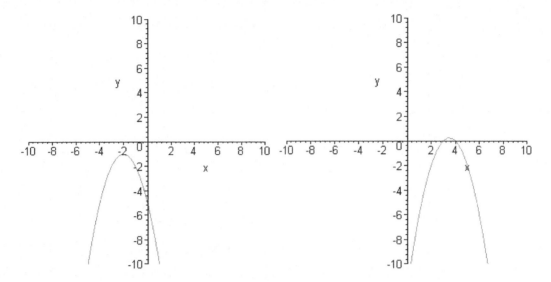

Range: ____$f(x) \in (-\infty, -1]$____ Range: ____$f(x) \in (-\infty, \frac{1}{4}]$____

Vertex form: ____$f(x) = -(x+2)^2 - 1$____ Vertex form: ____$f(x) = -\left(x - \frac{7}{2}\right)^2 + \frac{1}{4}$____

Factorized form: ____None____ Factorized form: ____$f(x) = -(x-3)(x-4)$____

Standard form: ____$f(x) = -x^2 - 4x - 5$____ Standard form: ____$f(x) = -x^2 - 7x - 12$____

24. Write the expression of the function in all possible forms, indicate the range assume $a = 1$ or -1 in both cases:

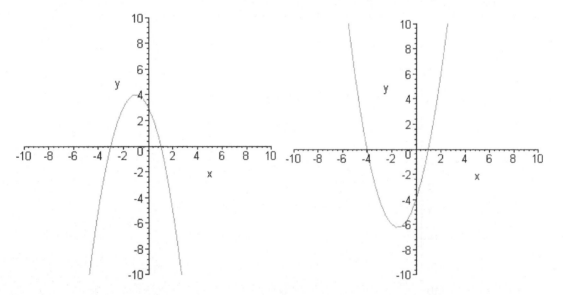

Range: ____$f(x) \in (-\infty, 4]$____ Range: ____$f(x) \in (-\frac{25}{4}, \infty]$____

Vertex form: ____$f(x) = -(x+1)^2 + 4$____ Vertex form: ____$f(x) = \left(x + \frac{3}{2}\right)^2 - \frac{25}{4}$____

Factorized form: ____$f(x) = -(x-1)(x+3)$____ Factorized form: ____$f(x) = (x-1)(x+4)$____

Standard form: ____$f(x) = -x^2 - 2x + 3$____ Standard form: ____$f(x) = x^2 + 3x - 4$____

25. Write the expression of the function in all possible forms, indicate the range assume $a = 1$ or -1 in both cases:

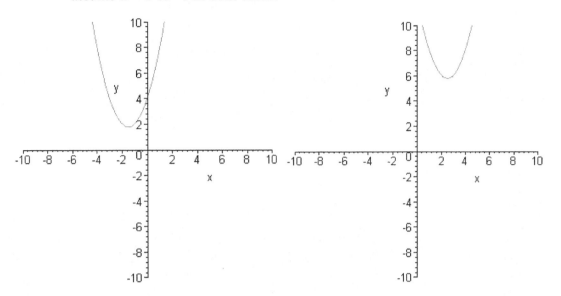

Range: _____ $f(x) \in [\frac{7}{4}, \infty)$ _____   Range: _____ $f(x) \in [\frac{23}{4}, \infty)$ _____

Vertex form: _____ $f(x) = \left(x + \frac{3}{2}\right)^2 + \frac{7}{4}$ _____   Vertex form: _____ $f(x) = \left(x + \frac{5}{2}\right)^2 + \frac{23}{4}$ _____

Factorized form: _____ None _____   Factorized form: _____ None _____

Standard form: _____ $f(x) = x^2 + 3x + 4$ _____   Standard form: _____ $f(x) = x^2 + 5x + 12$ _____

Analyze the following functions:

26. $f(x) = -3$

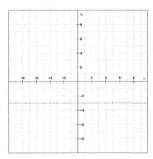

$Vertex\ \ Form : None(Linear)$

$Factorized\ \ Form : None(Linear)$

$Domain : x \in R \quad Range : f(x) \in \{-3\}$

$y\,int : (0, -3) \quad Vertex : None$

$x\,int : None$

$Increase : Never \quad Decrease : Never$

27. $f(x) = 5x$

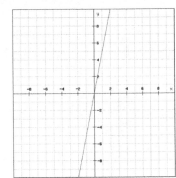

Vertex Form : *None*(*Linear*)

Factorized Form : *None*(*Linear*)

Domain : $x \in R$ *Range* : $f(x) \in R$

y int : $(0,0)$ *Vertex* : *None*

x int : $(0,0)$

Increase : $x \in R$ *Decrease* : *Never*

28. $f(x) = x^2 + 8x + 19$

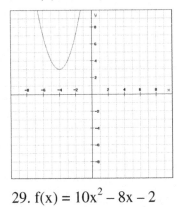

Vertex Form : $f(x) = (x+4)^2 + 3$

Factorized Form : *None*

Domain : $x \in R$ *Range* : $f(x) \in [3, \infty)$

y int : $(0,19)$ *Vertex* : $(-4,3)$

x int : *None*

Increase : $x \in (-4, \infty)$ *Decrease* : $x \in (-\infty, 4)$

29. $f(x) = 10x^2 - 8x - 2$

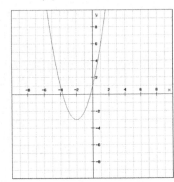

Vertex Form : $f(x) = 10\left(x - \dfrac{2}{5}\right)^2 - \dfrac{90}{25}$

Factorized Form : $f(x) = 10\left(x + \dfrac{1}{5}\right)(x-1)$

Domain : $x \in R$ *Range* : $f(x) \in [-\dfrac{90}{25}, \infty)$

y int : $(0,-2)$ *Vertex* : $(\dfrac{2}{5}, -\dfrac{90}{25})$

x int : $(-\dfrac{1}{5}, 0), (1,0)$

Increase : $x \in (\dfrac{2}{5}, \infty)$ *Decrease* : $x \in (-\infty, \dfrac{2}{5})$

30. $f(x) = x^2 + 4x + 1$

Vertex Form : $f(x) = (x+2)^2 - 3$

Factorized Form : $f(x) = \left(x - (\sqrt{3} - 2)\right)\left(x - (-\sqrt{3} - 2)\right)$

Domain : $x \in R$ *Range* : $f(x) \in [-3, \infty)$

y int : $(0,1)$ *Vertex* : $(-2,-3)$

x int : $(\sqrt{3} - 2, 0), (-\sqrt{3} - 2, 0)$

Increase : $x \in (-2, \infty)$ *Decrease* : $x \in (-\infty, -2)$

31. $f(x) = 4x^2 - 14x + 6$

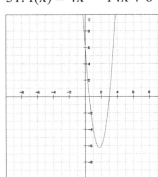

$Vertex\ Form: f(x) = 4\left(x - \dfrac{7}{4}\right)^2 - \dfrac{25}{4}$

$Factorized\ Form: f(x) = 2\left(x - \dfrac{1}{2}\right)(x - 3)$

$Domain: x \in R\quad Range: f(x) \in [-\dfrac{25}{4}, \infty)$

$y\,int: (0,6)\quad Vertex: (\dfrac{7}{4}, -\dfrac{25}{4})$

$x\,int: (\dfrac{1}{2}, 0), (3, 0)$

$Increase: x \in (\dfrac{7}{4}, \infty)\quad Decrease: x \in (-\infty, \dfrac{7}{4})$

32. $f(x) = 2x^2 - 3x - 5$

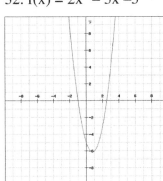

$Vertex\ Form: f(x) = 2\left(x - \dfrac{3}{4}\right)^2 - \dfrac{49}{8}$

$Factorized\ Form: f(x) = 2\left(x - \dfrac{5}{2}\right)(x + 1)$

$Domain: x \in R\quad Range: f(x) \in [-\dfrac{49}{8}, \infty)$

$y\,int: (0, -5)\quad Vertex: (\dfrac{3}{4}, -\dfrac{49}{8})$

$x\,int: (\dfrac{5}{2}, 0), (-1, 0)$

$Increase: x \in (\dfrac{3}{4}, \infty)\quad Decrease: x \in (-\infty, \dfrac{3}{4})$

33. $f(x) = x^2 + 3x - 10$

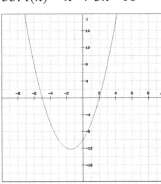

$Vertex\ Form: f(x) = \left(x + \dfrac{3}{2}\right)^2 - \dfrac{49}{4}$

$Factorized\ Form: f(x) = (x + 5)(x - 2)$

$Domain: x \in R\quad Range: f(x) \in [-\dfrac{49}{4}, \infty)$

$y\,int: (0, -10)\quad Vertex: (-\dfrac{3}{2}, -\dfrac{49}{4})$

$x\,int: (-5, 0), (2, 0)$

$Increase: x \in (-\dfrac{3}{2}, \infty)\quad Decrease: x \in (-\infty, -\dfrac{3}{2})$

34. $f(x) = x^2 + 7x - 1$

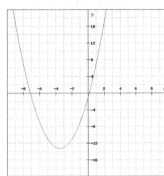

Vertex Form: $f(x) = \left(x + \dfrac{7}{2}\right)^2 - \dfrac{53}{4}$

Factorized Form: $f(x) = \left(x - \left(\sqrt{\dfrac{53}{5}} - \dfrac{7}{2}\right)\right)\left(x - \left(-\sqrt{\dfrac{53}{5}} - \dfrac{7}{2}\right)\right)$

Domain: $x \in R$ Range: $f(x) \in [-\dfrac{53}{4}, \infty)$

y int: $(0, -1)$ Vertex: $(-\dfrac{7}{2}, -\dfrac{53}{4})$

x int: $(\sqrt{\dfrac{53}{5}} - \dfrac{7}{2}, 0), (-\sqrt{\dfrac{53}{5}} - \dfrac{7}{2}, 0)$

Increase: $x \in (-\dfrac{7}{2}, \infty)$ Decrease: $x \in (-\infty, -\dfrac{7}{2})$

35. $f(x) = x^2 + 2x + 7$

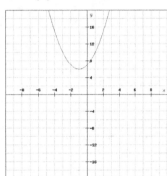

Vertex Form: $f(x) = (x + 1)^2 + 6$

Factorized Form: None

Domain: $x \in R$ Range: $f(x) \in [6, \infty)$

y int: $(0, 7)$ Vertex: $(-1, 6)$

x int: None

Increase: $x \in (-1, \infty)$ Decrease: $x \in (-\infty, -1)$

36. $f(x) = x^2 + x - 1$

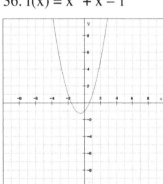

Vertex Form: $f(x) = \left(x + \dfrac{1}{2}\right)^2 - \dfrac{5}{4}$

Factorized Form: $f(x) = \left(x - \left(\sqrt{\dfrac{5}{4}} - \dfrac{1}{2}\right)\right)\left(x - \left(-\sqrt{\dfrac{5}{4}} - \dfrac{1}{2}\right)\right)$

Domain: $x \in R$ Range: $f(x) \in [-\dfrac{5}{4}, \infty)$

y int: $(0, -1)$ Vertex: $(-\dfrac{1}{2}, -\dfrac{5}{4})$

x int: $(\sqrt{\dfrac{5}{4}} - \dfrac{1}{2}, 0), (-\sqrt{\dfrac{5}{4}} - \dfrac{1}{2}, 0)$

Increase: $x \in (-\dfrac{1}{2}, \infty)$ Decrease: $x \in (-\infty, -\dfrac{1}{2})$

37. $f(x) = x^2 + 2x + 1$

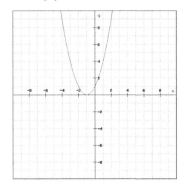

Vertex Form: $f(x) = (x+1)^2$

Factorized Form: $f(x) = (x+1)(x+1)$

Domain: $x \in R$ *Range*: $f(x) \in [0, \infty)$

y int: $(0,1)$ *Vertex*: $(-1,0)$

x int: $(-1,0)$

Increase: $x \in (-1, \infty)$ *Decrease*: $x \in (-\infty, -1)$

38. $f(x) = x^2 + 1$

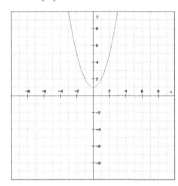

Vertex Form: $f(x) = x^2 + 1$

Factorized Form: *None*

Domain: $x \in R$ *Range*: $f(x) \in [1, \infty)$

y int: $(0,1)$ *Vertex*: $(0,1)$

x int: *None*

Increase: $x \in (0, \infty)$ *Decrease*: $x \in (-\infty, 0)$

39. $f(x) = x^2 - 1$

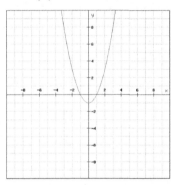

Vertex Form: $f(x) = x^2 - 1$

Factorized Form: $f(x) = (x+1)(x-1)$

Domain: $x \in R$ *Range*: $f(x) \in [-1, \infty)$

y int: $(0,-1)$ *Vertex*: $(0,-1)$

x int: $(-1,0),(1,0)$

Increase: $x \in (0, \infty)$ *Decrease*: $x \in (-\infty, 0)$

40. $f(x) = x^2 + 3x$

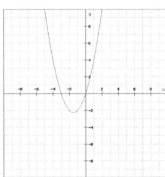

Vertex Form: $f(x) = \left(x+\dfrac{3}{2}\right)^2 - \dfrac{9}{4}$

Factorized Form: $f(x) = x(x+3)$

Domain: $x \in R$ *Range*: $f(x) \in [-\dfrac{9}{4}, \infty)$

y int: $(0,0)$ *Vertex*: $(-\dfrac{3}{2}, -\dfrac{9}{4})$

x int: $(-3,0),(0,0)$

Increase: $x \in (-\dfrac{3}{2}, \infty)$ *Decrease*: $x \in (-\infty, -\dfrac{3}{2})$

41. $f(x) = x^2 + 5x$

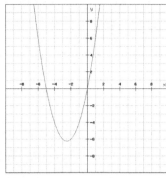

$Vertex\ Form: f(x) = \left(x + \dfrac{5}{2}\right)^2 - \dfrac{25}{4}$

$Factorized\ Form: f(x) = x(x+5)$

$Domain: x \in R \quad Range: f(x) \in [-\dfrac{25}{4}, \infty)$

$y\,int: (0,0) \quad Vertex: (-\dfrac{5}{2}, -\dfrac{25}{4})$

$x\,int: (-5,0), (0,0)$

$Increase: x \in (-\dfrac{5}{2}, \infty) \quad Decrease: x \in (-\infty, -\dfrac{5}{2})$

42. $f(x) = x^2 - 3x$

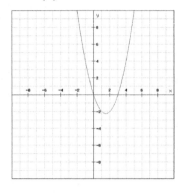

$Vertex\ Form: f(x) = \left(x - \dfrac{3}{2}\right)^2 - \dfrac{9}{4}$

$Factorized\ Form: f(x) = x(x-3)$

$Domain: x \in R \quad Range: f(x) \in [-\dfrac{9}{4}, \infty)$

$y\,int: (0,0) \quad Vertex: (\dfrac{3}{2}, -\dfrac{9}{4})$

$x\,int: (0,0), (3,0)$

$Increase: x \in (\dfrac{3}{2}, \infty) \quad Decrease: x \in (-\infty, \dfrac{3}{2})$

43. $f(x) = x^2 - 7x$

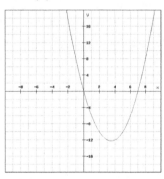

$Vertex\ Form: f(x) = \left(x - \dfrac{7}{2}\right)^2 - \dfrac{49}{4}$

$Factorized\ Form: f(x) = x(x-7)$

$Domain: x \in R \quad Range: f(x) \in [-\dfrac{49}{4}, \infty)$

$y\,int: (0,0) \quad Vertex: (\dfrac{7}{2}, -\dfrac{49}{4})$

$x\,int: (0,0), (7,0)$

$Increase: x \in (\dfrac{7}{2}, \infty) \quad Decrease: x \in (-\infty, \dfrac{7}{2})$

44. $f(x) = x^2 + 4x + 6$

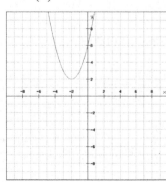

$Vertex\ Form: f(x) = \left(x+2\right)^2 + 2$

$Factorized\ Form: None$

$Domain: x \in R \quad Range: f(x) \in [2, \infty)$

$y\,int: (0,6) \quad Vertex: (-2,2)$

$x\,int: None$

$Increase: x \in (-2, \infty) \quad Decrease: x \in (-\infty, -2)$

45. $f(x) = -2x^2 - 16x - 29$

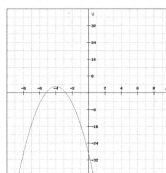

$Vertex \quad Form: f(x) = -2(x+4)^2 + 3$

$Factorized \quad Form: f(x) = -2\left(x - \left(\sqrt{\dfrac{3}{2}} - 2\right)\right)\left(x - \left(-\sqrt{\dfrac{3}{2}} - 2\right)\right)$

$Domain: x \in R \quad Range: f(x) \in (-\infty, 3]$

$y\,int: (0, -29) \quad Vertex: (-4, 3)$

$x\,int: (\sqrt{\dfrac{3}{2}} - 2, 0), (-\sqrt{\dfrac{3}{2}} - 2, 0)$

$Increase: x \in (-\infty, -4) \quad Decrease: x \in (-4, \infty)$

46. $f(x) = x^2 - 6x + 4$

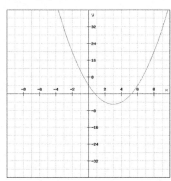

$Vertex \quad Form: f(x) = (x-3)^2 - 5$

$Factorized \quad Form: f(x) = \left(x - (\sqrt{5} + 3)\right)\left(x - (-\sqrt{5} + 3)\right)$

$Domain: x \in R \quad Range: f(x) \in [-5, \infty)$

$y\,int: (0, 4) \quad Vertex: (3, -5)$

$x\,int: (\sqrt{5} + 3, 0), (-\sqrt{5} + 3, 0)$

$Increase: x \in (3, \infty) \quad Decrease: x \in (-\infty, 3)$

47. $f(x) = x^2 - 7x + 2$

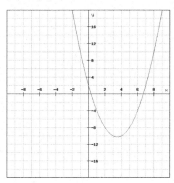

$Vertex \quad Form: f(x) = \left(x - \dfrac{7}{2}\right)^2 - \dfrac{41}{4}$

$Factorized \quad Form: f(x) = \left(x - \left(\sqrt{\dfrac{41}{4}} + \dfrac{7}{2}\right)\right)\left(x - \left(-\sqrt{\dfrac{41}{4}} + \dfrac{7}{2}\right)\right)$

$Domain: x \in R \quad Range: f(x) \in [-\dfrac{41}{4}, \infty)$

$y\,int: (0, 2) \quad Vertex: (\dfrac{7}{2}, -\dfrac{41}{4})$

$x\,int: (\sqrt{\dfrac{41}{4}} + \dfrac{7}{2}, 0), (-\sqrt{\dfrac{41}{4}} + \dfrac{7}{2}, 0)$

$Increase: x \in (\dfrac{7}{2}, \infty) \quad Decrease: x \in (-\infty, \dfrac{7}{2})$

48. $f(x) = x^2 + 3x + 10$

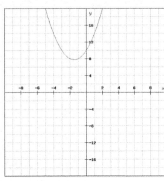

$Vertex\ \ Form: f(x) = \left(x + \dfrac{3}{2}\right)^2 + \dfrac{49}{4}$

$Factorized\ \ Form: None$

$Domain: x \in R\ \ Range: f(x) \in [\dfrac{49}{4}, \infty)$

$y\,int: (0,10)\ \ Vertex: (-\dfrac{3}{2}, \dfrac{49}{4})$

$x\,int: None$

$Increase: x \in (-\dfrac{3}{2}, \infty)\ \ Decrease: x \in (-\infty, -\dfrac{3}{2})$

49. $f(x) = x^2 + 5$

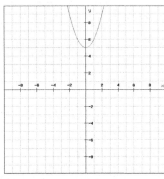

$Vertex\ \ Form: f(x) = x^2 + 5$

$Factorized\ \ Form: None$

$Domain: x \in R\ \ Range: f(x) \in [5, \infty)$

$y\,int: (0,5)\ \ Vertex: (0,5)$

$x\,int: None$

$Increase: x \in (0, \infty)\ \ Decrease: x \in (-\infty, 0)$

50. $f(x) = x^2 - 3$

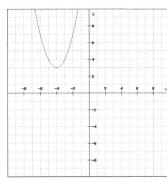

$Vertex\ \ Form: f(x) = x^2 - 3$

$Factorized\ \ Form: f(x) = (x + \sqrt{3})(x - \sqrt{3})$

$Domain: x \in R\ \ Range: f(x) \in [-3, \infty)$

$y\,int: (0,-3)\ \ Vertex: (0,-3)$

$x\,int: (-\sqrt{3}, 0), (\sqrt{3}, 0)$

$Increase: x \in (0, \infty)\ \ Decrease: x \in (-\infty, 0)$

51. $f(x) = x^2 - 7x$

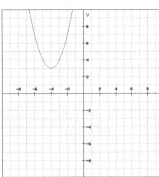

$Vertex\ \ Form: f(x) = \left(x - \dfrac{7}{2}\right)^2 - \dfrac{49}{4}$

$Factorized\ \ Form: f(x) = x(x - 7)$

$Domain: x \in R\ \ Range: f(x) \in [-\dfrac{49}{4}, \infty)$

$y\,int: (0,0)\ \ Vertex: (\dfrac{7}{2}, -\dfrac{49}{4})$

$x\,int: (0,0), (7,0)$

$Increase: x \in (\dfrac{7}{2}, \infty)\ \ Decrease: x \in (-\infty, \dfrac{7}{2})$

52. $f(x) = x^2 + 3x - 5$

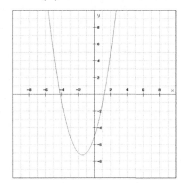

$Vertex\ \ Form: f(x) = \left(x + \dfrac{3}{2}\right)^2 - \dfrac{29}{4}$

$Factorized\ \ Form: f(x) = \left(x - \left(\sqrt{\dfrac{29}{4}} - \dfrac{3}{2}\right)\right)\left(x - \left(-\sqrt{\dfrac{29}{4}} - \dfrac{3}{2}\right)\right)$

$Domain: x \in R\ \ Range: f(x) \in [-\dfrac{29}{4}, \infty)$

$y\,int: (0, -5)\ \ Vertex: (-\dfrac{3}{2}, -\dfrac{29}{4})$

$x\,int: (\sqrt{\dfrac{29}{4}} - \dfrac{3}{2}, 0), (-\sqrt{\dfrac{29}{4}} - \dfrac{3}{2}, 0)$

$Increase: x \in (-\dfrac{3}{2}, \infty)\ \ Decrease: x \in (-\infty, -\dfrac{3}{2})$

53. $f(x) = 5x^2 - 3$

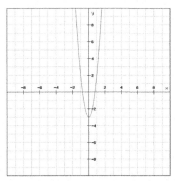

$Vertex\ \ Form: f(x) = 5x^2 - 3$

$Factorized\ \ Form: f(x) = 5\left(x - \sqrt{\dfrac{3}{5}}\right)\left(x + \sqrt{\dfrac{3}{5}}\right)$

$Domain: x \in R\ \ Range: f(x) \in [-3, \infty)$

$y\,int: (0, -3)\ \ Vertex: (0, -3)$

$x\,int: (-\sqrt{\dfrac{3}{5}}, 0), (\sqrt{\dfrac{3}{5}}, 0)$

$Increase: x \in (0, \infty)\ \ Decrease: x \in (-\infty, 0)$

54. $f(x) = 5x^2 - 10x$

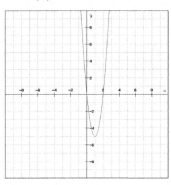

$Vertex\ \ Form: f(x) = 5(x-1)^2 - 5$

$Factorized\ \ Form: f(x) = 5x(x-2)$

$Domain: x \in R\ \ Range: f(x) \in [-5, \infty)$

$y\,int: (0, 0)\ \ Vertex: (1, -5)$

$x\,int: (0, 0), (2, 0)$

$Increase: x \in (1, \infty)\ \ Decrease: x \in (-\infty, 1)$

55. $f(x) = -5x^2$

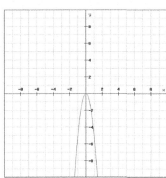

$Vertex\ \ Form: f(x) = -5x^2$

$Factorized\ \ Form: f(x) = -5x^2$

$Domain: x \in R\ \ Range: f(x) \in (-\infty, 0]$

$y\,int: (0, 0)\ \ Vertex: (0, 0)$

$x\,int: (0, 0)$

$Increase: x \in (-\infty, 0)\ \ Decrease: x \in (0, \infty)$

56. $f(x) = -x^2 + 6x - 8$

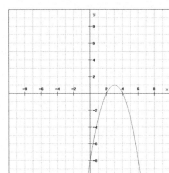

Vertex Form: $f(x) = -(x-3)^2 + 1$

Factorized Form: $f(x) = -(x-2)(x-4)$

Domain: $x \in R$ *Range*: $f(x) \in (-\infty, 1]$

$y$int: $(0, -8)$ *Vertex*: $(3, -1)$

$x$int: $(2, 0), (4, 0)$

Increase: $x \in (-\infty, 3)$ *Decrease*: $x \in (3, \infty)$

57. $f(x) = -x^2 - 6x + 2$

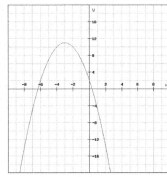

Vertex Form: $f(x) = -(x+3)^2 + 11$

Factorized Form: $f(x) = -\left(x - \left(\sqrt{11} - 3\right)\right)\left(x - \left(-\sqrt{11} - 3\right)\right)$

Domain: $x \in R$ *Range*: $f(x) \in (-\infty, 11]$

$y$int: $(0, 2)$ *Vertex*: $(-3, 11)$

$x$int: $(\sqrt{11} - 3, 0), (-\sqrt{11} - 3, 0)$

Increase: $x \in (-\infty, -3)$ *Decrease*: $x \in (-3, \infty)$

58. $f(x) = -x^2 + x - 5$

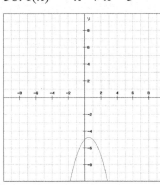

Vertex Form: $f(x) = -\left(x - \dfrac{1}{2}\right)^2 - \dfrac{19}{4}$

Factorized Form: *None*

Domain: $x \in R$ *Range*: $f(x) \in (-\infty, -\dfrac{19}{4}]$

$y$int: $(0, -5)$ *Vertex*: $(\dfrac{1}{2}, -\dfrac{19}{4})$

$x$int: *None*

Increase: $x \in (-\infty, \dfrac{1}{2})$ *Decrease*: $x \in (\dfrac{1}{2}, \infty)$

59. $f(x) = -x^2 - 4x - 4$

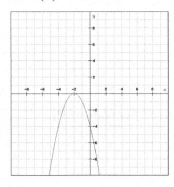

Vertex Form: $f(x) = -(x+2)^2$

Factorized Form: $f(x) = -(x+2)(x+2)$

Domain: $x \in R$ *Range*: $f(x) \in (-\infty, 0]$

$y$int: $(0, -4)$ *Vertex*: $(-2, 0)$

$x$int: $(-2, 0)$

Increase: $x \in (-\infty, -2)$ *Decrease*: $x \in (-2, \infty)$

60. $f(x) = -x^2 + 3$

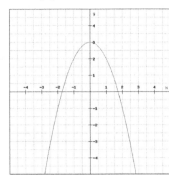

$Vertex\ \ Form: f(x) = -x^2 + 3$

$Factorized\ \ Form: f(x) = -(x + \sqrt{3})(x - \sqrt{3})$

$Domain: x \in R\ \ Range: f(x) \in (-\infty, 3]$

$y\,int: (0,3)\ \ Vertex: (0,3)$

$x\,int: (\sqrt{3}, 0), (-\sqrt{3}, 0)$

$Increase: x \in (-\infty, 0)\ \ Decrease: x \in (0, \infty)$

61. $f(x) = 3x^2$

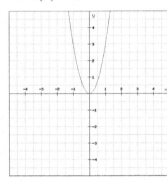

$Vertex\ \ Form: f(x) = 3x^2$

$Factorized\ \ Form: f(x) = 3x^2$

$Domain: x \in R\ \ Range: f(x) \in [0, \infty)$

$y\,int: (0,0)\ \ Vertex: (0,0)$

$x\,int: (0,0)$

$Increase: x \in (0, \infty)\ \ Decrease: x \in (-\infty, 0)$

62. $f(x) = 2((x + 3)x + 4) = 2x^2 + 6x + 8 = 2(x^2 + 3x + 4)$

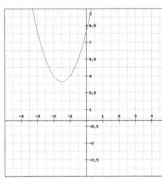

$Vertex\ \ Form: f(x) = 2\left(x + \dfrac{3}{2}\right)^2 + \dfrac{7}{2}$

$Factorized\ \ Form: None$

$Domain: x \in R\ \ Range: f(x) \in [\dfrac{7}{2}, \infty)$

$y\,int: (0,8)\ \ Vertex: (-\dfrac{3}{2}, \dfrac{7}{2})$

$x\,int: None$

$Increase: x \in (-\dfrac{3}{2}, \infty)\ \ Decrease: x \in (-\infty, -\dfrac{3}{2})$

63. $f(x) = \dfrac{2x - 4x^2}{2} = -2x^2 + x$

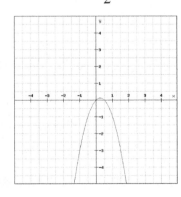

$Vertex\ \ Form: f(x) = -2\left(x - \dfrac{1}{4}\right)^2 + \dfrac{1}{8}$

$Factorized\ \ Form: f(x) = -x(2x - 1)$

$Domain: x \in R\ \ Range: f(x) \in (-\infty, \dfrac{1}{8}]$

$y\,int: (0,0)\ \ Vertex: (\dfrac{1}{4}, \dfrac{1}{8})$

$x\,int: (0,0), (\dfrac{1}{2}, 0)$

$Increase: x \in (-\infty, \dfrac{1}{4})\ \ Decrease: x \in (\dfrac{1}{4}, \infty)$

64. $f(x) = \dfrac{4x^2 + 8x}{4} - 2 = x^2 + 2x - 2$

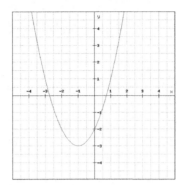

$Vertex\ Form: f(x) = (x+1)^2 - 3$

$Factorized\ Form: f(x) = (x-(\sqrt{3}-1))(x-(-\sqrt{3}-1))$

$Domain: x \in R\quad Range: f(x) \in [-3, \infty)$

$y\,int: (0, -2)\quad Vertex: (-1, 3)$

$x\,int: (\sqrt{3}-1, 0), (-\sqrt{3}-1, 0)$

$Increase: x \in (-1, \infty)\quad Decrease: x \in (-\infty, -1)$

65. $f(x) = \dfrac{(x-3)(x+4)}{2} - 1 = \dfrac{1}{2}x^2 + \dfrac{1}{2}x - 7$

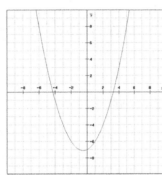

$Vertex\ Form: f(x) = \dfrac{1}{2}\left(x + \dfrac{1}{2}\right)^2 - \dfrac{57}{8}$

$Factorized\ Form: f(x) = \dfrac{1}{2}\left(x - \left(-\dfrac{1}{2} + \dfrac{\sqrt{57}}{2}\right)\right)\left(x - \left(-\dfrac{1}{2} - \dfrac{\sqrt{57}}{2}\right)\right)$

$Domain: x \in R\quad Range: f(x) \in [-1, \infty)$

$y\,int: (0, -7)\quad Vertex: (-\dfrac{1}{2}, -\dfrac{57}{8})$

$x\,int: (-\dfrac{1}{2} + \dfrac{\sqrt{57}}{2}, 0), (-\dfrac{1}{2} - \dfrac{\sqrt{57}}{2}, 0)$

$Increase: x \in (-\dfrac{1}{2}, \infty)\quad Decrease: x \in (-\infty, -\dfrac{1}{2})$

66. Vertex of $y = 7(x+3)^2 + 4$? (–3, 4), its axes of symmetry: x = –3

67. Vertex of $y = -2(x-4)^2 + 2$? (4, 2), its axes of symmetry: x = 4

68. The graph of the relation $x = -5(y+2)^2 + 6$ opens to the left.

69. b = 16, x = 4

70. When a quadratic function can be written as a perfect square on the graph it means that its vertex is on the x axis and it has a single x intercept.

71. The zeros: x = 0, x = 2, axis of symmetry x = 1

72. The roots: $x = -\dfrac{6}{5}, x = 12,$ axis of symmetry: $x = \dfrac{27}{5}$

73. The quadratic equation is used to find the zeros (x intercepts) of the quadratic function. in case this equation has no solutions it means the quadratic function is completely above or below the x axis and the value of $b^2 - 4ac$ is negative. In case $b^2 - 4ac$ is positive the quadratic function will have 2 zeros (2 x intercepts) and lastly if $b^2 - 4ac$ is zero the quadratic function will have 1 zero.

If $b^2 - 4ac > 0$ there are 2 zeros (2 x intercepts) Example: $f(x) = x^2 - 10x + 2$

If $b^2 - 4ac = 0$ there are 1 zero (1 x intercept) Example: $f(x) = x^2 - 6x + 9$

If $b^2 - 4ac < 0$ there are <u>no zeros (no x intercepts)</u> Example: $f(x) = x^2 + 4x + 1$

74. What values of b make the relation $y = 6x^2 + bx + 5$ have no zeros?

   $Discri\min ant = b^2 - 120 < 0; b \in (-\sqrt{120}, \sqrt{120})$

75. Under what conditions will the parabola with equation $y = a(x - h)^2 + k$ have

   two x–intercepts? <u>$k < 0$</u>

76. $y = -1.7(x + 13.2)^2 - 3.1$ <u>Opens down, vertex below x axes so no zeros</u>

77. A parabola has its vertex in the third quadrant and opens down. A possible

   value for $b^2 - 4ac$ can be -4

78. The equation, $f(x) = -2(x + 2)^2 + 3$
   _____

79. The equation $f(x) = \frac{1}{2}(x + 2)^2 - 3$
   _____

80. Give   the relation $y = -4(x - 2)^2 + 7$, state its axis of symmetry: <u>x = 2</u>

81. The vertex of the relation $y = -(x - 3)(x + 1)$.

   <u>Maximum: (1, 4), axis of symmetry x = 1</u>

82.   T   he parabola $y = 4(x - 2)^2 - 7$ is the image parabola.

83. The discriminant is: <u>$\Delta = b^2 - 4ac$</u> .

84. If <u>$\Delta > 0$</u> , then, <u>the quadratic equation has 2 solutions</u>

85. If <u>$\Delta = 0$</u> , then, <u>the quadratic equation has 1 solution</u>

86. If <u>$\Delta < 0$</u>   , then, <u>the quadratic equation has 0 solutions</u>

87. Write down 2 quadratic equations with 0 solutions:

   <u>$x^2 + 1 = 0$ $x^2 + 3x + 10 = 0$</u>

88. Write down 2 quadratic equations with 1 solution:

   <u>$x^2 + 2x + 1 = 0$ $x^2 - 4x + 4 = 0$</u>

89. Write down 2 quadratic equations with 2 solutions:

   <u>$x^2 - 1 = 0$ $x^2 - x - 6 = 0$</u>

Use the discriminant to determine the <u>number of solutions</u> to the following equations

90. $x^2 - 4x + 1 = 3$

   $\Delta = 16 - 16 = 0$

   <u>1 solution</u>

91. $2x^2 - 4x + 1 = -3$

   $\Delta = 16 - 32 < 0$

   <u>0 solutions</u>

92. $3x^2 - 4x + 1 = -1$

$\Delta = 16 - 24 < 0$

0 *solutions*

_____

93. $x^2 + 6x + 11 = 2$

$\Delta = 36 - 36 = 0$

1 *solution*

_____

94. $-2x^2 + 6x + 2 = -10$

$\Delta = 36 + positive > 0$

2 *solutions*

_____

95. $-3x^2 - 3x - 5 = 3$

$\Delta = 9 - 96 < 0$

0 *solutions*

_____

96. $3x^2 - 3x - 3 = -3$

$\Delta = 9 > 0$

2 *solutions*

_____

97. $x^2 - 3x - 4 = -1$

$\Delta = 9 + positive > 0$

2 *solutions*

_____

98. $x^2 - 7x - 5 = 3$

$\Delta = 49 + positive > 0$

2 *solutions*

_____

99. $2x^2 + 4x + 2 = 0$

$\Delta = 16 - 16 = 0$

1 *solution*

_____

100. $x^2 - 2x + 4 = 5$

$\Delta = 4 - 4 = 0$

1 *solution*

_____

101. $-3x^2 + 3x - 1 = 3$

$\Delta = 9 - 48 < 0$

0 *solutions*

_____

102. $-2x^2 + 7x - 3 = 2$

$\Delta = 49 - 40 > 0$

2 *solutions*

_____

103. $-x^2 + 12x + 4 = -1$

$\Delta = 144 + positive > 0$

2 *solutions*

_____

104. $x^2 + x - 2 = -1$

$\Delta = 1 + 4 > 0$

2 *solutions*

_____

105. $-8x^2 + 3x + 2 = -1$

$\Delta = 9 + positive > 0$

2 *solutions*

_____

154

106. Given the equation $x^2 + 3bx + 4 = 0$. Determine the number of solutions as a function of b.

$$\Delta = 9b^2 - 16; 9b^2 - 16 = 0; b = \pm\frac{4}{3}$$

$$if \quad b \in (-\infty, -\frac{4}{3}) \cup (\frac{4}{3}, \infty) \quad 2 \ solutions$$

$$f \quad b = \pm\frac{4}{3} \quad 1 \ solution$$

$$f \quad b \in (-\frac{4}{3}, \frac{4}{3}) \quad 0 \ solutions$$

107. Given the equation $ax^2 + ax + a = 0$. Determine the number of solutions as a function of a.

$$\Delta = a^2 - 4a^2 = -3a^2 < 0$$
$$\forall a \in \mathfrak{R}, 0 \ solutions$$

108. Given the equation $2x^2 + bx + 3 = 0$. Find the value of b for which the following equation has 1 solution. Find that solution.

$$\Delta = b^2 - 24 = 0; b = \pm\sqrt{24}$$

$$2x^2 + \sqrt{24}x + 3 = 0$$

$$x = \frac{-\sqrt{24} \pm \sqrt{24-24}}{4} = \frac{-\sqrt{24}}{4}$$

109. Given the equation $ax^2 + bx + 1 = 0$. Find the value of b, in terms of a, for which the following equation has 1 solution. Find that solution.

$$\Delta = b^2 - 4a = 0; b = \pm 2\sqrt{a}$$

$$ax^2 + 2\sqrt{a}x + 1 = 0$$

$$x = \frac{-2\sqrt{a} \pm \sqrt{4a-4a}}{2a} = \frac{-\sqrt{a}}{a} = \frac{-1}{\sqrt{a}}$$

QUADRATIC INEQUALITIES

1. $x^2 > 0$ $x \in \mathfrak{R}, x \neq 0$

2. $x^2 \geq 0$ $x \in \mathfrak{R}$

3. $x^2 < 0$ No Solution

4. $x^2 \leq 0$ $x = 0$

5. $x^2 - 1 > 0$
    $x \in (-\infty, -1) \cup (1, \infty)$

6. $x^2 - 1 \geq 0$
    $x \in (-\infty, -1] \cup [1, \infty)$

7. $x^2 - 1 < 0$ $x \in (-1, 1)$

8. $x^2 - 1 \leq 0$ $x \in [-1, 1]$

9. $x^2 + 2 > 0$ $x \in \mathfrak{R}$

10. $x^2 + 2 \geq 0$ $x \in \mathfrak{R}$

11. $x^2 + 2x + 1 \leq 0$ $x = -1$

12. $x^2 + 2 \leq 0$ No Solution

13. $6x^2 - 3x > 0$

    $x \in (-\infty, 0) \cup (\frac{1}{2}, \infty)$

14. $x^2 + 4x \geq 0$

    $x \in (-\infty, -4) \cup (0, \infty)$

15. $x^2 - 5x < 0$ $x \in (0, 5)$

16. $2x^2 + 6x \leq 0$ $x \in [-3, 0]$

17. $x^2 - 4x + 4 > 0$ $x \in \mathfrak{R}, x \neq 2$

18. $-x^2 + x + 2 > 0$ $x \in (-1, 2)$

19. $-x^2 - 6x - 9 < 0$ $x \in \mathfrak{R}, x \neq -3$

20. $-3x^2 + 7 \leq 0$

$$x \in (-\infty, -\sqrt{\frac{7}{3}}] \cup [\sqrt{\frac{7}{3}}, \infty)$$

21. $x^2 - 8x + 12 > 0$

$$x \in (-\infty, 2) \cup (6, \infty)$$

22. $-x^2 + 3x + 3 \leq 0$

$$x \in [\frac{3 - \sqrt{21}}{2}, \frac{3 + \sqrt{21}}{2}]$$

23. $-x^2 - 9x > 0$

$$x \in (-\infty, -9) \cup (0, \infty)$$

24. $-2x^2 - 3x + 10 > 0$

$$x \in [\frac{-3 - \sqrt{89}}{4}, \frac{-3 + \sqrt{89}}{4}]$$

25. $x^2 + 1 > 0$ $x \in \mathfrak{R}$

26. $-x^2 + 1 < 0$

$$x \in (-\infty, -1) \cup (1, \infty)$$

27. $-x^2 - 1 > 0$ No solution

28. $-x^2 + 1 \leq 0$

$$x \in (-\infty, -1] \cup [1, \infty)$$

29. $-x^2 + 3 \geq 0$ $x \in [-\sqrt{3}, \sqrt{3}]$

30. $-x^2 + 3 \leq 0$

$$x \in (-\infty, -\sqrt{3}] \cup [\sqrt{3}, \infty)$$

31. $x^2 - 3x > 0$

$$x \in (-\infty, 0) \cup (3, \infty)$$

32. $x^2 - 3x < 0$ $x \in (0, 3)$

33. $2x^2 + 4 > 0$ $x \in \mathfrak{R}$

34. $2x^2 + 4 < 0$ No Solution

35. $-x^2 - 3x + 2 >$

$$0 \; x \in (\frac{-3 - \sqrt{17}}{2}, \frac{-3 + \sqrt{17}}{2})$$

36. $x^2 - 3x + 2 < 0$ $x \in (1, 2)$

37. $x^2 + 2x - 3 > 0$

$$x \in (-\infty, -3) \cup (1, \infty)$$

38. $-x^2 + 2x - 3 < 0$

$$x \in (-\infty, \frac{-3 - \sqrt{17}}{2}) \cup (\frac{-3 + \sqrt{17}}{2}, \infty)$$

39. $-2x^2 + 8x - 10 > 0$ No
solution

40. $-2x^2 + 8x - 10 < 0$ $x \in \mathfrak{R}$

Applications

1. The height of a ball kicked upwards is given by $h(t) = 40t - 16t^2$ meters, $t \in [0, 2.5]$ where t is measured in seconds.

    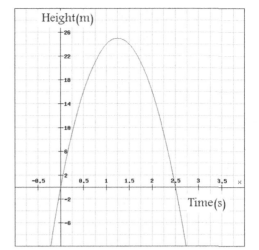

    a. The corresponding function, label the axes.

    b. Calculate h(1) and give a practical interpretation to your answer.

        h(1) = 24m, the height of the ball after 1 second.

    c. Calculate the zeros of h(t) and explain the meaning in the context of the problem.

        t = 0s, t = 2.5s, the instants in which the height of the ball is kicked. Right in the beginning and after it fell back.

    d. Solve the equation h(t) = 10 and explain the meaning of the solutions in the context of the problem.

        $h(t) = 40t - 16t^2 = 10$; $t \approx 0.28s$, $t \approx 2.22s$ the instants in which the height of the ball is 10m once on the way up and once on the way down.

        The maximum height of the ball and the instant in which it reaches it.

        The vertex of the parabola is (1.25, 25) so the maximum height is 25m

2. The width of a rectangle is three times is length, its area is 243 m². Find its perimeter. $x \cdot 3x = 243; x = 9; Perimeter = 18 + 6 = 24m$

3. Find 2 consecutive even numbers that when their sum is squared 100 is obtained. $(2x + 2)^2 = 100; x = 4$ The numbers are 4 and 6

157

4. The efficiency of an engine as a function of the concentration of a certain chemical component is given by $f(x) = -0.5x^2 + x$, $0 \le x \le 2$.

    a. Sketch the function in its domain.

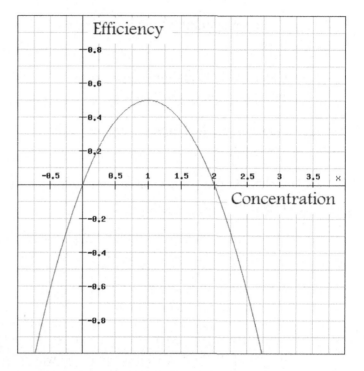

    b. Find the concentration of the chemical for which the efficiency is maximized. What is the efficiency in this case?

       The vertex of the parabola is (1, 0.5) so the concentration required is 1 and the efficiency is 0.5

5. A hundred meters of fencing is available to enclose a rectangular field along side of a River, What dimensions will produce the maximum area that can be enclosed?

$A(x) = x(100 - 2x)$

Parabola whose maximum is

(25, 1250) so the dimensions are:

25m width and 50m length

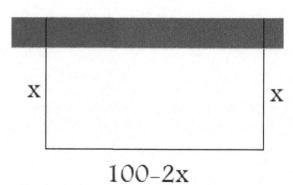

$100-2x$

CHAPTER 4 – TRIGONOMETRIC FUNCTIONS

4.1. – DEGREES AND RADIANS

. If we go back to the definition of an angle in a circle it is the following:

$$X = \frac{\text{Length of Arc}}{\text{Radius}}$$, In case that S is the entire circle we obtain:

$$X = \frac{S}{R} = \frac{Length - of - circumfernece}{Radius - of - circumfernece} = 6.2831... = 2\pi$$

So what we see is that the angle of the entire circle is approximately 6.28 or exactly 2π.

That means: $2\pi_{rad} = 360°$; $1° = \frac{2\pi}{360} rad \approx 0.017_{rad}$; $1_{rad} = \left(\frac{360}{2\pi}\right)^0 \approx 57.3°$

Exercises:

1. Complete the table:

Degrees	360°	-180°	90°	45°	22.5°
Radians	2π	$-\pi$	$\dfrac{\pi}{2}$	$\dfrac{\pi}{4}$	$\dfrac{\pi}{8}$

2. Complete the table:

Degrees	0°	30°	60°	-120°	150°
Radians	0	$\dfrac{\pi}{6}$	$\dfrac{\pi}{3}$	$-\dfrac{2\pi}{3}$	$\dfrac{5\pi}{6}$

3. Complete the table:

Degrees	315°	-225°	135°	330°	420°
Radians	$\dfrac{7\pi}{4}$	$-\dfrac{5\pi}{4}$	$\dfrac{3\pi}{4}$	$\dfrac{11\pi}{6}$	$\dfrac{7\pi}{3}$

4. Complete the table:

Degrees	54°	18°	-36°	15°	75°
Radians	$\dfrac{3\pi}{10}$	$\dfrac{\pi}{10}$	$-\dfrac{\pi}{5}$	$\dfrac{\pi}{12}$	$\dfrac{5\pi}{12}$

5. Complete the table:

Degrees	54°	-18°	36°	15°	75°
Radians	$\dfrac{3\pi}{10}$	$-\dfrac{\pi}{10}$	$\dfrac{\pi}{5}$	$\dfrac{\pi}{12}$	$\dfrac{5\pi}{12}$

6. Complete the table:

Degrees	5°	1°	-10°	660°	540°
Radians	$\dfrac{\pi}{36}$	$\dfrac{\pi}{180}$	$-\dfrac{\pi}{18}$	$\dfrac{11\pi}{3}$	3π

7. Complete the table:

Degrees	180°	18°	-300°	$\dfrac{2160°}{7}$	792°
Radians	π	$\dfrac{\pi}{10}$	$-\dfrac{5\pi}{3}$	$\dfrac{12\pi}{7}$	$\dfrac{22\pi}{5}$

8. Complete the table:

Degrees	$\dfrac{180}{\pi}$	$2.4\cdot\dfrac{180}{\pi}$	$3.5\cdot\dfrac{180}{\pi}$	$-\dfrac{360}{\pi}$	$-3.1\cdot\dfrac{180}{\pi}$
Radians	1	2.4	3.5	-2	-3.1

9. Given the following circles, find θ or L in each one of the cases (in degrees and radians):

$\theta = \dfrac{6}{2} = 3 Rad = \left(\dfrac{540}{\pi}\right)^{\circ}$

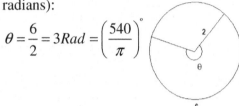

$\theta = \dfrac{2}{3} Rad = \left(\dfrac{120}{\pi}\right)^{\circ}$

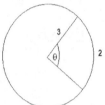

L = 3

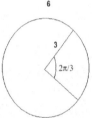

$L = \dfrac{7\pi}{18}\cdot 3 = \dfrac{7\pi}{6}$

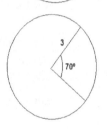

10. The length of the perimeter of a circle with radius r is $2\pi r$. The length of the arc that corresponds an angle x° is $\dfrac{x°}{360}2\pi r$. In case the angle x is measured in radians it would be $\dfrac{x}{2\pi}2\pi r = xr$

11. The area of a circle with radius r is πr^2 The area of the sector that corresponds an angle x° is $\dfrac{x°}{360}\pi r^2$ In case the angle x is measured in radians it would be $\dfrac{x}{2\pi}\pi r^2 = \dfrac{x}{2}r^2$

12. Given the circle with r = 2cm :
   a. Show the arc corresponding an angle of 45°.
   b. Calculate its length. $L = \dfrac{\pi}{4}2 = \dfrac{\pi}{2}cm$

   c. Shade the corresponding sector area.
   d. Calculate it. $A = \dfrac{\pi}{8}2^2 = \dfrac{\pi}{4}cm^2$

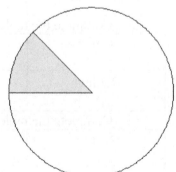

13. Given the circle with r = 3.2m:
    a. Show Shade the arc corresponding an angle of 20°.
    b. Calculate its length.

    $$L = \frac{\pi}{9} \cdot 3.2 = \frac{3.2\pi}{9} cm$$

    c. Shade the corresponding sector area.
    d. Calculate it.

    $$A = \frac{\pi}{18}(3.2)^2 \approx 1.79 cm^2$$

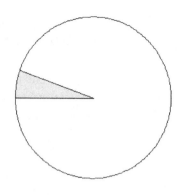

14. Given the circle with r = 3.2m:

    a. Show Shade the arc corresponding an angle of $\frac{\pi}{10} rad$.

    b. Calculate its length.

    $$L = \frac{\pi}{10} \cdot 3.2 = 0.32\pi cm$$

    c. Shade the corresponding sector area.
    d. Calculate it.

    $$A = \frac{\pi}{20}(3.2)^2 \approx 1.61 cm^2$$

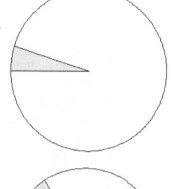

15. Given the circle with r = 3.2m:
    a. Show Shade the arc corresponding an angle of 1 radian.
    b. Calculate its length.
        $$L = 1 \cdot 3.2 = 3.2 cm$$
    c. Shade the corresponding sector area.
    d. Calculate it.

    $$A = \frac{1}{2}(3.2)^2 \approx 5.12 cm^2$$

16. Given the following concentric circles with radii 3 cm and 5 cm correspondingly. Calculate the shaded area.
    $$A = \pi 5^2 - \pi 3^2 = 16\pi cm^2$$

17. Given the following concentric circles with radii 10m and 14m correspondingly. Calculate the shaded area.

    $$A = \frac{40}{360}\left(\pi(14)^2 - \pi(10)^2\right) = \frac{32\pi}{3} cm^2$$

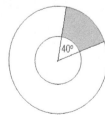

161

4.2. – TRIGONOMETRIC FUNCTIONS

Definition: The trigonometric functions are defined using the so called "unit circle" which is simply a circle with radius 1.
In consequence:

$$\left(Sin(x)\right)^2 + \left(Cos(x)\right)^2 = 1$$ This is called the Pythagorean identity

Use your calculator to find:

$$\left(Sin(10^\circ)\right)^2 + \left(Cos(10^\circ)\right)^2 = 1$$

$$\left(Sin(1_{rad})\right)^2 + \left(Cos(1_{rad})\right)^2 = 1$$

Definition of Sin(x):
As can be deduced from the unit circle in the <u>first</u> and <u>second</u> quadrants the Sin(x) function is <u>positive</u>, while in the <u>third</u> and <u>forth</u> quadrants it is <u>negative</u>.

Definition of Cos(x):
As can be deduced from the unit circle in the <u>first</u> and <u>forth</u> quadrants the Cos(x) function is <u>positive</u>, while in the <u>second</u> and <u>third</u> quadrants it is <u>negative</u>

Exercises:
In each one of the cases sketch the unit circle and the corresponding angle and then find the corresponding value:

1. $Sin(0^\circ) = 0$
2. $Cos(0_{rad}) = 1$
3. $Sin(0_{rad}) = 0$
4. $Cos(0^\circ) = 1$
5. $Sin(90^\circ) = 1$
6. $Cos(\pi_{rad}) = -1$
7. $Sin(3\pi/4_{\;rad}) = \dfrac{1}{\sqrt{2}}$
8. $Cos(225^\circ) = -\dfrac{1}{\sqrt{2}}$
9. $Sin(225^\circ) = -\dfrac{1}{\sqrt{2}}$
10. $Cos(4\pi/3_{\;rad}) = -\dfrac{1}{2}$
11. $Sin(4\pi/3_{\;rad}) = -\dfrac{\sqrt{3}}{2}$
12. $Cos(210^\circ) = -\dfrac{\sqrt{3}}{2}$
13. $Sin(210^\circ) = -\dfrac{1}{2}$
14. $Sin(3\pi/4_{\;rad}) = \dfrac{1}{\sqrt{2}}$

15. $Cos(225^\circ) = -\dfrac{1}{\sqrt{2}}$
16. $Sin(-225^\circ) = \dfrac{1}{\sqrt{2}}$
17. $Cos(4\pi/3_{\;rad}) = -\dfrac{1}{2}$
18. $Sin(4\pi/3_{\;rad}) = -\dfrac{\sqrt{3}}{2}$
19. $Cos(210^\circ) = -\dfrac{\sqrt{3}}{2}$
20. $Sin(-210^\circ) = \dfrac{1}{2}$
21. $Sin(-\pi_{rad}) = 0$
22. $Cos(90^\circ) = 0$
23. $Sin(270^\circ) = -1$
24. $Cos(\pi/2_{rad}) = 0$
25. $Sin(3\pi/2_{rad}) = -1$
26. $Cos(270^\circ) = 0$
27. $Sin(360^\circ) = 0$
28. $Cos(-\pi/2_{rad}) = 0$
29. $Sin(2\pi_{rad}) = 0$
30. $Cos(180^\circ) = -1$

31. $\text{Sin}(180°) = 0$

32. $\text{Cos}(\pi/3_{rad}) = \dfrac{1}{2}$

33. $\text{Sin}(\pi/4_{rad}) = \dfrac{1}{\sqrt{2}}$

34. $\text{Cos}(-45°) = \dfrac{1}{\sqrt{2}}$

35. $\text{Sin}(3\pi/2_{rad}) = -1$

36. $\text{Cos}(-2\pi/3_{rad}) = -\dfrac{1}{2}$

37. $\text{Sin}(2\pi/3_{rad}) = \dfrac{\sqrt{3}}{2}$

38. $\text{Cos}(3\pi/4_{rad}) = -\dfrac{1}{\sqrt{2}}$

39. $\text{Cos}(300°) = \dfrac{1}{2}$

40. $\text{Sin}(300°) = -\dfrac{\sqrt{3}}{2}$

41. $\text{Cos}(2\pi_{rad}) = 1$

42. $\text{Sin}(2\pi_{rad}) = 0$

43. $\text{Sin}(330°) = -\dfrac{1}{2}$

44. $\text{Cos}(390°) = \dfrac{\sqrt{3}}{2}$

45. $\text{Cos}(135°) = -\dfrac{1}{\sqrt{2}}$

46. $\text{Sin}(135°) = \dfrac{1}{\sqrt{2}}$

47. $\text{Sin}(45°) = \dfrac{1}{\sqrt{2}}$

48. $\text{Cos}(-3\pi/2_{rad}) = 0$

49. $\text{Cos}(70°) \approx 0.342$

50. $\text{Cos}(130°) \approx -0.642$

51. $\text{Cos}(1°) \approx 0.999$

52. $\text{Cos}(3_{rad}) \approx -0.990$

53. $\text{Sin}(1_{rad}) \approx 0.841$

54. $\text{Cos}(\Pi/5_{rad}) \approx 0.809$

55. $\text{Sin}(2\Pi/7_{rad}) \approx 0.782$

An angle between 0° and 360° different than the first one.

56. $\text{Sin}(25°) = \text{Sin}(155°)$

57. $\text{Sin}(145°) = \text{Sin}(35°)$

58. $\text{Sin}(70°) = \text{Sin}(110°)$

59. $\text{Sin}(-20°) = \text{Sin}(200°)$

60. $\text{Sin}(-30°) = \text{Sin}(210°)$

61. $\text{Sin}(225°) = \text{Sin}(315°)$

62. $\text{Sin}(250°) = \text{Sin}(290°)$

63. $\text{Cos}(250°) = \text{Cos}(110°)$

64. $\text{Cos}(350°) = \text{Cos}(10°)$

65. $\text{Cos}(450°) = \text{Cos}(90°)$

66. $\text{Cos}(-250°) = \text{Cos}(250°)$

67. $\text{Cos}(-50°) = \text{Cos}(50°)$

68. $\text{Cos}(-73°) = \text{Cos}(73°)$

Definitions of Tan (x), Cot(x), Sec(x) Cosec(x)

$$Tan(x) = \left(\frac{Sin(x)}{Cos(x)}\right), Cos(x) \neq 0 \qquad Cot(x) = \left(\frac{Cos(x)}{Sin(x)}\right), Sin(x) \neq 0$$

$$Sec(x) = \left(\frac{1}{Cos(x)}\right), Cos(x) \neq 0 \qquad Csc(x) = \left(\frac{1}{Sin(x)}\right), Sin(x) \neq 0$$

In Consequence:

Tan(x) = tg(x) is positive in the 1st and 3rd quadrants and negative in the 2nd and 4th quadrants. Cotg(x) = Cot(x) =Cotan(x) is positive in the 1st and 3rd quadrants and negative in the 2nd and 4th quadrants.

163

69. The following trigonometric functions in terms of a and b:

a. $\text{Sin}(\theta) = b$ $\text{Cos}(\theta) = a$
b. $\text{Sin}(\theta + 360°) = b$
c. $\text{Sin}(\theta + 180°) = -b$
d. $\text{Sin}(180° - \theta) = b$
e. $\text{Cos}(180° - \theta) = -a$
f. $\text{Sin}(360° - \theta) = -b$
g. $\text{Cos}(360° - \theta) = a$
h. $\text{Sin}(90° - \theta) = a$
i. $\text{Cos}(90° - \theta) = b$

j. $\text{Tan}(\theta) = \dfrac{b}{a}$

k. $\text{Cotan}(\theta) = \dfrac{a}{b}$

l. $\text{Sec}(\theta) = \dfrac{1}{a}$

m. $\text{Csc}(\theta) = \dfrac{1}{b}$

n. $\text{Tan}(\theta + 180°) = \dfrac{b}{a}$

o. $\text{Tan}(\theta + 90°) = \dfrac{Sin(\theta + 90°)}{Cos(\theta + 90°)} = \dfrac{a}{-b}$

p. $\text{Cos}(270° - \theta) = -b$
q. $\text{Sin}(270° + \theta) = -a$

r. $\text{Sec}(\theta + 180°) = \dfrac{1}{\cos(\theta + 180)} = \dfrac{1}{-a}$

s. $\text{Csc}(270° + \theta) = \dfrac{1}{\sin(\theta + 270)} = \dfrac{1}{-a}$

t. $\text{Cot}(\theta) = \dfrac{a}{b}$

u. $\text{Cot}(\theta - 180°) = \dfrac{-a}{-b} = \dfrac{a}{b}$

v. $\text{Sec}(\theta + 720°) = \text{Sec}(\theta) = \dfrac{1}{\cos(\theta)} = \dfrac{1}{a}$

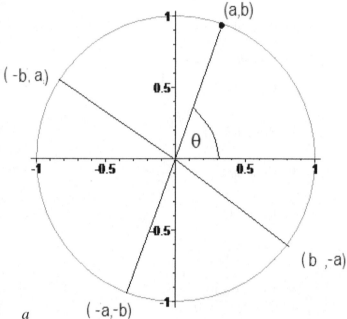

Complete the following table:

Angle in degrees	Angle in Radians	Sin(x)	Cos(x)	Tan(x)	Cot(x)	Sec(x)	Csc(x)
0	0	0	1	0	D.E.	1	D.E.
30°	$\dfrac{\pi}{6}$	$\dfrac{1}{2}$	$\dfrac{\sqrt{3}}{2}$	$\dfrac{1}{\sqrt{3}}$	$\sqrt{3}$	$\dfrac{2}{\sqrt{3}}$	2
45°	$\dfrac{\pi}{4}$	$\dfrac{1}{\sqrt{2}}$	$\dfrac{1}{\sqrt{2}}$	1	1	$\sqrt{2}$	$\sqrt{2}$
60°	$\dfrac{\pi}{3}$	$\dfrac{\sqrt{3}}{2}$	$\dfrac{1}{2}$	$\sqrt{3}$	$\dfrac{1}{\sqrt{3}}$	2	$\dfrac{2}{\sqrt{3}}$
90°	$\dfrac{\pi}{2}$	1	0	D.E.	0	D.E.	1
120°	$\dfrac{2\pi}{3}$	$\dfrac{\sqrt{3}}{2}$	$-\dfrac{1}{2}$	$-\sqrt{3}$	$-\dfrac{1}{\sqrt{3}}$	-2	$\dfrac{2}{\sqrt{3}}$
135°	$\dfrac{3\pi}{4}$	$\dfrac{1}{\sqrt{2}}$	$-\dfrac{1}{\sqrt{2}}$	-1	-1	$-\sqrt{2}$	$\sqrt{2}$
150°	$\dfrac{5\pi}{6}$	$\dfrac{1}{2}$	$-\dfrac{\sqrt{3}}{2}$	$-\dfrac{1}{\sqrt{3}}$	$-\sqrt{3}$	$-\dfrac{2}{\sqrt{3}}$	2
180°	π	0	-1	0	D.E.	-1	D.E.
210°	$\dfrac{7\pi}{6}$	$-\dfrac{1}{2}$	$-\dfrac{\sqrt{3}}{2}$	$\dfrac{1}{\sqrt{3}}$	$\sqrt{3}$	$-\dfrac{2}{\sqrt{3}}$	-2
225°	$\dfrac{5\pi}{4}$	$-\dfrac{1}{\sqrt{2}}$	$-\dfrac{1}{\sqrt{2}}$	1	1	$-\sqrt{2}$	$-\sqrt{2}$
240°	$\dfrac{4\pi}{3}$	$-\dfrac{\sqrt{3}}{2}$	$-\dfrac{1}{2}$	$\sqrt{3}$	$\dfrac{1}{\sqrt{3}}$	-2	$-\dfrac{2}{\sqrt{3}}$
270°	$\dfrac{3\pi}{2}$	-1	0	D.E.	0	D.E.	-1
300°	$\dfrac{5\pi}{3}$	$-\dfrac{\sqrt{3}}{2}$	$\dfrac{1}{2}$	$-\sqrt{3}$	$-\dfrac{1}{\sqrt{3}}$	2	$-\dfrac{2}{\sqrt{3}}$
315°	$\dfrac{7\pi}{4}$	$-\dfrac{1}{\sqrt{2}}$	$\dfrac{1}{\sqrt{2}}$	-1	-1	$\sqrt{2}$	$-\sqrt{2}$
330°	$\dfrac{11\pi}{6}$	$-\dfrac{1}{2}$	$\dfrac{\sqrt{3}}{2}$	$-\dfrac{1}{\sqrt{3}}$	$-\sqrt{3}$	$\dfrac{2}{\sqrt{3}}$	-2
360°	2π	0	1	0	D.E.	1	D.E.
390°	$\dfrac{13\pi}{6}$	$\dfrac{1}{2}$	$\dfrac{\sqrt{3}}{2}$	$\dfrac{1}{\sqrt{3}}$	$\sqrt{3}$	$\dfrac{2}{\sqrt{3}}$	2

Exercises:

1. Given that $\sin(x) = \dfrac{2}{7}$ and $0 < x < \dfrac{\pi}{2}$, find:

a. $\text{Cos}(x) = \dfrac{\sqrt{45}}{7}$

b. $\text{Tan}(x) = \dfrac{2}{\sqrt{45}}$

c. $\text{Cot}(x) = \dfrac{\sqrt{45}}{2}$

d. $\text{Csc}(x) = \dfrac{7}{2}$

e. $\text{Sin}(2x) = \dfrac{4\sqrt{45}}{49}$

f. $\text{Cos}(2x) = \dfrac{51}{49}$

g. $\text{Sin}(3x) = \dfrac{262}{343}$

h. $\text{Cos}(3x) = \dfrac{99\sqrt{5}}{343}$

i. $\text{Sin}(\pi - x) = \dfrac{2}{7}$

j. $\text{Cos}(\pi - x) = -\dfrac{\sqrt{45}}{7}$

k. $\text{Sin}(2\pi - x) = -\dfrac{2}{7}$

l. $\text{Cos}(2\pi - x) = \dfrac{\sqrt{45}}{7}$

m. $\text{Sin}(x + \dfrac{\pi}{2}) = \dfrac{\sqrt{45}}{7}$

2. Given that $\text{Cos}(x) = -\dfrac{1}{6}$ and $\pi < x < \dfrac{3\pi}{2}$, find:

a. $\text{Sin}(x) = -\dfrac{\sqrt{35}}{6}$

b. $\text{Tan}(x) = \sqrt{35}$

c. $\text{Cot}(x) = \dfrac{1}{\sqrt{35}}$

d. $\text{Csc}(x) = -\dfrac{6}{\sqrt{35}}$

e. $\text{Sin}(2x) = \dfrac{\sqrt{35}}{18}$

f. $\text{Cos}(2x) = -\dfrac{17}{18}$

g. $\text{Sin}(4x) = \dfrac{17\sqrt{35}}{162}$

h. $\text{Cos}(4x) = \dfrac{127}{162}$

i. $\text{Sin}(\pi - x) = -\dfrac{\sqrt{35}}{6}$

j. $\text{Cos}(\pi - x) = \dfrac{1}{6}$

k. $\text{Sin}(2\pi - x) = \dfrac{\sqrt{35}}{6}$

l. $\text{Cos}(2\pi - x) = -\dfrac{1}{6}$

m. $\text{Cos}(x + \dfrac{\pi}{2}) = \dfrac{\sqrt{35}}{6}$

3. Given that $\text{Tan}(x) = 3$ and $\pi < x < 2\pi$, so x is in the 3rd quadrant. find:

a. $\text{Cos}(x) = -\dfrac{\sqrt{10}}{10}$

b. $\text{Tan}(x) = 3$

c. $\text{Cot}(x) = \dfrac{1}{3}$

d. $\text{Csc}(x) = \dfrac{10}{3\sqrt{10}}$

e. $\text{Tan}(2x) = -\dfrac{3}{4}$

f. $\text{Sin}(3x) = -\dfrac{9\sqrt{10}}{50}$

g. $\text{Cos}(3x) = -\dfrac{13\sqrt{10}}{50}$

4. Given that $\sin(x) = -\dfrac{1}{3}$ and $\pi < x < \dfrac{3}{2}\pi$, x is in the 3rd quadrant. Find:

a. $\text{Cos}(x) = -\dfrac{\sqrt{8}}{3}$

b. $\text{Tan}(x) = \dfrac{1}{\sqrt{8}}$

c. $\text{Cot}(x) = \sqrt{8}$

d. $\text{Csc}(x) = -3$

e. $\text{Sin}(2x) = \dfrac{2\sqrt{8}}{9}$

f. $\text{Cos}(2x) = \dfrac{7}{9}$

g. $\text{Sin}(3x) = \text{Sin}(2x + x) = -\dfrac{23}{27}$

h. $\text{Cos}(3x) = = -\dfrac{10\sqrt{2}}{27}$

i. $\text{Sin}(\pi - x) = -\dfrac{1}{3}$

j. $\text{Cos}(\pi - x) = \dfrac{\sqrt{8}}{3}$

k. $\text{Sin}(2\pi - x) = \dfrac{1}{3}$

l. $\text{Cos}(2\pi - x) = -\dfrac{\sqrt{8}}{3}$

m. $\text{Sin}(x + \dfrac{\pi}{2}) = -\dfrac{\sqrt{8}}{3}$

5. Given that $\text{Cos}(x) = \dfrac{1}{5}$ and $0 < x < \pi$, x is in the $\underline{1^{\text{st}}}$ quadrant. Find:

a. $\text{Sin}(x) = \dfrac{\sqrt{24}}{5}$

b. $\text{Tan}(x) = \sqrt{24}$

c. $\text{Cot}(x) = \dfrac{1}{\sqrt{24}}$

d. $\text{Csc}(x) = \dfrac{5}{\sqrt{24}}$

e. $\text{Sin}(2x) = \dfrac{2\sqrt{24}}{25}$

f. $\text{Cos}(2x) = -\dfrac{23}{25}$

g. $\text{Sin}(4x) = 2\sin(2x)\cos(2x) = -\dfrac{184\sqrt{6}}{625}$

h. $\text{Cos}(4x) = 2\cos^2(2x) - 1 = \dfrac{433}{625}$

i. $\text{Sin}(\pi - x) = \dfrac{\sqrt{24}}{5}$

j. $\text{Cos}(\pi - x) = -\dfrac{1}{5}$

k. $\text{Sin}(2\pi - x) = -\dfrac{\sqrt{24}}{5}$

l. $\text{Cos}(2\pi - x) = \dfrac{1}{5}$

m. $\text{Cos}(x + \dfrac{\pi}{2}) = -\dfrac{\sqrt{24}}{5}$

6. Given that $\text{Cotan}(x) = -2$ and $\pi < x < 2\pi$, so x is in the $\underline{4^{\text{th}}}$ quadrant. Find:

$$1 + \cot^2(x) = \dfrac{1}{\sin^2(x)} ; 5 = \dfrac{1}{\sin^2(x)} ; \sin(x) = -\dfrac{1}{\sqrt{5}}$$

a. $\text{Cos}(x) = \dfrac{2}{\sqrt{5}}$

b. $\text{Tan}(x) = -\dfrac{1}{2}$

c. $\text{Csc}(x) = -\sqrt{5}$

d. $\text{Tan}(2x) = \dfrac{\sin(2x)}{\cos(2x)} = \dfrac{-20}{15} = -\dfrac{4}{3}$

e. $\text{Sin}(3x) = -\dfrac{11\sqrt{5}}{25}$

f. $\text{Cos}(3x) = \dfrac{2\sqrt{5}}{25}$

167

4.3. – TRIGONOMETRIC FUNCTIONS

1. Write next to each one of the functions if it's periodic or not. Determine the period of the periodic ones.

    a.   No   b. Yes   c. Yes   d. Yes

2. Given the function $f(x) = \operatorname{Sin}(x)$, $g(x) = \cos(x)$, Complete the following table:

x°	0	15	30	45	60	75	90	105	120	135	150	165	180
Rad	0	$\dfrac{\pi}{12}$	$\dfrac{\pi}{6}$	$\dfrac{\pi}{4}$	$\dfrac{\pi}{3}$	$\dfrac{5\pi}{12}$	$\dfrac{\pi}{2}$	$\dfrac{7\pi}{12}$	$\dfrac{2\pi}{3}$	$\dfrac{3\pi}{4}$	$\dfrac{5\pi}{6}$	$\dfrac{11\pi}{12}$	π
f(x)	0	≈ 0.259	$\dfrac{1}{2}$	$\dfrac{1}{\sqrt{2}}$	$\dfrac{\sqrt{3}}{2}$	≈ 0.966	1	$\dfrac{\sqrt{3}}{2}$	$\dfrac{\sqrt{3}}{2}$	$\dfrac{1}{\sqrt{2}}$	$\dfrac{1}{2}$	≈ 0.259	0
g(x)	1	$\dfrac{\sqrt{3}}{2}$	$\dfrac{\sqrt{3}}{2}$	$\dfrac{1}{\sqrt{2}}$	$\dfrac{1}{2}$	≈ 0.259	0	≈ -0.259	$-\dfrac{1}{2}$	$-\dfrac{1}{\sqrt{2}}$	$-\dfrac{\sqrt{3}}{2}$	≈ -0.966	-1

195	210	225	240	255
$\dfrac{13\pi}{12}$	$\dfrac{7\pi}{6}$	$\dfrac{5\pi}{4}$	$\dfrac{4\pi}{3}$	$\dfrac{17\pi}{12}$
≈ -0.259	$-\dfrac{1}{2}$	$-\dfrac{1}{\sqrt{2}}$	$-\dfrac{\sqrt{3}}{2}$	≈ -0.966
≈ -0.966	$-\dfrac{\sqrt{3}}{2}$	$-\dfrac{1}{\sqrt{2}}$	$-\dfrac{1}{2}$	≈ -0.259

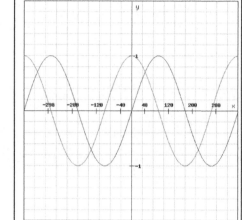

- The domain of the function: $x \in R$
- The y intercept: $f(x):(0,0); g(x):(0,1)$
- The x intercept(s): $f(x):(0+\pi k,0); g(x):(\dfrac{\pi}{2}+\pi k,0), k \in \mathbb{Z}$
- The corresponding limits and the equation of the vertical asymptote: <u>None</u>
- The corresponding limits and the equation of the horizontal asymptote: <u>None</u>
- Increasing: $f(x):x \in (-\dfrac{\pi}{2},\dfrac{\pi}{2}); g(x):(\pi,2\pi)$, and in the corresponding intervals
- Decreasing: $f(x):x \in (\dfrac{\pi}{2},\dfrac{3\pi}{2}); g(x):(0,\pi)$, and in the corresponding intervals
- Max: $f(x):x \in (\dfrac{\pi}{2}+2\pi k,1); g(x):(2\pi k,1), k \in \mathbb{Z}$

    Min: $f(x):x \in (-\dfrac{\pi}{2}+2\pi k,-1); g(x):(\pi+2\pi k,-1), k \in \mathbb{Z}$

- State the range of the function: $f(x) \in [-1,1]; g(x) \in [-1,1]$

3. Given the function f(x) = Sin(x)
   a. The function translated 2 positions up. f(x) = Sin(x) + 2
   b. The function translated 3 positions left. f(x) = Sin(x+3)
   c. The function translated 3 positions left and 1 up. f(x) = Sin(x+3) + 1
   d. The function translated 4 positions right and 1 up. f(x) = Sin(x – 4) + 1
   e. Change the function so that the period would be 2. $f(x) = Sin(\pi x)$

   f. The period is 3 and the amplitude 2. $f(x) = 2Sin(\frac{2\pi}{3} x)$

   g. The period would is π and the amplitude 4. $f(x) = 4Sin(2x)$

   h. The period is $\frac{\pi}{3}$ and the amplitude k. $f(x) = kSin(6x)$

   i. The period would be 6, the amplitude 3, then shift the function 2 positions
      right and 1 down. $f(x) = 3Sin\left(\frac{\pi}{3}(x-2)\right) - 1$

   j. The period would be $\frac{\pi}{3}$, the amplitude 1.3, then shift the function 4 positions
      left and 2 down. $f(x) = 1.3Sin(6(x+4)) - 2$

   k. The period would be $\frac{\pi}{5}$, the amplitude 4, then shift the function π positions
      left and 5 down. $f(x) = 4Sin(10(x+\pi)) - 5$

4. Given the function f(x) = 3Sin(5(x – 2)) + 3
   a. Amplitude = 5
   b. Period = $\frac{2\pi}{5}$
   c. Horizontal Translation: 2 Right with respect to 3Sin(5x) + 3
   d. Vertical Translation: 3 up with respect to 3Sin(5(x – 2))   Midline: y = 3
   e. Range: $f(x) \in [0,6]$

5. Given the function f(x) = –5Cos(3x – 2) – 3.4 = –5Cos(3(x – $\frac{2}{3}$)) – 3.4

   a. Amplitude = 5
   b. Period = $\frac{2\pi}{3}$

   c. Horizontal Translation: $\frac{2}{3}$ Right with respect to –5Cos(3x) – 3.4

   d. Vertical Translation: 3.4 down with respect to –5Cos(3(x– $\frac{2}{3}$)),

      midline: y=–3.4
   e. Range: $f(x) \in [-8.4, 1.6]$

6. Given the function $f(x) = 2.4\text{Sin}(\pi x - \frac{\pi}{2}) - 3 = 2.4\text{Sin}(\pi(x - \frac{1}{2})) - 3$

    a. Amplitude = 2.4

    b. Period = 2

    c. Horizontal Translation: $\frac{1}{2}$ Right with respect to $2.4\text{Sin}(\pi x) - 3$

    d. Vertical Translation: 3 down with respect to $2.4\text{Sin}(\pi(x - \frac{1}{2}))$

       midline: y = –3

    e. Range: $f(x) \in [-5.4, -0.6]$

7. Given the function $f(x) = 4 - (2.4)\text{Cos}(2\pi x - \frac{\pi}{3}) = -(2.4)\text{Cos}(2\pi(x - \frac{1}{6})) + 4$

    a. Amplitude = 4

    b. Period = 1

    c. Horizontal Translation : $\frac{1}{6}$ Right with respect to $-(2.4)\text{Cos}(2\pi x) + 4$

    d. Vertical Translation: 4 up with respect to $-(2.4)\text{Cos}(2\pi(x - \frac{1}{6}))$

       midline: y = 4

    e. Range: $f(x) \in [1.6, 6.4]$

8. Given the function $f(x) = 1 + 4\text{Sin}(\frac{\pi}{3}x - 3) = 4\text{Sin}(\frac{\pi}{3}(x - \frac{9}{\pi})) + 1$

    a. Amplitude = 4

    b. Period = 6

    c. Horizontal Translation; $\frac{9}{\pi}$ Right with respect to $4\text{Sin}(\frac{\pi}{3}x) + 1$

    d. Vertical Translation: 1 up with respect to $4\text{Sin}(\frac{\pi}{3}(x - \frac{9}{\pi}))$

       midline: y = 1

    e. Range: $f(x) \in [-3, 5]$

9. Given the function $f(x) = -\text{Sin}(\frac{\pi}{5}x - 1) + 1 = -\text{Sin}(\frac{\pi}{5}(x - \frac{5}{\pi})) + 1$

    a. Amplitude = 1

    b. Period = 10

    c. Horizontal Translation: $\frac{5}{\pi}$ Right with respect to $-\text{Sin}(\frac{\pi}{5}(x - \frac{5}{\pi})) + 1$

    d. Vertical Translation: 1 up with respect to $-\text{Sin}(\frac{\pi}{5}(x - \frac{5}{\pi}))$ midline: y = 1

    e. Range: $f(x) \in [0, 2]$

10. Given the function f(x) = 4 – 3Cos(3x°)
    a. Amplitude = 3
    b. Period = 120°
    c. Horizontal Translation: None with respect to 4 – 3Cos(3x°)
    d. Vertical Translation: 4 up with respect to – 3Cos(3x°)
       Midline: y = 4
    e. Range: $f(x) \in [1,7]$

11. Given the function $f(x) = -Sin(\frac{x^o}{10}) + 1$

    a. Amplitude = 1
    b. Period = 3600°

    c. Horizontal Translation: None with respect to $-Sin(\frac{x^o}{10}) + 1$

    d. Vertical Translation: 1 up with respect to $-Sin(\frac{x^o}{10})$

       Midline: y = 1

    e. Range: $f(x) \in [0,2]$

12. Given the graph, complete:
    a. Amplitude = 1
    b. Period = π
    c. Horizontal Translation: Depends (sin or cos)
    d. Midline: y = 0

    e. $f(x) = Sin(2x) = Cos\left(2\left(x - \frac{\pi}{4}\right)\right)$

    f. Range: $f(x) \in [-1,1]$

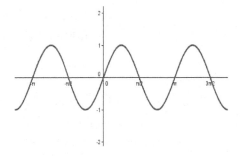

13. Given the graph, complete:
    a. Amplitude = 2

    b. Period = $\frac{2\pi}{3}$

    c. Horizontal Translation: Depends (sin or cos)
    d. Midline: y = 1

    e. $f(x) = 2Sin(\frac{3}{2\pi}x) + 1 = 2Cos\left(3\left(x - \frac{\pi}{6}\right)\right) + 1$

    f. Range: $f(x) \in [-1,3]$

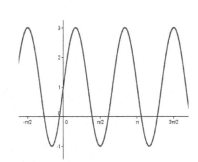

14. Given the graph, complete:
    a. Amplitude = 2
    b. Period = 4π
    c. Horizontal Translation: Depends (sin or cos)
    d. Midline: y = –2

    e. $f(x) = 2Sin(\frac{1}{2}x) - 2 = 2Cos\left(\frac{1}{2}(x-\pi)\right) - 2$

    f. Range: $f(x) \in [-4, 0]$

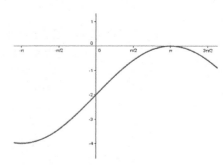

15. Given the graph, complete:
    a. Amplitude = 2
    b. Period = 2
    c. Horizontal Translation: Depends (sin or cos)
    d. Midline: y = 0

    e. $f(x) = 2Sin(\pi x) = 2Cos\left(\pi\left(x - \frac{1}{2}\right)\right)$

    f. Range: $f(x) \in [-2, 2]$

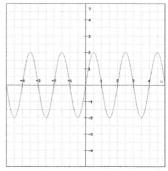

16. Given the graph, complete:
    a. Amplitude = 3
    b. Period = 6
    c. Horizontal Translation: Depends (sin or cos)
    d. Midline: y = 1

    e. $f(x) = 3Sin(\frac{\pi}{3}x) + 1 = 3Cos\left(\frac{\pi}{3}\left(x - \frac{3}{2}\right)\right) + 1$

    f. Range: $f(x) \in [-2, 4]$

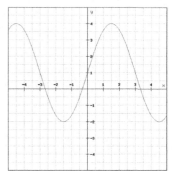

17. Given the graph, complete:
    a. Amplitude = 1
    b. Period = 4
    c. Horizontal Translation: Depends (sin or cos)
    d. Midline: y = 3

    e. $f(x) = -Sin(\frac{\pi}{2}x) + 3 = Cos\left(\frac{\pi}{2}(x+1)\right) + 3$

    f. Range: $f(x) \in [2, 4]$

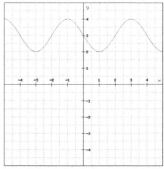

18. Given the graph, complete:
    a. Amplitude = 2
    b. Period = 0.5
    c. Horizontal Translation: Depends (sin or cos)
    d. Midline: y = –2

    e. $f(x) = 2Sin(4\pi x) - 2 = 2Cos\left(4\pi\left(x - \frac{1}{8}\right)\right) - 2$

    f. Range: $f(x) \in [-4, 0]$

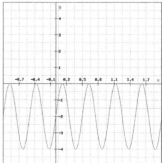

19. Given the graph, complete:
   a. Amplitude = 2
   b. Period = 8
   c. Horizontal Translation = Depends (sin or cos)
   d. Midline: y = 2

   e. $f(x) = 2Sin\left(\dfrac{\pi}{4}(x-1)\right) + 2 = 2Cos\left(\dfrac{\pi}{4}(x-3)\right) + 2$

   f. Range: $f(x) \in [0,4]$

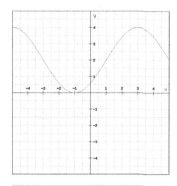

20. Given the graph, complete:
   a. Amplitude = 3
   b. Period = 1
   c. Horizontal Translation = Depends (sin or cos)
   d. Midline: y = −1

   e. $f(x) = 3Sin(2\pi x) - 1 = 3Cos\left(2\pi\left(x - \dfrac{1}{4}\right)\right) - 1$

   f. Range: $f(x) \in [-4,2]$

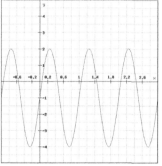

21. Given the graph, complete:
   a. Amplitude = 3
   b. Period = 6
   c. Horizontal Translation: Depends (sin or cos)
   d. Midline: y = 4

   e. $f(x) = 3Sin\left(\dfrac{\pi}{3}(x+1)\right) + 4 = 3Cos\left(\dfrac{\pi}{3}(x - \dfrac{1}{2})\right) + 4$

   f. Range: $f(x) \in [1,7]$

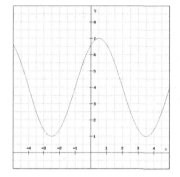

22. Given the graph, complete:
   a. Amplitude = 3
   b. Period = 8
   c. Horizontal Translation: Depends (sin or cos)
   d. Midline: y = 4

   e. $f(x) = 3Sin\left(\dfrac{\pi}{4}(x-1)\right) + 4 = 3Cos\left(\dfrac{\pi}{4}(x-3)\right) + 4$

   f. Range: $f(x) \in [1,7]$

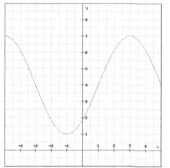

23. Given the graph, complete:
   a. Amplitude = 5
   b. Period = 2
   c. Horizontal Translation: Depends (sin or cos)
   d. Midline: y = −1

   e. $f(x) = 5Sin\left(\pi\left(x - \dfrac{1}{2}\right)\right) - 1 = -5Cos(\pi x) - 1$

   f. Range: $f(x) \in [-6,4]$

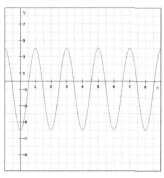

24. Given the function $f(x) = -2 + \text{Cos}(\dfrac{\pi}{2}x)$

    a. Amplitude = 1
    b. Period = 4
    c. Horizontal Translation: None

       with respect to $\text{Cos}(\dfrac{\pi}{2}x)$

    d. Vertical Translation: 2 down

       with respect to $\text{Cos}(\dfrac{\pi}{2}x)$

    e. Midline: y = –2
    f. Range: $f(x) \in [-3, -1]$

    g. Sketch the 2 periods of the function, include maximums and minimums.

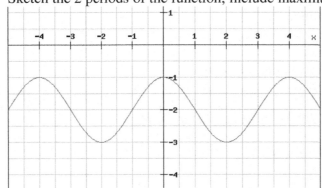

25. Given the function $f(x) = 2\text{Sin}(\dfrac{2\pi}{3}x) - 1$

    a. Amplitude = 2
    b. Period = 3
    c. Horizontal Translation:
       None with respect to

       $2\text{Sin}(\dfrac{2\pi}{3}x) - 1$

    d. Vertical Translation: 1 down
       with respect to

       $2\text{Sin}(\dfrac{2\pi}{3}x)$

    e. Midline: : y = –1
    f. Range: $f(x) \in [-3, 1]$

    g. Sketch the 2 periods of the function, include maximums and minimums.

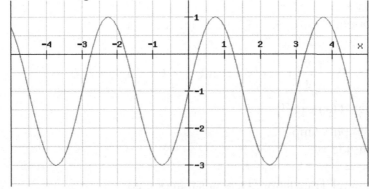

26. Given the function $f(x) = 3 - 2Cos(\pi x - \frac{\pi}{2}) = 3 - 2Cos(\pi(x - \frac{1}{2}))$

   a. Amplitude = 3

   b. Period = 3

   c. Horizontal Translation:
$\frac{1}{2}$ right with respect to
$3 - 2Cos(\pi x)$

   d. Vertical Translation: 3 up with respect to
$-2Cos(\pi x - \frac{\pi}{2})$

   e. Midline: y = 3

   f. Range: $f(x) \in [1,5]$

   g. Sketch the 2 periods of the function, include maximums and minimums.

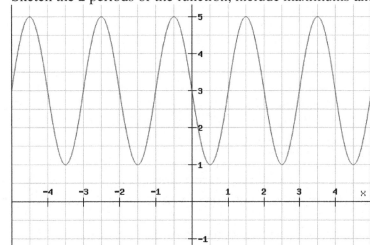

27. Given the function $f(x) = -2Sin(\pi x - \frac{\pi}{2}) + 1 = -2Sin(\pi(x - \frac{1}{2})) + 1$

   a. Amplitude = 2

   b. Period = 2

   c. Horizontal Translation:
$\frac{1}{2}$ right with respect to
$-2Sin(\pi x) + 1)$

   d. Vertical Translation: 1 up with respect to $-2Sin(\pi(x - \frac{1}{2}))$

   e. Midline: y = 1

   f. Range: $f(x) \in [-1,3]$

   g. Sketch the 2 periods of the function, include maximums and minimums.

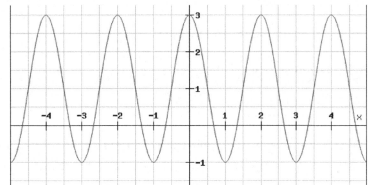

28. Given the function f(x) = Tan(x), Complete the following table:

x°	0	15	30	45	60	75	90	105	120	135	150	165	180
Rad	0	$\dfrac{\pi}{12}$	$\dfrac{\pi}{6}$	$\dfrac{\pi}{4}$	$\dfrac{\pi}{3}$	$\dfrac{5\pi}{12}$	$\dfrac{\pi}{2}$	$\dfrac{7\pi}{12}$	$\dfrac{2\pi}{3}$	$\dfrac{3\pi}{4}$	$\dfrac{5\pi}{6}$	$\dfrac{11\pi}{12}$	π
f(x)	0	≈0.268	$\dfrac{1}{\sqrt{3}}$	1	$\sqrt{3}$	≈3.73	D.E.	≈−3.73	$-\sqrt{3}$	−1	$-\dfrac{1}{\sqrt{3}}$	≈−0.268	0

195	210	225	240	255
$\dfrac{13\pi}{12}$	$\dfrac{7\pi}{6}$	$\dfrac{5\pi}{4}$	$\dfrac{4\pi}{3}$	$\dfrac{17\pi}{12}$
≈0.268	$\dfrac{1}{\sqrt{3}}$	1	$\sqrt{3}$	≈3.73

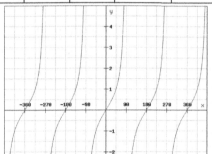

- State the domain of the function: $x \notin (\dfrac{\pi}{2} + \pi k), k \in \mathbb{Z}$

- State the y intercept: $f(x):(0,0)$

- State the x intercept(s): $f(x):(0 + \pi k, 0), k \in \mathbb{Z}$

- The corresponding limits and equation of vertical asymptotes: $x = \dfrac{\pi}{2} + \pi k, k \in \mathbb{Z}$

- The corresponding limits and the equation of the horizontal asymptote: None

- Increasing on the interval: $x \notin (\dfrac{\pi}{2} + \pi k), k \in \mathbb{Z}$, decreasing on the interval: None

- Find the max/min point(s): None
- State the range of the function: $f(x):x \in (-\infty, \infty)$

29. Given the function f(x) = Tan(x)
    a. The same function translated 2 positions up. f(x) = Tan(x) +2
    b. The same function translated 3 positions left. f(x) = Tan(x + 3)
    c. The same function translated 3 positions left and 1 up. f(x) = Tan(x + 3) + 1
    d. The same function translated 4 positions right and 1 up. f(x) = Tan(x – 4) + 1

    e. Period is 2. $f(x) = \tan(\dfrac{\pi}{2}x)$

    f. Period is 3 and the amplitude 2. $f(x) = \tan(\dfrac{\pi}{2}x)$. Tan has no amplitude!

    g. The period is π. $f(x) = \tan(x)$

    h. The period is $\dfrac{\pi}{3}$. $f(x) = \tan(3x)$

    i. The period is 6, 2 positions right and 1 down. $f(x) = \tan\left(\dfrac{\pi}{6}(x-2)\right) - 1$

176

j. The period is $\dfrac{\pi}{3}$, 4 positions left and 2 down. $f(x) = \tan(3(x+4)) - 2$

k. The period is $\dfrac{\pi}{5}$, π positions left and 5 down. $f(x) = \tan(4(x+\pi)) - 5$

30. Given the graph, complete:
    a. Amplitude = None
    b. Period = π
    c. Horizontal Translation: None
    d. Midline: y = 0
    e. $f(x) = \tan(x)$
    f. Range: $f(x): x \in (-\infty, \infty)$

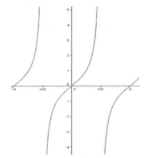

31. Given the graph, complete:
    a. Amplitude = None
    b. Period = $\dfrac{\pi}{3}$
    c. Horizontal Translation: None
    d. Midline: y = 0
    e. $f(x) = \tan(3x)$
    f. Range: $f(x): x \in (-\infty, \infty)$

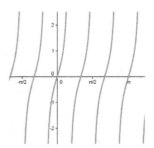

32. Given the graph, complete:
    a. Amplitude = None
    b. Period = 2
    c. Horizontal Translation: None
    d. Midline: y = 0
    e. $f(x) = \tan(\dfrac{\pi}{2}x)$
    f. Range: $f(x): x \in (-\infty, \infty)$

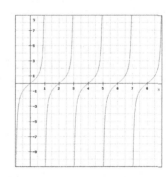

4.4. – SINE AND COSINE RULE

The sine rule: For any triangle, given the sides a, b and c and their corresponding opposite angles, A, B and C:

$$\frac{Sin(A)}{a} = \frac{Sin(B)}{b} = \frac{Sin(C)}{c}$$

How many equations are written above? 3

$$\frac{Sin(A)}{a} = \frac{Sin(B)}{b} \qquad \frac{Sin(A)}{a} = \frac{Sin(C)}{c} \qquad \frac{Sin(B)}{b} = \frac{Sin(C)}{c}$$

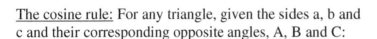

The cosine rule: For any triangle, given the sides a, b and c and their corresponding opposite angles, A, B and C:

$$a^2 = b^2 + c^2 - 2bc\cos(A)$$

$$b^2 = a^2 + c^2 - 2ac\cos(B)$$

$$c^2 = a^2 + b^2 - 2ab\cos(C)$$

Given the following triangle:

a. Find AD in terms of AC and the angle C. $AD = AC\sin(C)$

b. Find the Area of the triangle in terms of BC, AC and the angle C.

$$S_{ABC} = \frac{BC \cdot AC\sin(C)}{2}$$

c. Conclusion: **Area of any triangle is given by half of the product of 2 of its sides multiplied by the sine of the angle between those sides**

$$S_{ABC} = \frac{a \cdot b\sin(\alpha)}{2}$$

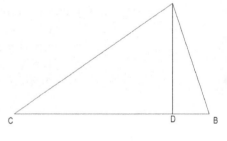

Exercises

1. Sketch a triangle with angles: 20°, 80°, C and sides 10, b, c .Write the Sine and Cosine rule for this triangle.

$$\frac{Sin(20°)}{10} = \frac{Sin(80°)}{b} = \frac{Sin(80°)}{c}$$

$$10^2 = b^2 + c^2 - 2bc\cos(20°)$$
$$b^2 = 10^2 + c^2 - 20c\cos(80°)$$
$$c^2 = 10^2 + b^2 - 20b\cos(80°)$$

2. Find all the missing sides, angles and area of the triangles below. If there is more than one set of solutions, try to find them all.

$$12^2 = 8^2 + 10^2 - 2 \cdot 8 \cdot 10 \cos(G)$$

$$G \approx 82.8°$$

$$10^2 = 8^2 + 12^2 - 2 \cdot 8 \cdot 12 \cos(S)$$

$$S \approx 55.8°$$

$$M = 180° - 82.8° - 55.8° = 41.4°$$

$$Area = \frac{10 \cdot 12 \cdot \sin(41.4°)}{2} \approx 36.7 cm^2$$

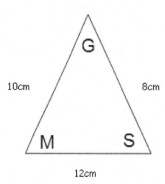

$$x^2 = 11^2 + 10^2 - 2 \cdot 11 \cdot 10 \cos(30)$$

$$x \approx 5.52 cm$$

$$11^2 = (5.52)^2 + 10^2 - 2 \cdot 11 \cdot 10 \cos(G)$$

$$G \approx 87.5°$$

$$M = 180° - 30° - 87.5° = 62.5°$$

$$Area = \frac{10 \cdot 11 \cdot \sin(30°)}{2} \approx 27.5 cm^2$$

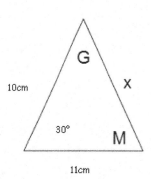

Conclusion: The cosine rule must be used in the following cases:
    I.   <u>All sides are known and no angle</u>
    II.   <u>2 sides are know and only the angle between them</u>

3. Find all the sides, angles and the area of the following triangles:
<u>Ambiguous Case (2 possible solutions)</u>

$$6^2 = 8^2 + x^2 - 2 \cdot x \cdot 8 \cos(40°)$$

$$x_1 \approx 3.04 cm \quad ; x_2 \approx 9.22 cm$$

$$8^2 = 6^2 + 3.04^2 - 2 \cdot 3.04 \cdot 8 \cos(G)$$

$$G_1 \approx 121°$$

$$M_1 = 180° - 121° - 40° = 19°$$

$$8^2 = 6^2 + 9.22^2 - 2 \cdot 9.22 \cdot 8 \cos(G)$$

$$G_2 \approx 59.0°$$

$$M_2 = 180° - 59° - 40° = 81°$$

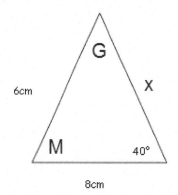

$$Area_1 = \frac{6 \cdot 8 \cdot \sin(19°)}{2} \approx 7.81 cm^2 \qquad Area_2 = \frac{6 \cdot 8 \cdot \sin(81°)}{2} \approx 23.7 cm^2$$

$$\frac{\sin(20°)}{10} = \frac{\sin(G)}{15}$$

$$G_1 \approx 30.9° \quad ; G_2 \approx 141°$$

$$M_1 = 180° - 30.9° - 20° = 129.1°$$

$$M_2 = 180° - 141° - 20° = 19°$$

$$x_1^2 = 10^2 + 15^2 - 2 \cdot 10 \cdot 15 \cos(129.1°)$$

$$x_1 \approx 22.7cm$$

$$x_2^2 = 10^2 + 15^2 - 2 \cdot 10 \cdot 15 \cos(19°)$$

$$x_2 \approx 6.43cm$$

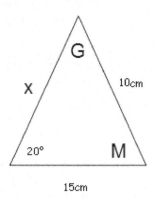

$$Area_1 = \frac{15 \cdot 22.7 \cdot \sin(20°)}{2} \approx 58.2cm^2 \quad Area_2 = \frac{15 \cdot 6.43 \cdot \sin(20°)}{2} \approx 16.5cm^2$$

Conclusion: <u>The ambiguous case appears when 2 sides are known and the angle opposite to the shorter of those sides</u>

4. Find all the sides, angles and the area of the following triangles:

$$M = 180° - 20° - 50° = 110°$$

$$\frac{\sin(110°)}{15} = \frac{\sin(20°)}{x} \quad ; x \approx 5.45cm$$

$$\frac{\sin(110°)}{15} = \frac{\sin(50)}{y} \quad ; y \approx 12.2cm$$

$$Area = \frac{15 \cdot 5.45 \cdot \sin(50°)}{2} \approx 31.3cm^2$$

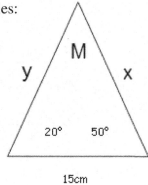

5. Find all the sides, angles and the area of the triangle:
<u>This triangle can have any size as only angles are given</u>

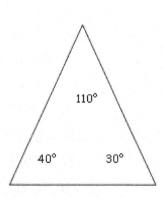

6. Find all the sides, angles and the area of the triangle:

<u>Ambiguous Case (2 possible solutions)</u>
$$5^2 = 9^2 + x^2 - 2 \cdot x \cdot 9 \cos(20°)$$
$$x_1 \approx 4.52cm$$
$$x_2 \approx 12.4cm$$
$$\frac{\sin(20°)}{5} = \frac{\sin(G)}{9}$$
$$G_1 \approx 28.6°$$
$$G_2 \approx 180 - 28.6° = 151°$$
$$M_1 = 180° - 20° - 28.6° = 131°$$
$$M_2 = 180° - 20° - 151.4° = 8.6°$$
$$Area = \frac{9 \cdot 5 \cdot \sin(50°)}{2} \approx 36.4cm^2$$

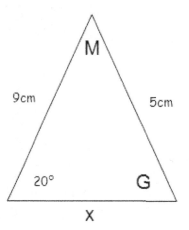

7. Find all the sides, angles and the area of the triangle:

<u>This triangle cannot exist as the sum 5 + 6 is smaller than 13</u>

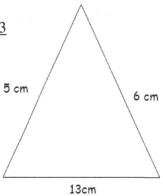

8. Find all the sides, angles and the area of the triangle:

$$\frac{\sin(50°)}{15} = \frac{\sin(G)}{12}$$

$G \approx 37.8°$

$M = 180° - 37.8° - 50° = 92.2°$

$x^2 = 12^2 + 15^2 - 2 \cdot 12 \cdot 15 \cos(92.2°)$

$x \approx 19.6cm$

$$Area = \frac{15 \cdot 12 \cdot \sin(50°)}{2} \approx 48.2cm^2$$

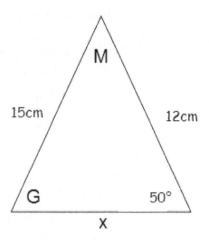

9. Find all the sides, angles and the area of the triangle:

$$x^2 = 12^2 + 8^2 - 2 \cdot 12 \cdot 8 \cos(40°)$$

$x \approx 7.81cm$

$$\frac{7.81}{Sin(40°)} = \frac{8}{Sin(G)}$$

$G \approx 41.2°$

$M = 180° - 41.2° - 40° = 98.8°$

$$Area = \frac{8 \cdot 12 \cdot \sin(40°)}{2} \approx 30.9cm^2$$

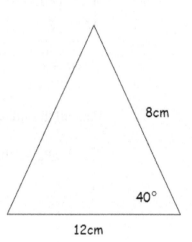

10. Find all the sides, angles and the area of the triangle:

$$x^2 = 13^2 + 6^2 - 2 \cdot 13 \cdot 6 \cos(20°)$$

$x \approx 7.64cm$

$$\frac{7.64}{Sin(20°)} = \frac{6}{Sin(G)}$$

$G \approx 15.6°$

$M = 180° - 15.6° - 40° = 134.4°$

$$Area = \frac{6 \cdot 13 \cdot \sin(20°)}{2} \approx 13.3cm^2$$

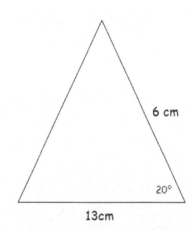

11. Can you identify how many triangles (not to scale) you could draw using the given information? In which example could you find the ambiguous case? Sketch (to scale as possible) both triangles in that case.

a. Ambiguous case – 2 triangles

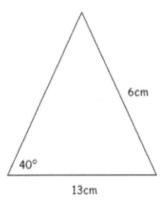

b. 1 triangle

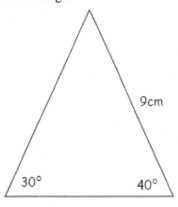

c. 1 triangle

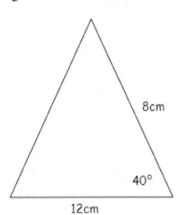

d. No triangle, 5+6 < 13

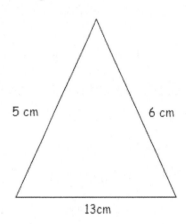

e. 1 triangle

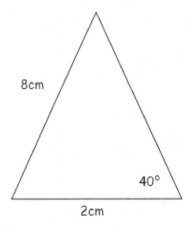

f. Ambiguous case – 2 triangles

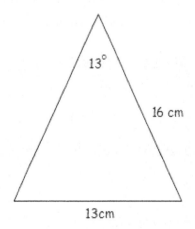

4.5. – TRIGONOMETRIC RATIOS

Following directly from the unit circle are the trigonometric ratios:

$$Sin(x) = \frac{a}{c} \qquad Cos(x) = \frac{b}{c} \qquad Tan(x) = \frac{Sin(x)}{Cos(x)} = \frac{a}{b}$$

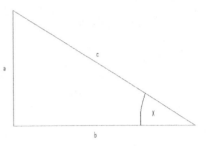

Exercises:

1. Find x and y in the following cases:

a.

$$\sin(25°) = \frac{5}{y}$$

$$y \approx 11.8$$

$$\tan(25°) = \frac{5}{x}$$

$$\underline{x \approx 10.7}$$

b.

$$\sin(20°) = \frac{y}{8}$$

$$y \approx 2.74$$

$$\cos(20°) = \frac{x}{8}$$

$$\underline{x \approx 7.52}$$

2. Find all the missing sides, angles, area and perimeter of the following triangle:

$$AB = \sqrt{36+49} = \sqrt{85}$$

$$C = 90°$$

$$\tan(A) = \frac{6}{7}; A \approx 40.6°$$

$$B \approx 90 - 40.6 = 39.4°$$

$$Area = \frac{6 \cdot 7}{2} = 21$$

$$\underline{Perimeter = 6+7+\sqrt{85} = 13+\sqrt{85}}$$

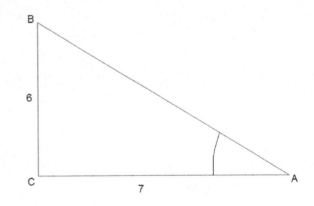

3. Find all the missing sides, angles, area and perimeter of the following triangle:

$$CB = \sqrt{64-49} = \sqrt{15}$$

$$C = 90°$$

$$\cos(A) = \frac{7}{8}; A \approx 29.0°$$

$$B \approx 90 - 29.0 = 61.0°$$

$$Area = \frac{\sqrt{15} \cdot 7}{2}$$

$$\underline{Perimeter = 8+7+\sqrt{15} = 15+\sqrt{15}}$$

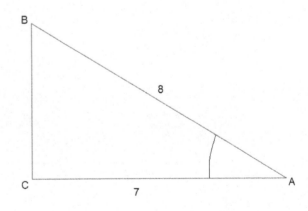

184

4. Find all the missing sides, angles, area and perimeter of the following triangle:

$$\cos(30°) = \frac{7}{AB}; AB = \frac{14}{\sqrt{3}}$$

$$CB = \sqrt{\left(\frac{14}{\sqrt{3}}\right)^2 - 49} = \frac{7}{\sqrt{3}}$$

$$C = 90°; B = 60°$$

$$Area = \frac{\left(\frac{7}{\sqrt{3}} \cdot 7\right)}{2} = \frac{49}{2\sqrt{3}}$$

$$Perimeter = 7 + \frac{14}{\sqrt{3}} + \frac{7}{\sqrt{3}} = 7 + \frac{21}{\sqrt{3}}$$

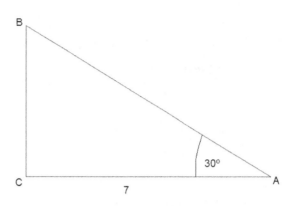

5. Find all the missing sides, angles, area and perimeter of the following triangle:

$$x^2 + 4x^2 = 225; x = \sqrt{45}$$

$$AC = 2\sqrt{45}; BC = \sqrt{45}$$

$$\cos(A) = \frac{2\sqrt{45}}{15}; A \approx 26.6°$$

$$C = 90°; B \approx 63.4°$$

$$Area = \frac{2\sqrt{45} \cdot \sqrt{45}}{2} = 45$$

$$Perimeter = 2\sqrt{45} + \sqrt{45} + 15 = 15 + 3\sqrt{45}$$

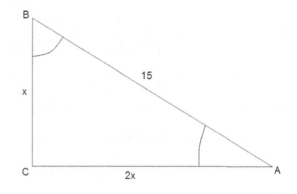

6. Find all the missing sides, angles, area and perimeter of the following triangle:

$$3x = 90°; x = 30°$$

$$C = 90°; B \approx 60°; A = 30°$$

$$\sin(30°) = \frac{10}{AB}; AB = 20$$

$$AC = \sqrt{400 - 100} = \sqrt{300}$$

$$Area = \frac{\sqrt{300} \cdot 10}{2} = 5\sqrt{300}$$

$$Perimeter = 10 + 20 + \sqrt{300} = 30 + \sqrt{300}$$

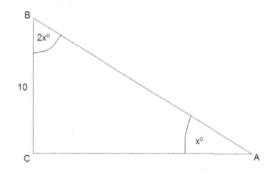

7. Find all the missing sides, angles, area and perimeter of an equilateral triangle with length side 10cm.

$A = B = C = 60°$

$AB = AC = BC = 10cm$

$Perimeter = 10 + 10 + 10 = 30cm$

$BD = \sqrt{100 - 25} = \sqrt{75}cm$

$Area = \dfrac{\sqrt{75} \cdot 10}{2} = 5\sqrt{75}cm^2$

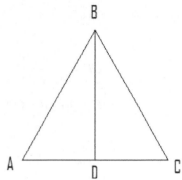

8. Find all the angles in an isosceles triangle whose base length is 20 cm and it is half its side length.

$AB = AC = 40cm$

$Perimeter = 40 + 40 + 20 = 100cm$

$Cos(B) = \dfrac{10}{40}; B = C \approx 75.5°$

$A \approx 180° - 151° = 29°$

$AD = \sqrt{400 - 100} = \sqrt{300}cm$

$Area = \dfrac{\sqrt{300} \cdot 20}{2} = 10\sqrt{300}cm^2$

9. The Triangle in the diagram (not to scale) is <u>not</u> right angled, find x and y.

$Y^2 = 40^2 + 10^2 - 2 \cdot 40 \cdot 10 \cos(35)$

$Y \approx 32.3$

$\dfrac{10}{Sin(x)} = \dfrac{32.3}{Sin(35)}$

$x \approx 10.2°$

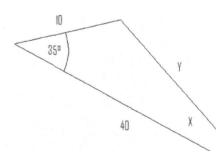

10. The shade formed by building is 100m long. The depression angle of the light as it approaches the ground is 40°.
    a. Sketch a diagram that describes the situation.
    b. Find the height of the building.

$\tan(40°) = \dfrac{h}{100}$

$h \approx 83.9m$

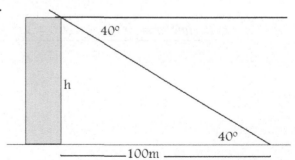

11. The height of building is 120m. The depression angle of the light as it approaches the ground is 30°.
    a. Sketch a diagram that describes the situation.
    b. Find the length of the shade on the ground.

$$\tan(30°) = \frac{120}{L}$$

$$L = 120 \cdot \sqrt{3} m$$

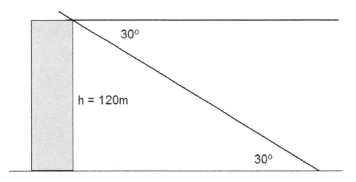

12. In its search for food the 1.5m tall lion is observing a certain prey located 2 m above the ground. The lion's head forms an angle of 12° as he looks at his prey.
    a. Sketch a diagram that describes the situation.
    b. Find the distance from the lion's mouth to its prey.

$$\sin(12°) = \frac{0.5}{L}$$

$$L = 2.40 m$$

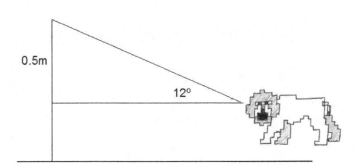

13. Measuring the height and distance of objects:

    x = 20°. AB = 4m, y = 18°. Find AD, AC, CD.

$$\tan(20°) = \frac{h}{AD} \quad ; \tan(18°) = \frac{h}{AD + 4}$$

$$x \approx 33.3m \quad h \approx 12.1m$$

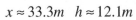
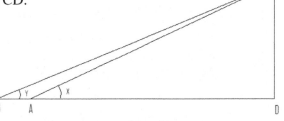

4.6. – INVERSE TRIGONOMETRIC FUNCTIONS

Give your answer(s) in radians and
degrees, use a calculator if necessary:

1. $\text{Arcsin}(0) = 0 = 0°$

2. $\text{Arcos}(0) = \dfrac{\pi}{2} = 90°$

3. $\text{Arcsin}(1) = \dfrac{\pi}{2} = 90°$

4. $\text{Arcos}(2) = \text{D.E.}$

5. $\text{Arcsin}(0.5) = \dfrac{\pi}{6} = 30°$

6. $\text{Arcos}(-0.5) = -\dfrac{\pi}{3} = -60°$

7. $\text{Arcsin}(\dfrac{\sqrt{3}}{2}) = \dfrac{\pi}{3} = 60°$

8. $\text{Arcos}(-\dfrac{\sqrt{3}}{2}) = -\dfrac{\pi}{6} = -30°$

9. $\text{Arcsin}(\dfrac{\sqrt{2}}{2}) = \dfrac{\pi}{4} = 45°$

10. $\text{Arcos}(-\dfrac{\sqrt{2}}{2}) = \dfrac{\pi}{4} = 45°$

11. $\text{Arcsin}(\dfrac{\sqrt{2}}{2}) = \dfrac{\pi}{4} = 45°$

12. $\text{Arcsin}(-1) = -\dfrac{\pi}{2} = -90°$

13. $\text{Arcos}(-1) = \pi = 180°$
14. $\text{Arcsin}(0.2) \approx 0.201 \approx 11.5°$
15. $\text{Arcos}(-0.4) \approx 1.98 \approx 114°$
16. $\text{Arcsin}(1/5) \approx 0.201 \approx 11.5°$
17. $\text{Arcos}(-5) = \text{D.E.}$
18. $\text{Arcsin}(0.9) \approx 1.12 \approx 65.2°$
19. $\text{Arcsin}(-2.4) = \text{D.E.}$
20. $\text{Arcos}(0.05) \approx 1.52 \approx 87.1°$
21. $\text{Arctan}(-5) \approx -1.37 \approx -78.7°$

22. $\text{Arctan}(1) = \dfrac{\pi}{4} = 45°$

23. $\text{Arctan}(-2.4) \approx -1.18 \approx -67.4°$

24. $\text{Arctan}(\dfrac{1}{\sqrt{3}}) = \dfrac{\pi}{6} = 30°$

25. $\text{Arctan}(-\sqrt{3}) = -\dfrac{\pi}{3} = -60°$

26. $\text{Arctan}(\sqrt{3}) = \dfrac{\pi}{3} = 60°$

27. $\text{Arctan}(-1) = -\dfrac{\pi}{4} = -45°$

Evaluate:

28. $Arc\sin\left(\dfrac{-1}{2}\right) = -\dfrac{\pi}{6} = -30°$

29. $Arc\cos\left(\dfrac{\sqrt{3}}{2}\right) = \dfrac{\pi}{6} = 30°$

30. $Arc\tan(0) = 0 = 0°$

31. $\cos\left(arc\sin\left(\dfrac{\sqrt{3}}{2}\right)\right) = \cos(60°) = \dfrac{1}{2}$

32. $\cos\left(\arcsin\left(\dfrac{2}{5}\right)\right) = \sqrt{1 - \sin^2\left(\arcsin\left(\dfrac{2}{5}\right)\right)} = \sqrt{\dfrac{1}{5}}$

33. $\sin\left(\arcsin\left(\dfrac{\pi}{5}\right)\right) = \dfrac{\pi}{5}$

34. $\csc\left(\arcsin\left(-\dfrac{2}{7}\right)\right) = -\dfrac{7}{2}$

35. $\cos\left(\arctan\left(\dfrac{3}{4}\right)\right) = \sqrt{\dfrac{1}{1 + \tan^2\left(\arctan\left(\dfrac{3}{4}\right)\right)}} = \dfrac{4}{5}$

36. $\csc\left(\arccos\left(\dfrac{2\sqrt{5}}{5}\right)\right) = \dfrac{1}{\sin\left(\arccos\left(\dfrac{2\sqrt{5}}{5}\right)\right)} = $

$= \dfrac{1}{\sqrt{1 - \cos^2\left(\arccos\left(\dfrac{2\sqrt{5}}{5}\right)\right)}} = \sqrt{5}$

CHAPTER 5 – SETS

5.1. – SETS

1. A set is <u>a collection of different objects</u>

2. Give 3 examples of sets:
    a. {chair, table, shelf}
    b. {1, 2, 3...}
    c. {Jeff, Ron, Alex, ...}

3. Consider the set {2, 4, 6, ...}
    a. This is the set of <u>even numbers</u>. The next element is <u>8</u>
    b. In this set the number of elements is <u>infinite</u>. It is an <u>infinite</u> set

4. Consider the set {1, 8, 27, ...}
    a. This is the set of <u>perfect cubes</u>. The next element is <u>64</u>
    b. In this set the number of elements is <u>infinite</u>. It is an <u>infinite</u> set

5. Consider the set {Asia, Africa, ...}
    a. This is the set of <u>continents</u>. The next element is <u>America</u>.
    b. In this set the number of elements is <u>6</u>. It is a <u>finite</u> set

6. A **subset** is <u>a set such that each of its elements is contained in a bigger (or equal) set</u>. It is denoted by $A \subseteq B$

7. Given the set L = {A, B, C}
    a. State all the possible subsets of L. include the empty set.
        <u>L1 = {A, B, C}</u>
        <u>L2 = {A, B}</u>
        <u>L3 = {A, C}</u>
        <u>L4 = {B, C}</u>
        <u>L5 = {A}</u>
        <u>L6 = {B}</u>
        <u>L7 = {C}</u>
        <u>L8 = {}</u>
    b. All the subsets except <u>L1</u> are called **proper subsets denoted by**
        $A \subset B$
    c. Explain the difference between a subset and a proper subset.
        <u>A proper subset is smaller than the original set, a subset may be equal (like L1)</u>
    d. $A \not\subset B$ means <u>not a proper subset</u>
    e. $A \not\subseteq B$ means that A is NOT a subset of B

8. M is the set of perfect square smaller than a 100.
    a. List the elements of M <u>{1, 4, 9, 16, 25, 36, 49, 64, 81}</u>
    b. List the subset Q of even numbers in M <u>{4, 16, 36, 64}</u>

9. N is the set of prime numbers between 10 and 30.
   a. List the elements of M {11, 13, 17, 19, 23, 29}
   b. List the subset Q of even numbers in M {}

10. The **<u>universal set</u>** is particular for <u>each problem</u> and contains <u>all the relevant objects</u> for the problem. Usually it is denoted by the letter <u>U</u>.

11. The universal set for the students in the classroom is
    U = {____, ____, ____, ____, ...} fill the names of the students in your classroom.

12. Given the sets U = {John, Raquel, Felix, Shan, Mila, Jessy, Pamela} and the subset of U: B = {Shan, Mila}.
    State the complement of the set B' = {John, Raquel, Felix, Jessy, Pamela}

13. The **<u>complement of a</u>** <u>set A is the set that contains all the elements of U that are not in A.</u>

14. The **<u>intersection</u>** of 2 sets is <u>the set that contains all the elements that belong to both of them at the same time.</u> It is denoted by $A \cap B$.

15. The **<u>union</u>** of 2 sets is <u>the set that contains all the elements that belong to either A or B or both.</u> It is denoted by $A \cup B$

16. For example if S = {1, 2, 3, 4, 5, 6, 7, 8, 9} and M = {2, 6, 10, 12}
    a. $S \cap M$ = {2, 6}
    b. $S \cup M$ = {1, 2, 3, 4, 5, 6, 7, 8, 9, 10, 12}

17. Given the sets U = {John, Raquel, Felix, Shan, Mila, Jessy, Pamela} and the subset of U: B = {Shan, Mila}.
    a. $U \cap B$ = {Shan, Mila}.
    b. $U \cup B$ = {John, Raquel, Felix, Shan, Mila, Jessy, Pamela}

18. Two set are said to be "**<u>disjoint</u>**" <u>in case they have no intersection</u>
    <u>Example: the Set "red cars" and the set "Yellow cars" are disjoint</u>

19. Two set are equal in case all of their elements are equal
    <u>Example: The set "positive integers" and the set "Natural numbers"</u>

<u>Venn diagrams</u>

Event	Set Language	Venn diagram	Probability result
Complementary event (A')	Not A		$P(A') = 1 - P(A)$
The <u>intersection</u> of A and B (A∩B)	Set of elements that belongs to A <u>and</u> B		$P(A \cup B) = P(A) + P(B) - P(A \cup B)$
The <u>union</u> of A and B (A∪B)	Set of elements that belongs to A <u>or</u> B <u>or</u> both		
If (A∩B) = ∅ A and B are said to be: mutually exclusive	The sets A and B are Mutually exclusive		$P(A \cup B) = P(A) + P(B)$ $P(A \cap B) = 0$

20. The **<u>commutative</u>** property of a set means that: <u>order does not change result</u>
    Example: $A \cup B = \underline{B \cup A}$

21. The **<u>associative</u>** property of a set means that: <u>Change the order</u>
    Example: $(A \cup B) \cup C = A \cup (B \cup C)$

22. The **<u>distributive</u>** property of a set means that: <u>we can "expand"</u>
    Example: $C \cup (A \cap B) = (C \cup A) \cap (C \cap B)$
    $C \cap (A \cup B) = (C \cap A) \cup (C \cap B)$

23. Given N, the set of natural numbers, Z the set of integers, Q the set of rationals and R the set of Real numbers.
    a. Write down an element of the set N∩Z: <u>1</u>
    b. Write down an element of the set Q∩Z: <u>0</u>
    c. Write down an element of the set Q∩Z': <u>0.5</u>
    d. Write down an element of the set Q'∩Z: <u>not possible</u>
    e. Write down an element of the set R∩Q: <u>2</u>
    f. Write down an element of the set R∩Q': <u>π</u>
    g. Write down an element of the set N∩N': <u>Not possible</u>

24. Consider the sets: $U = \{x \in N\}$

$A = \{x \in N | 11 < x < 21\}$, B={multiples of 4}, and C ={13, 16, 18, 20}

    a. Write all the elements of the set $A \cap B$: {12, 16, 20}
    b. Write all the elements of the set $A \cap C$: {13, 16, 18, 20}
    c. Write all the elements of the set $B \cap C$: {16, 20}
    d. Write all the elements of the set $B \cup C$: {multiples of 4, 13, 18}
    e. Write all the elements of the set $A \cap (B' \cup C)$: {13, 14, 15, 16, 17, 18, 19, 20}
    f. Write all the elements of the set $A \cap (B \cup C')$: {12, 14, 15, 16, 17, 19, 20}
    g. Write all the elements of the set $A \cap B \cap C'$): {12}

h.	True/**False**: $11 \in A$	**True**/False: $11 \in A'$
i.	**True**/False: $13 \in A \cap C$	**True**/False: $30 \notin B$
j.	**True**/False: $12 \in A \cap B$	**True**/False: $30 \notin C$
k.	True/**False**: $B \subset A$	**True**/False: $C \subset A$

25. Given the Venn diagram. Shade $A \cap B$

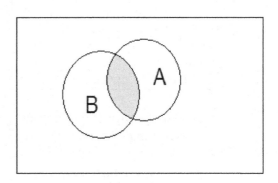

26. Given the Venn diagram. Shade $A \cap B'$

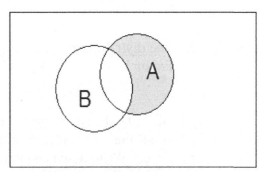

27. Given the Venn diagram. Shade B'

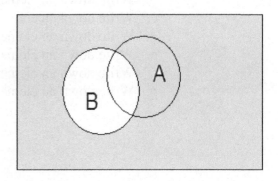

28. Given the Venn diagram. Shade A' ∩ B'

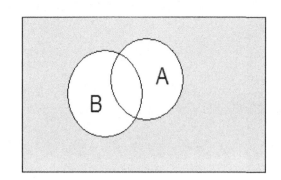

29. Given the Venn diagram. Shade A ∪ B

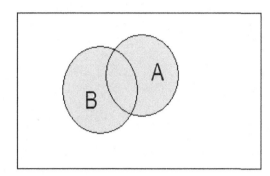

30. Given the Venn diagram. Shade A' ∪ B

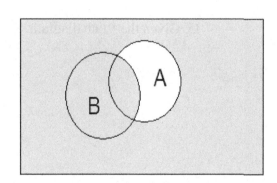

31. Given the Venn diagram. Shade A' ∪ B'

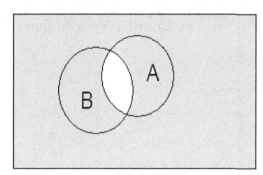

32. Given the Venn diagram. Shade A ∪ B

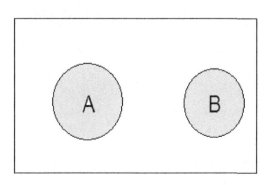

33. Given the Venn diagram. Shade A ∪ B'

34. Given the Venn diagram. Shade A ∩ B'

35. Given the Venn diagram. Shade A ∩ B   (None - Empty)

36. Given the Venn diagram. Shade A ∩ B ∩ C   (None - Empty)

37. Given the Venn diagram. Shade (A ∪ B) ∩ C

38. Given the Venn diagram. Shade (A' ∪ B) ∩ C

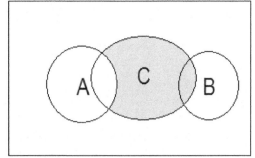

39. Given the Venn diagram. Shade (A ∪ B) ∩ C'

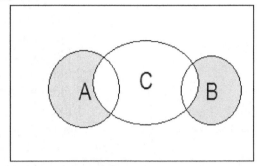

40. Given the Venn diagram. Shade A ∩ B ∩ C

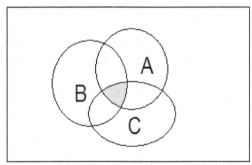

41. Given the Venn diagram. Shade (A ∩ B) ∩ C'

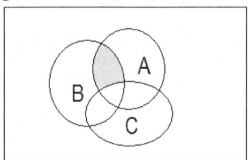

42. Given the Venn diagram. Shade (A' ∩ B) ∩ C

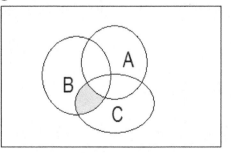

43. Given the Venn diagram. Shade $(A \cap B') \cap C$

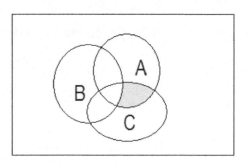

44. 50 drivers were asked about the favourite car colour. 3 choices were given: Red (X), Blue (Y) and White (Z). The results were:

          15 liked all three
          3 liked red and blue only
          9 liked red and white only
          7 liked blue and white only
          2 liked red only
          5 liked white only
          1 liked blue only

a. Represent this information in a Venn diagram. Fill the Venn diagram with all the corresponding numbers.

b. Write down the percentage of drivers that did not like any of the 3 colours. $\dfrac{8}{50} = 16\%$

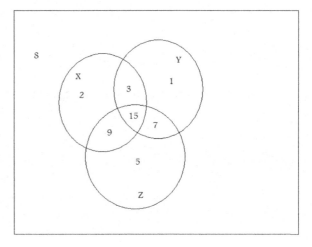

45. Given the sets U = {Real numbers}, A={Negative numbers}, Z={Integers}

Write the following numbers in the correct region: cos(0), 0.5, $-\pi$, 5^{-2}, -7, 0

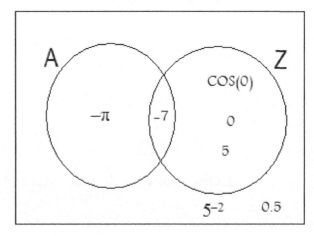

46. In a certain hospital in which there are 70 nurses, 20 work in cardiac surgery (C) and 15 others in the intensive care unit (I). 8 nurses work in both units.

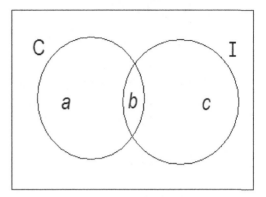

    a. $a = \underline{12}$ $b = \underline{8}$ $c = \underline{7}$

    b. Calculate the number of nurses that work outside of the cardiac surgery or intensive care units. <u>Nurses outside $= 70 - (20 + 35 - 8) = 23$</u>

47. Given the following sets:

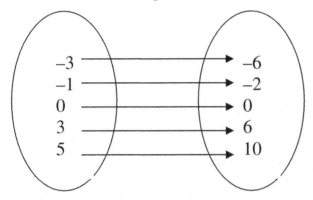

    a. Write down the paires created by this mapping from one set to another:
        (-3, -6), (-1, -2), (0, 0), (3, 6), (5, 10)
    b. Can you write a mathematical expression to express this mapping¿?
        <u>$x \to 2x$ or $f(x) = 2x$</u>

48. Given the following setts:

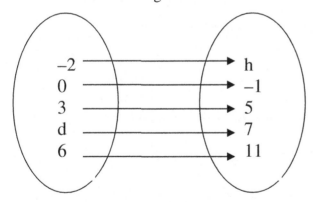

    a. Can you write a mathematical expression to express this mapping?

        <u>$x \to 2x - 1$ or $f(x) = 2x - 1$</u>

    b. Find h. Find d.   <u>$h = f(-2) = -5$</u>
        <u>$f(d) = -2d - 1 = 7; d = -4$</u>

CHAPTER 6 - STATISTICS

6.1. – STATISTICS

1. The set of objects that we are trying to study is called <u>population</u>. the number of elements in the population can be <u>finite</u> or <u>infinite</u>.
2. Usually the <u>population</u> is too big and therefore we obtain a <u>sample</u>. This process is called <u>sampling</u>.
3. We use the <u>sample</u> to obtain conclusions about the <u>population</u>.

Types of DATA

4. <u>Categorical</u> data.
5. <u>Numerical</u> data that can be divided to <u>continuous</u> or <u>discrete</u>.
6. <u>Numerical discrete</u> can be counted while <u>numerical continuous</u> data can be <u>measured</u>.

7. Give 3 examples of <u>Categorical</u> data:
    <u>Eye color (blue, green, brown etc.)</u>
    <u>Favorite food (meat, pasta, ice cream etc.)</u>
    <u>Preferred website (whatever.com, whatsup.com etc.)</u>

8. Give 3 examples of <u>numerical discrete</u> data:
    <u>Number of students in a classroom</u>
    <u>Shoe size</u>
    <u>Number of rabbits in the forest</u>

9. Give 3 examples of <u>numerical continuous</u> data:
    <u>Height of people</u>
    <u>Amount of energy in a laser beam</u>
    <u>CO_2 level in the atmosphere</u>

10. Given the following variables, classify them in the table:

Categorical	Numerical Discrete	Numerical Continuous
Eye color	Shoe size	Height
Type of fruit	Number of cars in a parking lot	Weight
Name of writer	Number of apples sold a day in a store	Velocity of the wind
	Numbers of pages in a book	Temperature
	Number of students in a school	

11. In a certain class the eye color of students was studied.
    a. How many students participated?   <u>14</u>
    b. Represent the information in a Bar Chart

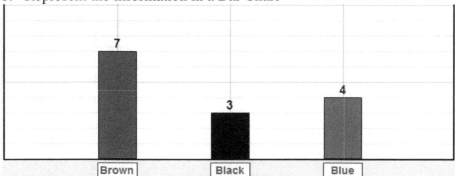

    c. Represent the information in a Pie Chart
    d. Represent the information in a Pie Chart (include the %)

$$\frac{7}{14} = 50\%$$

$$\frac{3}{14} \approx 21.4\%$$

$$\frac{4}{14} \approx 28.6\%$$

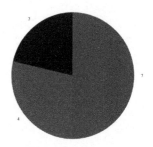

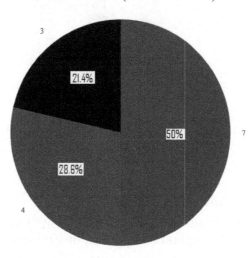

12. In a certain math class the following grades were obtained:

    65, 72, 85, 89, 52, 71, 89, 68, 63, 76, 61, 86, 98, 79, 79, 91, 74, 89, 77, 68, 78

    a. How many students participated? <u>21</u>
    b. What kind of data is this? <u>Numerical Discrete</u>
    c. Suggest a method to represent this information in a table.
    d. Use the table to create a bar graph

Grade	Frequency
[51, 60]	1
[61, 70]	5
[71, 80]	8
[81, 90]	5
[91, 100]	2

Grades

(bar graph: Frequency vs Grade; [51, 60]=1, [61, 70]=5, [71, 80]=8, [81, 90]=5, [91, 100]=2)

13. In a certain zoo the length of a certain type of animal (in meters) was studied.

a. How many animals participated? <u>14</u>
b. What kind of data is this? <u>Numerical continuous</u>
c. Suggest a method to represent this information in a table.

Length Interval (m)	Frequency
[1.50, 1.60)	3
[1.60, 1.70)	4
[1.70, 1.80)	4
[1.80, 1.90)	2
[1.90, 2.00)	1

d. Use the table to create a bar graph

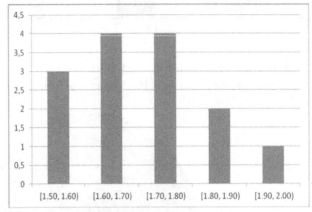

14. In a certain group shoe size was studied and the following results obtained:

45, 36, 44, 38, 41, 42, 48, 39, 40, 42, 43, 41, 38, 45, 41, 38, 42, 44, 41, 41, 46

a. How many students participated? <u>21</u>
e. What kind of data is this? <u>Numerical discrete</u>
b. Suggest a method to represent this information in a table.

c. Use the table to create a bar graph

Shoe size	Frequency
[36, 40]	6
[41, 45]	13
[46, 50]	2

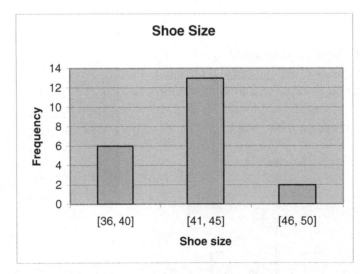

15. Choose a variable to collect information about in your classroom, state its kind, represent the information in a table and create a bar graph. <u>Should be done in class.</u>

6.2. – MEAN, MEDIAN, MODE AND FREQUENCY DIAGRAMS

1. In a certain club the number of visitors per day was studied during 1 week and the following results obtained: 58, 79, 66, 78, 23, 66, 63

   a. State the number of elements in the set: <u>7</u>
   b. What kind of data is this? <u>Numerical discrete</u>
   c. Find its mean: $\mu = \dfrac{383}{7} \approx 54.7$ Find its mode: <u>66</u>

   d. Write the information in an increasing order: 23, 58, 63, 66, 66, 78, 79
   e. Find its Median: 23, 58, 63, **66**, 66, 78, 79
      Q1 = <u>58</u> Q3 = <u>78</u>

2. In a certain restaurant the amount of meat (kg) consumed per day was studied and the following results obtained: 11.5, 12.2, 14.6, 15.0, 23.2, 21.2, 10.1, 13.1

   a. State the number of elements in the set: <u>8</u>
   b. What kind of data is this? <u>Numerical continuous</u>
   c. Find its mean: $\mu = \dfrac{120.9}{8} \approx 15.1$ <u>Kg</u> Find its mode: <u>None</u>.

   d. Write the information in an increasing order:
      10.1, 11.5, 12.2, **13.1, 14.6**, 15.0, 21.2, 23.2

   e. Find its Median: $= \dfrac{13.1 + 14.6}{2} = 13.85$ <u>Kg</u>

      Q1 $= = \dfrac{11.5 + 12.2}{2} = 11.85$ <u>Kg</u>   Q3 $= = \dfrac{15.0 + 21.2}{2} = 18.1$ <u>Kg</u>

3. In a certain math class the number of exercises per day given for HW is the following: 5, 6, 6, 6, 4, 4, 5, 5, 4, 5, 6, 6, 7, 3, 0, 3

   a. State the number of elements in the set: <u>16</u>
   b. What kind of data is this? <u>Numerical discrete</u>
   c. Find its mean: $\mu = \dfrac{75}{16} \approx 4.69$ Find its mode: <u>6</u>

   d. Write the information in an increasing order:
      0, 3, 3, 4, 4, 4, 5, **5, 5**, 5, 6, 6, 6, 6, 6, 7
   e. Find its Median: <u>5</u>   Q1 = <u>4</u>   Q3 = <u>6</u>

4. In the following data: 2, 2, 3, 3, 9, 9, 9 one natural number is missing. It is known that the median with the missing number is 3. Find all the possible values of the missing number.
   Adding the number 1:   1 ,2, 2, **3, 3**, 9, 9, 9   Median is 3, correct
   Adding the number 2:   2, 2, 2, **3, 3**, 9, 9, 9   Median is 3. correct
   Adding the number 3:   2, 2, 3, **3, 3**, 9, 9, 9   Median is 3. correct
   Adding the number 4 or any bigger: 2, 2, 3, **3, 4**, 9, 9, 9   Median is 3.5, incorrect
   The missing number can be 1, 2 or 3.

5. In a certain math class the following grades were obtained:
68, 79, 75, 89, 54, 81, 88, 62, 67, 75, 64, 85, 97, 77, 79, 90, 75, 89, 76, 68
   a. State the number of elements in the set: <u>20</u>

   b. What kind of data is this? <u>Numerical discrete</u>

   c. Find its mean: $\mu = \dfrac{1538}{20} \approx 76.9$ Find its mode: <u>75</u>

   d. Write the information in an increasing order:

   54, 62, 64, 67, 68, 68, 75, 75, 75, **76, 77**, 79, 79, 81, 85, 88, 89, 89, 90, 97

   e. Find its Median: $= \dfrac{76+77}{2} = 76.5$ Q1 = <u>68</u>   Q3 = $= \dfrac{85+88}{2} = 86.5$

   f. Fill the table:

Grade	Mid – Grade (Mi)	Frequency (fi)	fi · Mi	Cumulative Frequency (Fi)	Fi (%)
51 – 60	55.5	1	55.5	1	5
61 – 70	65.5	5	327.5	6	30
71 – 80	75.5	7	528.5	13	65
81 – 90	85.5	6	513	19	95
91 – 100	95.5	1	95.5	20	100
Total		20	1520		

   g. Use the table to find the mean: $\mu = \dfrac{1520}{20} = 76$ Comment on the result

   compared to the previous mean obtained. <u>The "price" for grouping the data is the error committed. 76 instead of 76.9 approx. 1.2% error.</u>

   h. Discuss the advantages and disadvantages of organizing information in a table. <u>In a table the information is much easier to perceive and analyze. It also occupies "less space". The big disadvantage is the error committed.</u>

   i. Is this the only possible choice for the left column of the table? Why? Discuss the advantages and disadvantages of organizing information in such a way.
   <u>No it is not the only possibility. Narrower or wider intervals can be chosen. Narrower interval implies higher accuracy but information may be harder to understand and/or analyze. It also implies more work. Wider interval implies lower level of accuracy but information may be easier to understand and/or analyze. It also implies less work.</u>

j. Design a new table with a different <u>interval</u>

Grade	Mid – Grade (Mi)	Frequency (fi)	fi · Mi	Cumulative Frequency (Fi)	Fi (%)
51 – 55	53	1	53	1	5
56 – 60	58	0	0	1	5
61 – 65	63	2	126	3	15
66 – 70	68	3	204	6	30
71 – 75	73	3	219	9	45
76 – 80	78	4	312	13	65
81 – 85	83	2	166	15	75
86 – 90	88	4	352	19	95
91 – 95	93	0	0	19	95
96 – 100	98	1	98	20	100
Total		20	1530		

k. Use the table to find the mean: $\mu = \dfrac{1530}{20} = 76.5$. Comment on the result compared to the previous mean obtained. <u>Since more intervals are used the approximation is closer to the real value.</u>

l. The mean of the <u>population</u> is denoted with the Greek letter mu: μ and typically it is <u>unknown</u>. The mean of the <u>sample</u> is denoted by $\overline{x}$

m. Find the modal interval in both tables: 1st: 71 – 80 2nd: <u>76 – 80, 86 – 90</u> <u>(bimodal)</u>

n. In general this method of organizing information is called <u>grouping</u>

o. The 1st column is called <u>class</u> with upper interval boundary and <u>Lower</u> interval boundary.

p. The 2nd column is called <u>Mid – Class</u>

q. On the following grid paper sketch the corresponding points.

OGIVE

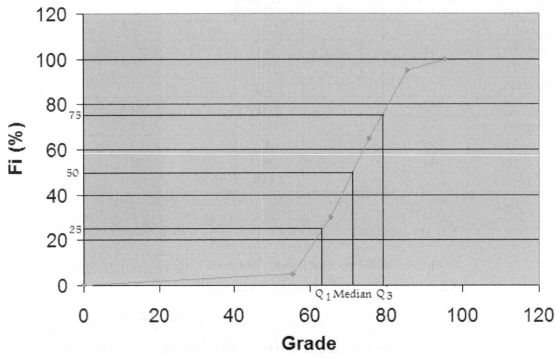

r. This graph is called cumulative frequency curve or <u>Ogive</u>

s. Find the median using the graph: <u>~ 72</u>

t. Find the first quartile (Q_1) using the graph: Q_1 = <u>~ 64</u>

u. Find the third quartile (Q_3) using the graph: Q_3 = <u>~ 79</u>

v. Find P_{30} using the graph: <u>~ 67</u> Find P_{65} using the graph: <u>~ 75</u>

w. The <u>Inter Quartile Range</u> is in general $Q_3 - Q_1$ in this case <u>86.5–68= 18.5</u>

x. Find the answers to all the different parts using your GDC.

6. In a certain class the following heights (in m) of students were collected:

1.77, 1.60, 1.89, 1.54, 1.77, 1.65, 1.86, 1.51, 1.67, 1.94, 1.73, 1.70, 1.66

a. State the number of elements in the set: 13
b. What kind of data is this? Numerical continuous
c. Find its mean: $\mu = \dfrac{22.29}{13} \approx 1.715m$ Find its mode: 1.77m

d. Write the information in an increasing order:
   1.51 1.54 1.60 1.65 1.66 1.67 **1.70** 1.73 1.77 1.77 1.86 1.89 1.94
e. Its Median: 1.70m   Q1 $= \dfrac{1.60+1.65}{2} = 1.625m$ Q3$= \dfrac{1.77+1.86}{2} = 1.815m$

f. Fill the table:

Height	Mid – Height (Mi)	Frequency (fi)	fi · Mi	Cumulative Frequency (Fi)	Fi (%)
[1.50 – 1.60)	1.55	2	3.1	2	15.4
[1.60 – 1.70)	1.65	4	6.6	6	46.2
[1.70– 1.80)	1.75	4	7	10	76.9
[1.80 – 1.90)	1.85	2	3.7	12	92.3
[1.90 – 2.00)	1.95	1	1.95	13	100
Total			22.35		

g. Use the table to find the mean: $\mu = \dfrac{22.35}{13} \approx 1.719m$ Comment on the result compared to the previous mean obtained. The "price" for grouping the data is the error committed. 1.719 instead of 1.715 approx. 0.23% error.

h. Discuss the advantages and disadvantages of organizing information in a table. In a table the information is much easier to perceive and analyze. It also occupies "less space". The big disadvantage is the error committed.

i. Is this the only possible choice for the left column of the table? Why? Discuss the advantages and disadvantages of organizing information in such a wayNo it is not the only possibility. Narrower or wider intervals can be chosen. Narrower interval implies higher accuracy but information may be harder to understand and/or analyze. It also implies more work. Wider interval implies lower level of accuracy but information may be easier to understand and/or analyze. It also implies less work.

j. On the following grid paper sketch the corresponding points.

OGIVE

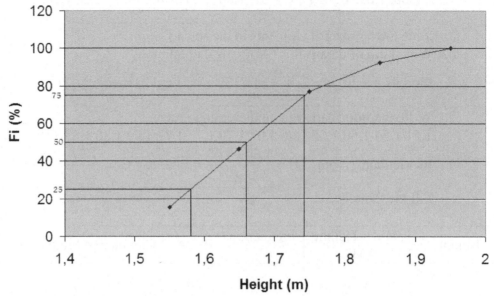

Height (m)

k. This graph is called cumulative frequency curve or <u>ogive</u>

l. Find the median using the graph: $\sim 1.66m$

m. Find the first quartile (Q_1) using the graph: $Q_1 = \sim 1.58m$

n. Find the third quartile (Q_3) using the graph: $Q_3 = \sim 1.74m$

o. Find P_{30} using the graph: $\sim 1.61m$ Find P_{70} using the graph: $\sim 1.71m$

p. The <u>Inter Quartile Range</u> is in general $Q_3 - Q_1$ in this case $\underline{1.815 - 1.625 = 0.190m}$

q. Find the answers to all the different parts using your GDC.

7. In a certain class students eye color was collected:

Brown, Black, Brown, Blue, Brown, Blue, Green, Brown, Black, Green

a. State the number of elements in the set: <u>10</u>

b. What kind of data is this? <u>Categorical</u>

c. Fill the table:

Eye Color	Mid – Color (Mi)	Frequency (fi)	Fi x Mi	Cumulative Frequency (Fi)	Fi (%)
Brown	N/A	4	N/A	N/A	N/A
Blue	N/A	2	N/A	N/A	N/A
Green	N/A	2	N/A	N/A	N/A
Black	N/A	2	N/A	N/A	N/A
Total	N/A	10	N/A	N/A	N/A

d. Obtain the mean: <u>N/A</u>

e. State the mode of the set: <u>Brown</u>

f. Find the modal interval: <u>N/A</u>

g. Find the Median using the original data: <u>N/A</u>

h. Find the median using the table, discuss your answer. <u>N/A</u>

i. Find the answers to all the different parts using your GDC. <u>N/A</u>

j. Represent the information in a histogram:

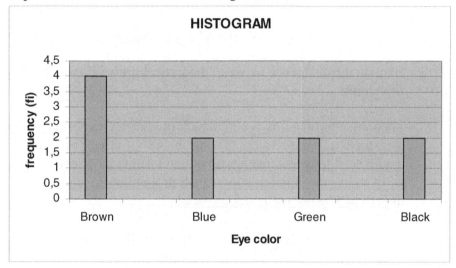

6.3. – PROBABILITY

Probability is the science of chance or likelihood of an event happening

If a random experiment is repeated <u>n</u> times in such a way that each of the trials is identical and independent, where n(A) is the number of <u>times</u> event A occurred,

then: Relative frequency of event A = $P(A) = \dfrac{n(A)}{N}$ $(N \rightarrow \infty)$

Exercises

1. In an unbiased coin what is P(head) ? <u>0.5</u>

    This probability is called "<u>theoretical probability</u>"

2. Explain the difference between theoretical probability and "experimental" probability.

    <u>Theoretical probability is calculated, predicted. "experimental" probability is measured in an experiment. The probability for head is theoretically 0.5, we would need to repeat an experiment an infinite number of times to make sure it is. In reality the coin has some small probability to lend on its thin side (more than 0) so it is not really 0.5 for head…</u>

3. Throw a drawing pin at least 15 times and fill the table:
    <u>This experiment should be done in class</u>

4. The definition of probability is:
    $$P(A) = \frac{\text{Number of times A ocurred}}{\text{Total numberof times experiment repeated}}$$

Properties of probability

1. $\underline{0} \leq P(A) \leq \underline{1}$
2. $P(U) = \underline{1}$

5. Given the sentence "Good morning everyone". Find the following probabilities in case the choices are being made in a random way:

    a. $P(\text{choosing a vowel}) = \dfrac{8}{19}$ c. $P(\text{choosing a "e"}) = \dfrac{3}{19}$

    b. $P(\text{choosing a "o"}) = \dfrac{4}{19}$ d. $P(\text{choosing a "z"}) = 0$

6. In case a student is chosen randomly in your classroom. Find the probability it´s a girl. <u>This should be done in class</u>

7. Find the probability of getting a prime number sum on tossing 2 dice. The primes are: 2, 3, 5, 7, 11: $\dfrac{1+2+4+6+2}{36} = \dfrac{15}{36}$

8. Find the probability of getting a sum of 17 on tossing 3 dice:
6,6,5; 6,5,6; 5,6,6;   Probability is $\dfrac{3}{216}$

9. Find the probability of being left handed in your classroom. <u>This should be done in class</u>

10. Find the probability of obtaining a sum of 5 on tossing 2 dice. $\dfrac{4}{36}$

11. Find the probability of obtaining 2 tails on tossing 2 coins. $\dfrac{1}{4}$

12. Find the probability that a 2 digit number divides by 3: $\dfrac{30}{90}$

13. Find the probability of choosing the letter b in the word probability: $\dfrac{2}{11}$

14. Find the probability of choosing a number that contains the digit 7 in the first hundred numbers (1 to 100). $\dfrac{19}{100}$

15. Find the probability of choosing a number that contains only even digits in the first thousand numbers (1 to 1000).
$$\left(\dfrac{\dfrac{50}{100}\cdot 5 + \dfrac{25}{100}\cdot 90 + \dfrac{12.5}{100}\cdot 1000}{1000}\right) = 0.15$$

16. Find the probability of obtaining a sum of 10 on tossing 2 dice. $\dfrac{3}{36}$

17. Find the probability of obtaining a sum of more than 5 on tossing 2 dice:
$\dfrac{5+6+5+4+3+2+1}{36} = \dfrac{26}{36}$

18. Knowing that the sum of 2 dice is more than 5, find the probability it's 10: $\dfrac{\left(\dfrac{3}{36}\right)}{\left(\dfrac{26}{36}\right)} = \dfrac{3}{26}$

19. In a bag with 5 red marbles and 6 white marbles find the probability of drawing:

    a. A red marble $\dfrac{5}{11}$

    b. 2 consecutive red marbles (without replacement) $\dfrac{5}{11}\cdot\dfrac{4}{10}=\dfrac{20}{110}=\dfrac{2}{11}$

    c. 2 consecutive white marbles (without replacement) $\dfrac{6}{11}\cdot\dfrac{5}{10}=\dfrac{30}{110}=\dfrac{3}{11}$

    d. Red and white marbles in any order (without replacement)
$$\dfrac{5}{11}\cdot\dfrac{6}{10}+\dfrac{6}{11}\cdot\dfrac{5}{10}=\dfrac{60}{110}=\dfrac{6}{11}$$

    e. Sum the results of parts b to d.
$$\dfrac{2}{11}+\dfrac{3}{11}+\dfrac{6}{11}=\dfrac{11}{11}=1,\ \text{The sum of probabilities of all options must be 1}$$

    f. 2 consecutive red marbles (with replacement): $\dfrac{5}{11}\cdot\dfrac{5}{11}=\dfrac{25}{121}$

    g. 2 consecutive white marbles (with replacement): $\dfrac{6}{11}\cdot\dfrac{6}{11}=\dfrac{36}{121}$

    h. Red and white marbles in any order (with replacement)
$$\dfrac{5}{11}\cdot\dfrac{6}{11}+\dfrac{6}{11}\cdot\dfrac{5}{11}=\dfrac{60}{121}$$

    i. Sum the results of parts f to h.
$$\dfrac{25}{121}+\dfrac{36}{121}+\dfrac{60}{121}=\dfrac{121}{121}=1,\ \text{Sum of probabilities of all options must be 1}$$

20. In a bag with 4 red marbles 3 white and 5 blue marbles find the probability of drawing:

    a. A red marble. $\dfrac{4}{12}$

    b. 2 consecutive red marbles (without replacement) $\dfrac{4}{12}\cdot\dfrac{3}{11}=\dfrac{12}{132}$

    c. 2 consecutive white marbles (without replacement) $\dfrac{3}{12}\cdot\dfrac{2}{11}=\dfrac{6}{132}$

    d. Red and blue marbles in any order (without replacement)
$$\dfrac{4}{12}\cdot\dfrac{5}{11}+\dfrac{5}{12}\cdot\dfrac{4}{11}=\dfrac{40}{132}$$

    e. White and blue marbles in any order (without replacement)
$$\dfrac{3}{12}\cdot\dfrac{5}{11}+\dfrac{5}{12}\cdot\dfrac{3}{11}=\dfrac{30}{132}$$

    f. 2 reds and 1 blue in any order (without replacement)
$$\dfrac{4}{12}\cdot\dfrac{3}{11}\cdot\dfrac{5}{10}+\dfrac{4}{12}\cdot\dfrac{5}{11}\cdot\dfrac{3}{10}+\dfrac{5}{12}\cdot\dfrac{4}{11}\cdot\dfrac{3}{10}=3\cdot\left(\dfrac{5}{12}\cdot\dfrac{4}{11}\cdot\dfrac{3}{10}\right)=\dfrac{180}{1320}$$
$$P(R,R,B)+P(R,B,R)+P(B,R,R)$$

    g. Red, White and Blue in any order (without replacement)
$$6\cdot\dfrac{4}{12}\cdot\dfrac{3}{11}\cdot\dfrac{5}{10}=\dfrac{360}{1320}$$
$$P(R,W,B)+P(R,B,W)+P(W,R,B)+P(W,B,R)+P(B,W,R)+P(B,R,W)$$

CHAPTER 7

7.1. – INTERNATIONAL SYSTEM OF UNITS

1. Meter (m) is a unit of <u>length/distance</u> Other units of <u>length/distance</u> are: <u>mile</u>.

2. Meter square (m^2) is a unit of <u>area</u> Other units of <u>area</u> are: <u>mile^2</u>

3. An area has units of m^2 A length has units of <u>m</u>

4. Kilo = <u>1000</u> Mili = $\dfrac{1}{1000}$

Convert the units, use scientific notation in at least one of each type of exercises:

5. How many metres in 2.5 km?

   <u>2500m</u>

6. How many metres in 0.5 km?

   <u>500m</u>

7. How many metres^2 in $\dfrac{1}{3}$ km^2?

   $\dfrac{1000000}{3} m^2$

   Ffg

8. How many metres in 56 km?

   <u>56000m</u>

9. How many metres in 2500 km?

   <u>2500000m</u>

10. How many km^2 in 26 m^2?

    $\dfrac{26}{1000000} km^2 = 0.000026 km^2$

11. How many km in 75 m?

    <u>0.075km</u>

12. How many km in 1000 m?

    <u>1km</u>

13. How many m in $5.2 \cdot 10^7$ km?

    $\underline{5.2 \cdot 10^{10} m}$

14. How many km^2 in $5.12 \cdot 10^8$ m^2?

    $\dfrac{5.12 \cdot 10^8}{10^6} = 512 km^2$

15. How many mm in 3.04 m?

    <u>3040mm</u>

16. How many mm^2 in 0.5 m^2?

    $\underline{0.5 m^2 = 0.5 \cdot 10^6 mm^2 = 5 \cdot 10^5 mm^2}$

17. How many mm^2 in 1 m^2?

    $\underline{1 m^2 = 10^6 mm^2}$

18. How many mm in 2 m?

    <u>2000mm</u>

19. How many mm in 2.5 m?

    <u>2500mm</u>

20. How many mm^2 are 1.35 m^2?

    $\underline{1.35 m^2 = 1.35 \cdot 10^6 mm^2}$

21. How many cm in $\frac{1}{3}$ m?

$\underline{33.3cm}$

22. How many cm^2 in 56 m^2?

$\underline{56m^2 = 56 \cdot 10^4 cm^2 = 5.6 \cdot 10^5 cm^2}$

23. How many cm in 3.1 km?

$\underline{310000cm}$

24. How many mm^2 in 0.5 cm^2?

$\underline{0.5cm^2 = 0.5 \cdot 10^2 mm^2 = 50mm^2}$

25. How many cm in in 120 m?

$\underline{12000cm}$

26. How many mm^2 in 5.1 cm^2?

$\underline{5.1cm^2 = 5.1 \cdot 10^2 mm^2 = 510mm^2}$

27. How many cm in 17 km?

$\underline{1700000cm}$

28. How many m in 12392 km?

$\underline{12392000m}$

29. How many mm^2 in 5.1 m^2?

$\underline{5.1m^2 = 5.1 \cdot 10^6 mm^2}$

30. How many m^2 in 2.2 mm^2?

$\underline{2.2mm^2 = 2.2 \cdot 10^{-6} m^2}$

31. How many cm in 13.12 m?

$\underline{1312cm}$

32. Complete the table:

mm	cm	m	km
14	1.4	0.014	0.000014
650	65	0.65	0.00065
3000	300	3	0.003
5000000	500000	5000	5
12.5	1.25	0.0125	0.0000125
37	3.7	0.037	0.000037
4780	478	4.78	0.00478
1310000	131000	1310	1.31
8000	800	8	0.008
mm^2	cm^2	m^2	km^2
14	0.14	$0.14 \cdot 10^{-4} = 1.4 \cdot 10^{-5}$	$0.14 \cdot 10^{-10} = 1.4 \cdot 10^{-11}$
6500	65	0.0065	$0.0065 \cdot 10^{-6} = 6.5 \cdot 10^{-9}$
3000000	30000	$3.$	$3 \cdot 10^{-6}$
$5 \cdot 10^{12}$	$5 \cdot 10^{10}$	$5 \cdot 10^6$	5
12.5	0.125	$0.125 \cdot 10^{-4} = 1.25 \cdot 10^{-5}$	$0.125 \cdot 10^{-10} = 1.25 \cdot 10^{-11}$
370	3.7	0.00037	$0.00037 \cdot 10^{-6} = 3.7 \cdot 10^{-10}$
4780000	47800	4.78	$4.78 \cdot 10^{-6}$
$1.31 \cdot 10^{12}$	$1.31 \cdot 10^{10}$	$1.31 \cdot 10^6$	1.31
$8 \cdot 10^9$	$8 \cdot 10^7$	8000	0.008

7.2. – COMMON ERRORS

1. $\sqrt{A+B} = \sqrt{A} + \sqrt{B}$

      $\sqrt{16+100} \neq \sqrt{16} + \sqrt{100}$

      True / **False**, Give an example to show your answer.

2. $\sqrt{A^2 + B^2} = A + B$

      $\sqrt{4^2 + 10^2} \neq 4 + 10$

      True / **False**, Give an example to show your answer.

3. $(A+B)^2 = A^2 + B^2$

      $(A+B)^2 = A^2 + B^2 + 2AB$

      True / **False**, if false write the correct version.

4. $(A+B)(A-B) = A^2 + B^2$

      $(3+7)(3-7) \neq 3^2 + 7^2$

      True / **False**, Give an example to show your answer.

5. $(A+B)(A-B) = A^2 - B^2$

      True / False, if false write the correct version..

6. $(x+2)^2 = x^2 + 4x + 2$

      $(x+2)^2 = x^2 + 4x + 4$

      True / **False**, if false write the correct version.

7. $(A-B)^2 = A^2 - B^2$

      $(3+7)^2 \neq 3^2 - 7^2$

      True / **False**, Give an example to show your answer.

8. $(2x-3)^2 = 4x^2 - 6x + 9$

      $(2x-3)^2 = 4x^2 - 12x + 9$

      True / **False**, if false write the correct version.

9. $(\sqrt{a} - 3)^2 = a^2 - 6a + 9$

      $(\sqrt{a} - 3)^2 = a^2 - 6\sqrt{a} + 9$

      True / **False**, if false write the correct version.

10. $x^2 x^3 = x^6$

      $x^2 x^3 = x^5$

      True / **False**, if false write the correct version.

11. $(x^2)^3 = x^{(2^3)}$

      $(x^2)^3 = x^6$

      True / **False**, if false write the correct version.

12. $\dfrac{x^{10}}{x^2} = x^5$ True / **False**, if false write the correct version.

$\dfrac{x^{10}}{x^2} = x^8$
<hr>

13. $x^1 = 1$ True / **False**, if false write the correct version.

$x^1 = x$
<hr>

14. $x^0 = 0$ True / **False**, if false write the correct version.

$x^0 = 1$
<hr>

15. $-3^2 = (-3)^2$ True / **False**, if false write the correct version.

$-3^2 = -3 \cdot 3 = -9; \quad (-3)^2 = (-3)(-3) = 9$
<hr>

16. $(4x^2) = (4x)^2$ True / **False**, if false write the correct version.

$(4x^2) \neq (4x)^2 = 16x^2$
<hr>

17. $\sqrt{7x} = 7x^{\frac{1}{2}}$ True / **False**, if false write the correct version.

$\sqrt{7x} = \sqrt{7} \cdot \sqrt{x} \neq 7x^{\frac{1}{2}} = 7 \cdot \sqrt{x}$
<hr>

18. $\dfrac{0}{2} = \dfrac{2}{0}$ True / **False**, if false write the correct version.

$\dfrac{0}{2} = 0 \neq \dfrac{2}{0} = Undefined!$
<hr>

19. $\dfrac{14+x}{14} = x$ True / **False**, if false write the correct version.

$\dfrac{14+x}{14} = \dfrac{14}{14} + \dfrac{x}{14} = 1 + \dfrac{x}{14} \neq x$
<hr>

20. $\dfrac{7-x}{7} = x - 1$ True / **False**, if false write the correct version.

$\dfrac{7-x}{7} = \dfrac{7}{7} - \dfrac{x}{7} = 1 - \dfrac{x}{7} \neq x - 1$
<hr>

21. $\dfrac{a+b}{a} = 1 + \dfrac{b}{a}$ **True** / False, if false write the correct version.

22. $\dfrac{14+x}{14} = x + \dfrac{x}{14}$ True / **False**, if false write the correct version.

$$\dfrac{14+x}{14} = \dfrac{14}{14} + \dfrac{x}{14} = 1 + \dfrac{x}{14} \neq x + \dfrac{x}{14}$$

23. $\dfrac{1}{x+y} = \dfrac{1}{x} + \dfrac{1}{y}$ True / **False**, if false write the correct version.

$$\dfrac{1}{x+y} \neq \dfrac{1}{x} + \dfrac{1}{y} = \dfrac{y+x}{xy}$$

24.   An **expression** and an **equation** is the same thing.   True / **False**

25. $\dfrac{\left(\dfrac{a}{b}\right)}{c} = \dfrac{a}{\left(\dfrac{b}{c}\right)}$ True / **False**, if false write the correct version.

$$\dfrac{\left(\dfrac{a}{b}\right)}{c} = \dfrac{a}{bc} \neq \dfrac{a}{\left(\dfrac{b}{c}\right)} = \dfrac{ac}{b}$$

26. $-a^2 = (-a)^2$ True / **False**, if false write the correct version.

$$-a^2 \neq (-a)^2 = a^2$$

27. $a^{-2} = (-a)^2$ True / **False**, if false write the correct version.

$$a^{-2} = \dfrac{1}{a^2} \neq (-a)^2 = a^2$$

28. $a^{-2} = -a^2$ True / **False**, if false write the correct version.

$$a^{-2} = \dfrac{1}{a^2} \neq -a^2$$

29. $a^{-2} = -\dfrac{1}{a^2}$ True / **False**, if false write the correct version.

$$a^{-2} = \dfrac{1}{a^2} \neq -\dfrac{1}{a^2}$$

30. $a^{-2} = \dfrac{1}{a^2}$ **True** / False, if false write the correct version.

31. $a^{-1} = -\dfrac{1}{a}$ True / **False**, if false write the correct version.

$$a^{-1} = \frac{1}{a} \neq -\frac{1}{a}$$

32. $\dfrac{1}{2} + \dfrac{1}{3} = \dfrac{1}{2+3}$ True / **False**, if false write the correct version.

$$\frac{1}{2} + \frac{1}{3} = \frac{5}{6} \neq \frac{1}{2+3} = \frac{1}{5}$$

33. $a^{-1} + a^{-1} = a^{-2}$ True / **False**, if false write the correct version.

$$a^{-1} + a^{-1} = \frac{1}{a} + \frac{1}{a} = \frac{2}{a} \neq a^{-2} = \frac{1}{a^2}$$

34. $a^{-1}a^{-1} = a^{-2}$ **True** / False, if false write the correct version.

35. $a^{-2}a^{-3} = a^{-6}$ True / **False**, if false write the correct version.

$$a^{-2}a^{-3} = \frac{1}{a^2} \cdot \frac{1}{a^3} = \frac{1}{a^5} = a^{-5} \neq a^{-6}$$

36. $a^{-2} + a^{-3} = a^{-5}$ True / **False**, if false write the correct version.

$$a^{-2} + a^{-3} = \frac{1}{a^2} + \frac{1}{a^3} = \frac{a+1}{a^3} \neq a^{-5} = \frac{1}{a^5}$$

7.3. – FRACTIONS REVIEW

1. Given the following circle, divide it to 2 equal pieces and shade $\frac{1}{2}$

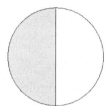

2. Given the following circle divide it to 3 equal pieces and shade $\frac{1}{3}$

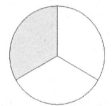

3. Given the following circle, divide it to 4 equal pieces and shade $\frac{1}{4}$

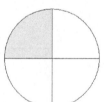

4. Given the following circle, divide it to 5 equal pieces and shade $\frac{1}{5}$

5. Given the following circle, divide it to 6 equal pieces and shade $\frac{1}{6}$

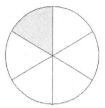

6. Given the following circle, divide it to 7 equal pieces and shade $\frac{1}{7}$

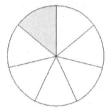

7. Given the following circle, divide it to 8 equal pieces and shade $\frac{1}{8}$

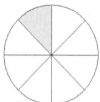

8. Given the following circle, divide it to 9 equal pieces and shade $\frac{1}{9}$

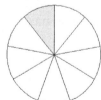

9. Given the following circle, divide it to 10 equal pieces and shade $\dfrac{1}{10}$

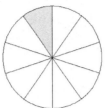

10. Given the following circle, divide it to 3 equal pieces and shade $\dfrac{2}{3}$

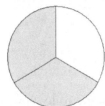

11. Given the following circle, divide it to 4 equal pieces and shade $\dfrac{2}{4}$

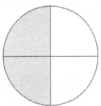

12. Given the following circle, divide it to 4 equal pieces and shade $\dfrac{3}{4}$

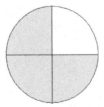

13. Given the following circle, divide it to 5 equal pieces and shade $\dfrac{2}{5}$

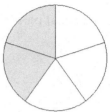

14. Given the following circle, divide it to 6 equal pieces and shade $\dfrac{5}{6}$

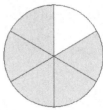

15. Given the following circle, divide it to 8 equal pieces and shade $\dfrac{5}{8}$

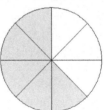

16. Given the following circle, divide it to 5 equal pieces and shade $\dfrac{4}{5}$

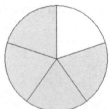

17. Given the following circle, divide it to 9 equal pieces and shade $\dfrac{4}{9}$

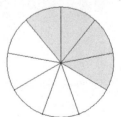

18. What fraction of the following circle is shaded: $\dfrac{5}{11}$

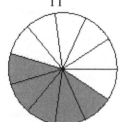

19. What fraction of the following circle is shaded: $\dfrac{2}{3}$

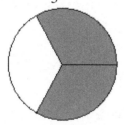

20. What fraction of the following circle is shaded: $\dfrac{5}{11}$

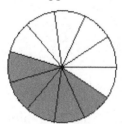

21. What fraction of the following circle is shaded: $\dfrac{12}{14} = \dfrac{6}{7}$

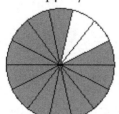

22. What fraction of the following circle is shaded: $\dfrac{7}{8}$

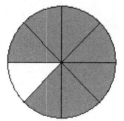

23. What fraction of the following circle is shaded: $\dfrac{1}{12}$

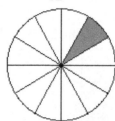

24. What fraction of the following table is shaded: $\dfrac{14}{64}$

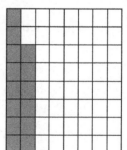

25. What fraction of the following table is shaded: $\dfrac{6}{35}$

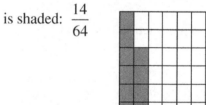

26. What fraction of the following table is shaded? $\dfrac{9}{24}$

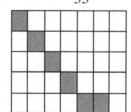

219

27. What fraction is shaded? $\dfrac{5}{16}$

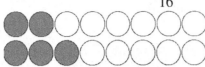

28. What fraction is shaded? $\dfrac{5}{12}$

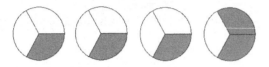

29. What fraction is shaded? $\dfrac{12}{24} = \dfrac{1}{2}$

30. What fraction is shaded? $\dfrac{8}{24}$

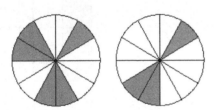

31. There were 12 cookies in the jar. John ate 5, write down the fraction of cookies john ate and the fraction that is left in the jar.

Eaten: $\dfrac{5}{12}$, Left $\dfrac{7}{12}$

32. Lia ate 3 cookies that represented $\dfrac{3}{4}$ of the cookies in the jar. Write down the number of cookies in the jar before she ate. Make a sketch to show answer.

4 cookies.

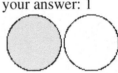

33. Rami ate $\dfrac{2}{5}$ of the cookies in the jar, Melissa ate $\dfrac{1}{4}$ of the cookies. Who ate more? Invent an imaginary jar with a number of cookies that will make the problem easy to solve.

With 20 cookies the problem is solved easily:

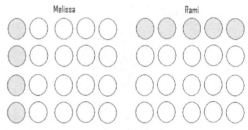

Rami ate more

34. How much is $\dfrac{1}{2}$ of 2? Shade to show your answer: 1

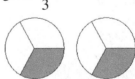

35. How much is $\dfrac{1}{3}$ of 2? Shade to show your answer: Shading a third of each gives $\dfrac{2}{3}$

36. How much is $\dfrac{1}{4}$ of 2? Shade to show your answer: Shading a quarter of each gives $\dfrac{2}{4}$

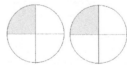

220

37. How much is $\frac{1}{5}$ of 2? Shade to show your answer: Shading a fifth of each gives $\frac{2}{5}$

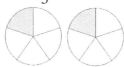

38. How much is $\frac{1}{3}$ of 5? In 2 different ways to show your answer: $\frac{5}{3}$

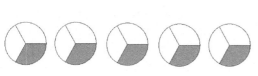

39. How much is $\frac{2}{5}$ of 4? In 2 different ways to show your answer: $\frac{8}{5}$

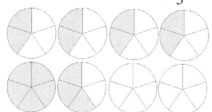

40. Sketch $\frac{3}{2}$ circles:

41. Sketch $\frac{5}{3}$ circles:

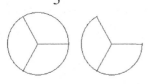

42. Sketch $\frac{7}{4}$ circles:

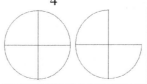

43. Sketch $\frac{8}{4}$ circles:

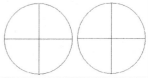

44. Sketch $\frac{7}{5}$ circles:

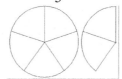

45. Sketch $\frac{8}{3}$ circles:

46. Nathan ate $\frac{2}{7}$ of the cookies in the jar, Melissa ate $\frac{1}{3}$ of the cookies.

Who ate more? Invent an imaginary jar with a number of cookies that will make the problem easy to solve. With 21 cookies the problem is easy to solve, Melissa ate more.

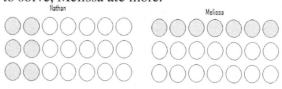

47. Write down the missing number(s) between 0 and 1: $\frac{1}{2}$

221

48. Write down the missing number(s) between 0 and 1: $\frac{1}{3}, \frac{2}{3}$

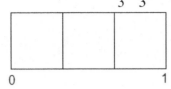

49. Write down the missing number(s) between 0 and 1: $\frac{1}{4}, \frac{2}{4}, \frac{3}{4}$

50. Write down the missing number(s) between 0 and 1: $\frac{1}{5}, \frac{2}{5}, \frac{3}{5}, \frac{4}{5}$

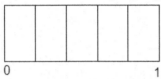

51. Write down the missing number(s) between 0 and 1: $\frac{1}{6}, \frac{2}{6}, \frac{3}{6}, \frac{4}{6}, \frac{5}{6}$

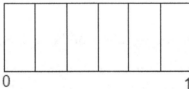

52. Write down the missing number(s) between 0 and 2: $\frac{1}{3}, \frac{2}{3}, 1, \frac{4}{3}, \frac{5}{3}$

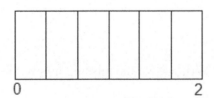

53. Write down the missing number(s) between 0 and 2: $\frac{1}{4}, \frac{2}{4}, \frac{3}{4}, 1, \frac{5}{4}, \frac{6}{4}, \frac{7}{4}$

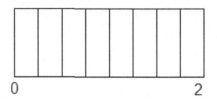

54. Write down the missing number(s) between 0 and 2:

$\frac{1}{5}, \frac{2}{5}, \frac{3}{5}, \frac{4}{5}, 1, \frac{6}{5}, \frac{7}{5}, \frac{8}{5}, \frac{9}{5}$

$0.2, 0.4, 0.6, 0.8, 1, 1.2, 1.4, 1.6, 1.8$

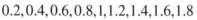
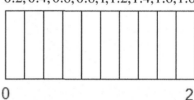

55. Write down the missing number(s) between 2 and 3:

$\frac{21}{10}, \frac{22}{10}, \frac{23}{10}, \frac{24}{10}, \frac{25}{10}, \frac{26}{10}, \frac{27}{10}, \frac{28}{10}, \frac{29}{10}$

$2.1, 2.2, 2.3, 2.4, 2.5, 2.6, 2.7, 2.8, 2.9$

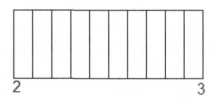

56. Write down the missing number(s) between 2 and 4:

$\frac{13}{6}, \frac{14}{6}, \frac{15}{6}, \frac{16}{6}, \frac{17}{6}, 3, \frac{19}{6}, \frac{20}{6}, \frac{21}{6}, \frac{22}{6}, \frac{23}{6}$

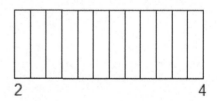

57. Write down the missing fractions(s): $-\dfrac{11}{5} = -2.2, \dfrac{3}{5} = 0.6$

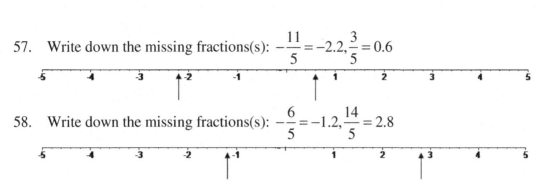

58. Write down the missing fractions(s): $-\dfrac{6}{5} = -1.2, \dfrac{14}{5} = 2.8$

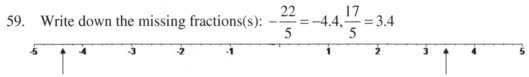

59. Write down the missing fractions(s): $-\dfrac{22}{5} = -4.4, \dfrac{17}{5} = 3.4$

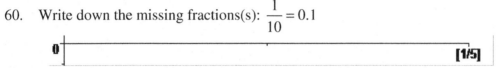

60. Write down the missing fractions(s): $\dfrac{1}{10} = 0.1$

0 |_____| [1/5]

61. Write down the missing fractions(s): $\dfrac{2}{8} = 0.25, \dfrac{3}{8} = 0.375$

[1/8] |_____| [1/2]

62. Write down the missing fractions(s): $\dfrac{7}{6}, \dfrac{8}{6} = \dfrac{4}{3}$

[1] |_____[3/2]___[5/3]|

63. Write down the missing fractions(s): $\dfrac{15}{7}, \dfrac{16}{7}, \dfrac{17}{7}, \dfrac{18}{7}, \dfrac{19}{7}$

[13/7] |_____[2]_____[20/7]|

64. Write down the missing fractions(s): $\dfrac{28}{9}, \dfrac{29}{9}$

[26/9] |_____[3]_____[10/3]|

65. Write down the missing fractions(s): $-\dfrac{8}{9}, -\dfrac{7}{9}, -\dfrac{6}{9}, -\dfrac{5}{9}$

[-10/9] |_____[-1]_____[-4/9]_____[-1/3]|

66. Write down the missing fractions(s): $-\dfrac{18}{5}, -\dfrac{16}{5}, -\dfrac{14}{5}, -\dfrac{12}{5}$

[-4] |_____[-2]____[-8/5]____[-6/5]|

67. Write down the missing fractions(s): $\dfrac{15}{4}, \dfrac{18}{4}, \dfrac{21}{4}$

[3/4] |____[3/2]____[9/4]____[3]_____[6]____[27/4]____[15/2]|

Made in United States
North Haven, CT
19 September 2022